CHILDREN OF SEPARATION AND DIVORCE

EDITED AND WITH NOTES AND INTRODUCTIONS

BY IRVING R. STUART, Ph. D.

AND LAWRENCE EDWIN ABT, Ph. D.

GROSSMAN PUBLISHERS, NEW YORK   1972

Children of
Separation
and Divorce

To Helen and Virginia,
whose sympathy for and
empathy with today's children
encouraged this collection.

I.R.S.

L.E.A.

CONTENTS

V. Socializing and Educating the Child

VI. Community Resources and Assistance Available for Parents and Children

PREFACE

When it is realized that of every three marriages contracted, approximately one ends in separation and divorce, the magnitude of this social problem in the United States becomes clearer. Moreover, current trends suggest that in the future an even larger percentage of marriages is likely to be terminated, with the result that the problem is almost certainly going to increase in importance and frequency.

Many disrupted marriages, of course, involve family units in which there are one or more children. When such a situation exists, grave new social, emotional, and personal problems are involved. This book is perhaps the first of its kind to attempt a thorough and systematic consideration of the whole range of such problems—with special emphasis on the new problems that develop for both children and their parents when marriages have been terminated.

This work seeks to take both a broad-gauged and deep look at a wide spectrum of the social and emotional issues and problems of divorce and separation. First, it seeks to set forth various current conceptions of parental responsibility in family situations in which a divorce has occurred. In doing so, the chapters that constitute Part I offer the reader a picture of some of the prevailing notions in our society about the importance of the family, how it functions, and what may occur when it has been disrupted by separation and divorce. To place these conceptions in a living frame of reference, the editors have conducted a series of interviews with divorced mothers and fathers who are struggling with the problems of their children. These reports have a familiar ring; and we think that they speak for themselves.

Just as it is important to know how divorced parents think and feel about their children, it is equally instructive to know how children from disrupted homes look at their parents. Again we have relied upon interviews, which are included in Part II of this work.

We are of the belief that religious feeling and experience are central to much of family life, whether it is intact or disrupted by separation and divorce. It is for this reason that it is important to know what the three principal religious faiths have to offer with respect to teachings of marital responsibility. In Part III we have been fortunate in obtaining brief but important statements from clergymen of wide experience in dealing with family life and its problems.

Our concerns for the large section of the American society that is economically and socially disadvantaged are great; some of these concerns find expression in Part IV. The social and emotional problems occasioned by divorce are no less real or significant for members of this important segment of our society, but the opportunities for their solution appear more limited.

It is the purpose of Part V to provide a wide range of information and points of view on how children develop, what educational opportunities can be afforded to them, and how to help parents deal with their responsibilities. Only when we can see a child in a longitudinal way, struggling to advance from one step to the next, can we begin to appreciate both the challenges he faces and the difficulties he must resolve. Some of these challenges—and many of the difficulties— unhappily become magnified for the child from a broken home.

Finally, we need to know something about how the community can help us with our problems and those of our children. Part VI, the final portion of this book, is offered as a beginning approach, through some agencies of community aid, to the resolution of problems that divorced parents and their children face.

We live in a time of rapid change—of the death of old values and the birth of new ones, of new conceptions of the role and function of the family, of increased responsibilities and opportunities for our young people. The trend today appears to be away from the family *as an institution,* but there are as yet no really viable alternatives or substitutes that enjoy general acceptance and approval, in spite of various experiments abroad. For some time to come, we are likely to have to work largely within the framework of the family as we know it today. Working within the family framework is the primary focus of this work, and we have tried to address problems of children of separation and divorce within this frame of reference. Many of the problems still run far ahead of their solutions, many views in this area are contradictory and conflicting. We have sought a middle way between the ideal and the practical.

We are deeply grateful to the contributors to this volume for sharing their views with us. But, as editors, we alone bear the responsibility for both the emphasis of this book and its outcome.

I. R. S. and L. E. A.

Parents' Views of Their Responsibilities Toward Their Children

Part One

INTRODUCTION

The chapters that constitute Part I are designed to provide the
reader with an understanding of the cultural and personality
forces that face family members in their interdependent relationships with each other and with the society and the community of which they are a part. Certain of these relationships
become modified and intensified when parents become separated and divorced. The material that follows seeks to indicate
the conditions under which these changes occur and the
consequences that may ensue both for parents and their children.

The primary focus of Part I is upon the changing roles of
the parents themselves rather than the effects upon the children. The new challenges and opportunities to separated and
divorced parents need to be seen against, and compared with,
existing family practices and relationships. This section offers
the reader much of the background and many of the insights
that need to be taken into account as parents examine their old
and new roles.

Dr. Myron Harris's paper, for example, discusses the role
of the parent as a member of a protective unit—the family—
and the physical and emotional dependency of his children. It
is also, we think, an exceptionally useful and helpful exploration of the wide range of interpersonal dynamics of family life,
with special emphasis on new problems that arise as a result

of family disruption through separation and divorce. Harris' chapter is instructive in affording us an understanding of the emotional and social factors that are peculiar to the family as a social unit.

The chapter by Dr. Benjamin Schlesinger and Eugene Stasiuk reviews the conclusions of their extensive research study of remarried couples and the effects of remarriage upon children. Through a presentation of excerpts from taped records, the authors illustrate vividly the emotional forces that operate upon and affect such couples, most of whom have brought to their new marital relationship children from an earlier union. We are in their debt for providing us with a body of information that formerly we could only speculate about. Their new material gives all of us much to reflect on.

Dr. Sally-Anne Milgrim provides us with an unusual series of taped interviews she conducted with prominent professionals who daily deal with divorced couples with adolescent children. From a background of many years' experience, the professional workers speak about their experiences with both parents and their children in many different divorce situations. It is enlightening to look at ourselves through the eyes of those who, in the course of their professional work, reach important decisions that affect our very ways of living, either as intact or separated family units.

In "The Scope of Legal Responsibility," Irving L. Golomb examines the current climate of opinion and practice in the legal profession concerning the responsibility of separated and divorced parents toward their children. It is a sobering experience to realize through Golomb's paper the limited rights and privileges that children from disrupted marital relationships have in the eyes of the law. It is our opinion that this is a whole new area for possible legal reform.

Helen D. Wargotz, in her consideration of the adjustment of children of divorced fathers, reports on a type of guidance service for teen-aged children from broken families that is becoming increasingly familiar, and necessary, in the larger metropolitan areas of the United States. Her experience as founder and director of one such agency in New York City is instructive, and this guidance center may serve as a presently existing model for other communities that seek to better meet the needs of teen-agers from disrupted homes.

Through taped interviews and discussions, the final section of Part I examines how divorced parents from different socioeconomic levels of American society view their situations and family relationships. The information from these interviews offers both an understanding of the multiple problems that divorced parents and their children face as well as a new frame of reference for looking at and coping with many of the difficulties that the dependent child faces in a world no longer secure for him. It is apparent to the editors—as we think it will be to the reader—that both the personal needs of the parents and their social backgrounds are important in shaping attitudes and ideas.

After taking a look at parental responsibilities toward their children, we are better prepared to move to a consideration of how children themselves view their parents, which is the scope of Part II.

MYRON W. HARRIS, Ph. D.

The Child as Hostage

In this chapter, Dr. Myron W. Harris, from a rich background not only in private practice of clinical psychology but also from the vantage point of a former school psychologist, provides an incisive and highly useful picture of how a child becomes a pawn in the power struggles of his parents and often serves as a hostage in the manipulations each parent uses against the other.

Dr. Harris examines some of the more common tactical operations of parents who seek to maintain or regain new sources of emotional security as their marriages become fragmented, and we understand more fully the effects of such tactical maneuvers upon children whose own security becomes threatened.

Human relationships are such that all of us operate on different levels of purpose and communication. There are culturally set and approved of patterns of thinking, feeling, and acting that become established for virtually all social roles, as, for example, the father, the mother, the eldest child, the youngest child, the grandmother, the employer, and the policeman. Much of what makes for security in each individual's life is the degree to which he has been able to recognize and follow the outlines and specific characteristics of the role that he has selected. This is the security that comes from fulfilling the expectations, requirements, and needs of those around us, a security which is gained from the messages of supportive encouragement and approval that we receive. In short, any social grouping—from a two-person dyad to a large societal mass—possesses an internal structure which wishes to hold itself together in its current organic posture. These are the elements that resist change, that praise maintenance of the *status quo*, and that reward continuity of action and life style.

In contrast to this means of gaining security is that which emanates more spontaneously from the essential qualities of the individual's needs before he becomes as socialized a being as customarily happens with chronological maturity. The process of growth has been portrayed as one in which a balance is continuously being struck and developed between one's internal needs as an individuated biological-psychological animal and one's needs to function effectively and acceptably as part of a social unit that involves interrelationships on a regular basis with other members. Thus, there is justification for conceiving of individual personality makeup as a product of the two interacting elements of security-attainment.

In marriage and family relationships, we find the most pressing emphases on role fulfillment—the husband or wife, father or mother, authority and complier, protector and agent for freedom. The father trying to do the proper things for his children must simultaneously be aware of his responsibilities as a husband to his wife. Yet these are the conscious and superficial aspects of responsibility and adaptation which pay little heed to the driving, compelling, unrelenting, sensual, stimulating, and exciting entreaties of the unsocialized narcissist that remains in all of us. It is difficult to portray that part of ourselves without arousing anxiety, guilt, denial, and expectations of opprobrium, for we all like to think of ourselves as rational human beings guided by reason, contemplative concern, deep understanding, and altruism. We may recognize that such less-favored impulses as selfishness, jealousy, vengefulness, desperate needs for being favored and loved, and sheer anger, may be present in our range of feelings. But we are generally compelled to believe that the actions that we finally do take with regard to others whom we profess to love and for whom we have taken on a protective stance, are based on reason, control of these more primitive impulses, and altruism over selfishness. But the fact is that we are still a combination of all the factors that have shaped us, and in the moments of greater stress there is the increased danger that we will be forced to respond with more primitive self-protective measures rather than with those that would stem from an individual whose greatest security came from his own internal sense of achievement, worthwhileness, and self-respect.

It is with this background in mind that we would consider the possibilities for use of the child as hostage in family relationships. A *hostage* is defined as "a person kept as a pledge pending the fulfillment of an agreement." That formalized structure occurs openly only when the circumstances are clearly those of combat, struggle for control, undisguised hostility. The use of hostages in personal relationships in which the conflicts between members are unadmitted or less apparent is, of course, more subtle and therefore more difficult to identify. But let us consider examples of hostaging with children as means of a parent struggling for the fulfillment of an agreement. There are, of course, conscious agreements regarding the rearing of the child—the religion into which he is to be raised, the responsibilities which each marriage partner may take on, the roles which mother and father alternately play in relationship to the child. But these are matters of open agreement and, because the primary communication about them may remain open and admitted, the likelihood of needing to use camouflaged methods of enforcing agreement is lessened.

But what of those cases in which the basis of agreement is unspoken, representing a bargain that has been recognized only in terms below the conscious awareness of both parties? For example, the woman who needs, for reasons bred of her own family background, to believe that she is performing an exceptionally good role as mother and whose criteria for such performance are so highly perfectionistic, so rigorously unwilling to allow any human error or flexibility, that she *must* always consider herself a success, yet always feels herself washed over by failure. For her the parental contract may include the unspoken vow that her husband will always support her every action in relationship to the children, and that he will do this as one facet of a continual recognition and praising of her maternal infallibility. She needs this, the family needs this if she is to continue to operate without excessive self-blame and anxiety, and she is likely to use whatever means are at her disposal to enforce the family's supplying of her requirements. We must realize, of course, that the major amount of this drive and structure to implement it is experienced and communicated at levels below specific verbal awareness.

If the father fails to fulfill his unwritten contract between himself and his wife and begins to criticize her as a mother, or if he begins to criticize her indirectly through criticism of the child, the mother may be unconsciously forced to enjoin the father from this contract-breaking through one of the most readily available methods, *i.e.*, capturing of the child and refusing to allow spontaneous or mutually supportive communication between child and father. She may do this by building up fears of the father ("Wait until your father gets home, he'll take care of you!"; "You had better be quiet, your father's coming up the walk and he can't stand that kind of noise"; "Let's all be careful and not tell Daddy anything about that because he might not understand"; "Your father was very angry at what you did last night, but we talked about it and he agreed not to punish you this time"). Sometimes this is effective, and the father, appreciating his wife's unceasing concern for his feelings and for keeping the children under sufficient control so that they do not irrationally upset him, begins to appreciate and praise the mother so fully that there is reestablished between them a mutually supporting neurotic contract that releases the child—now unneeded—from the position of hostage.

The perceptive reader has undoubtedly wondered what has happened to the child under such circumstances. The child is likely to react with precisely those same characteristics that develop in any individual who is looked upon or used as a device for the gaining of some other goal than his own welfare. He is likely to become distrustful of his parents and doubtful of his own independent worth and value as a person. He may develop symptoms designed to diminish the anxiety which would follow from the disillusionment of his belief that he lives in a comforting, all-protective family world—symptoms of a regressive nature, such as enuresis, infantile speech, diminution of learning ability in school and elsewhere, reduced capacity to socialize independently, etc. Or symptoms of an anger-expressing nature may be seen: explosiveness, constant irritability, withdrawal and depression, or persistently resistant refusals to go along with family-directed programs for his behavior.

Hostages do not generally feel security or faith in their captors and users. They may, if the period of hostaging has gone on for long enough in their lives, accept this as such an unquestioned reality that they adapt submissively, passively, dependently—and thereby lose their psychological lives in a torrent of retreat. The psychological and behavioral symptoms that flow from such submissive and compliant adaptations are in the range of lowered effectiveness. The intellectual functioning level drops, and parents become concerned about low I.Q. The drive for competitive achievement is assailed and often defeated—children avoid the give and take of free relationships with other children, seek to maintain parental protectiveness, and get along well with adults but poorly with children. A general abandonment of striving and self-induced growth activity takes place, and the child may progressively adapt himself more to passive and vegetating activity than to active, curiosity-spurred, adventurous, daring, explorative, expanding growth behavior.

And what of the hostager? We are portraying the behavior of such a parent as being motivated, often unwittingly, by the need to attain a sense of security through the domination and enforced knuckling-under of another person. And, further, the normal parental feelings of experiences of sheltering, nourishment, guiding, providing example and encouragement are infected by the excessive presence of another element that inevitably would be there but within tamed dimensions—the need to gain security through the actions or presence of one's child. When the child is used in this manner, there is frequently introduced a strong sense of guilt or inadequacy in the parent's conception of himself as a father or a mother, a matter which interrupts and roils the streams of parent-child development, so that both parent and child suffer.

IN DIVORCE

Because divorce has meant the breaking up of a relationship in which formerly were invested profound depths of affection, hope, needfulness, and mutually projected expectations of assurance, comfort, respect, and self-fulfillment, the disappointments, grief, and anger that result are inevitably high. The disturbances of self-esteem, the shock to each person's sense of interdependability, the fear that one has failed in a meaningful relationship all lead to an intensification of the struggle to find solace and security for one's self. One means of doing this, of course, is to project all blame and responsibility on the other partner. Fundamentally, however, it may ensue that the attacks on one's security systems are self-directed with feelings of worthlessness, failure, inadequacy, etc., even though these are defended against by powerful, vigorous, unrelenting attacks on the other party. The need for some reestablishment of assurance and respect for one's self is intensified, particularly so with respect to the degree of acrimony that has accompanied the separation and divorce, as well as with respect to the position of the particular parent with regard to the choice of separation and divorce. The motivation for retaliation may not be just an expression of anger but also a means of feeling that one has some degree of control rather than being simply a helpless victim.

The need to dominate the other partner, to prevent any further insult or injury to one's self taking place, is a manifestation of the same phenomenon. The need to find oneself loved and reassured as to being adequate or exceptional as a parent becomes particularly strong when all else is taken away. Thus, the opportunity for utilizing other individuals in this security-pursuing endeavor beckons most strongly—in fact, more strongly to the unconscious parts of ourselves than to the conscious, for the former are desperate, painfully needful, crying, and often panicked, while the latter have managed somehow to be more reasonable and socially restrained. It is obvious that the presence of children makes them an easily available commodity for use in whatever process of restabilization the individual selects.

In what ways, then, may the child be utilized in this parental effort at dealing with the injured tissues of the marriage relationship and of the weakened, damaged, and demeaned sense of self?

These are some possibilities:

1. The child is used as a means of depriving a parent of affection in retaliation for the deprivation of affection that the other parent experienced.

Jerry had been profoundly hurt when he discovered that his wife's reason for leaving him was not, as she had implied, because of their frequent arguments and sexual incompatibility, but rather because of a younger man whom she had met at the adult college classes she was attending, and with whom she had fallen in love in the course of a long clandestine affair. He felt displaced, rejected, and unwanted; and he reacted with all the rage which had been a recurrent problem for him since his early childhood years.

For him, Bea was "an immoral bitch," a woman whose concern for loved ones was so lacking that he could not dare to allow his children to remain dependent on her affection.

The only reasonable method of saving his children was to have his wife declared unfit and for him to take over the custody of the children. The fact that Bea was quite ready to continue in as responsible, caring, and trustworthy a maternal role as she had been before the separation meant little to Jerry, for he had to withdraw love from her as she had withdrawn it from him. He could not, of course, admit to himself that this was the motivation behind his move, and therefore he went to great efforts to establish her incompetence and unworthiness.

The children, torn between both parents, were forced into extreme positions for support of one or the other parent and were thus deprived of the opportunities for finding that both mothering and fathering needs could be met under the circumstances of divorce.

2. The child is used as a means of insuring continued attachment to the divorced spouse.

Elaine had sensed that a breakup was coming for some time. The mutual interests that had marked the early years of their marriage were a continuation of their sharing together as students in college, but soon Jeffrey expanded in his interests as his law practice led to participation in many community and business activities. Elaine was not interested in following this route with him, and she became increasingly separated from participation in what was important to Jeffrey. The result was that she was more often the quiet and discontented housewife than his companion.

When he asked for a divorce, she was torn apart and could not conceive of being able to live without Jeffrey's presence as husband and protector. She did not "fight" the divorce, although she struggled to understand why it was necessary, strove to make Jeffrey understand that they could make a go of life together, and that she would do everything in her power to preserve their marriage.

When the divorce was final, however, the recurrent circumstances were that their child, Hester, repeatedly came down with illnesses or periods of anxiety that necessitated the father's attention. With repeated apologies for disturbing him, Elaine would call Jeffrey and ask for his advice on what to do: Hester would not go to school, she had been sick all night and the doctors could not explain it, she could not go out with him that weekend because she was ill at home but would he come to see her, etc.

Hester was rapidly becoming a chronically sick or disturbed child—not because the mother wanted her to be, but because her own needs to hold onto her husband forced her to use the child as a figure to facilitate Jeffrey's return in some way to complete the marriage contract that had been broken.

3. Total allegiance to one parent is demanded with the concurrent total rejection of the other so that the child becomes the weakened puppet of parental needs.

David and Peggy tore their marriage apart in the divorce court with the same untempered fury that had ripped apart their home and intimacy during their seven years of marriage. They were both volatile and egocentric and seemed to have little capacity to react other than with rage at whatever circumstances of frustration or discomfort they found. Each shared the tendency to blame the other for whatever deprivation or unpleasantnesses life brought along.

There were two children from the marriage—Alan was five and his sister, Jody, was four. Both parents openly attacked the other in their presence, and in fact spoke with undisguised hostility about the other parent to the children. The effort to force them into the position of hostages, held in emotional bondage to the parent with whom they were spending time, was so persisting and unrelenting that the children were forced to alternately deny love to the opposing parent and avow loyalty only to the parent with whom they were currently spending time.

4. The child is used as direct hostage for payment of money or services.

When Joan and Harry divorced, she made certain that quite specific and rigid visitation privileges were spelled out in the agreement. Whenever Harry failed to fulfill his responsibility—being late in support payments, failing to pick up Billy at the designated hour, refusing to pay for extra clothing—Joan would refuse to allow Billy to see Harry at the next visiting time. The child was constantly and openly used as a bargaining device to force Harry to fulfill obligations, both those legally set, on which he was defaulting, and those which Joan herself established as necessary for her and the child's security.

THE CHILDREN

The child's processes of biological, social, and emotional growth continue to take place regardless of the tormented family circumstances. The needs which are present at the different stages of development still press upon him and seek gratification and understanding. The opportunities for the healthy and routine achievement of these gratifications, in ways that permit the child simultaneously to feel that his environment is concerned with his welfare and that he possesses self-generated powers to attain these conditions, become severely threatened. If he begins to be aware, consciously or unconsciously, that the surest route through which such growth-nourishing manifestations of parental caring may be attained is that of submitting himself to being manipulated as part of a power struggle between his parents, his security within his family and within himself becomes severely threatened. He may attempt restoration in various ways, consistent with the distress-reducing mechanisms that have been previously developed in his personality.

Among these possible maneuvers are the following:

1. He may attempt to establish his own countermethods of hostaging with the parents. For example, he may bargain his own spoken allegiance to one or the other parent in exchange for the opportunity of developing a sense of control over each of them, and therefore over the forces that affect his life. The parents may observe this as manipulative behavior designed to gain short-term satisfaction such as material objects, special treats, etc., but the underlying psychological motivation may often be that of gaining security through establishing control of parents as a substitute for the dissolved family stability.

2. Submissive compliance to each parent's pressure may become the method of calming anxiety and attaining immediate reassurance. The problem here, however, is that the only need of the child that is being answered is that of relief from current tension. The ease that is attained is temporary. The deeper needs are unexpressed and unanswered, the child may become accustomed to developing deafness to his own impulses and requirements, and symptoms of distress are certain to be experienced.

3. A continuing battle for self-survival may be expressed aggressively, explosively, and even violently. Jimmy's circumstances were characteristic of this. The angry breakup of his parents continued through the divorce proceedings and afterwards in untrammeled verbal attacks on each other, with Jimmy and his younger brother and sister being grasped as captured pawns by whichever parent was more impulsive and dominating at the moment. Anger would be directed at one of the children if his needs or worries got in the way of the desperate parental efforts to find some stability for themselves. Jimmy's customary responses were panic-driven—he would run out of the house and hide, tear into his mother's room and rip off the bedclothes, throw over tables or book shelves in fits of explosive fury, or shout outrageous curses at one of his parents as the external struggles and internal conflicts intensified.

4. Hostaging through guilt arousal may be utilized in order to remind the parent constantly that she or he is needed for the survival of the child. Kathy was a gentle and affectionate seven year old, the source for her father of considerable comfort and affection that could not be gleaned from his two other children who were already into adolescence by the time of the final breakup of the marriage. The father's departure from the household left Kathy feeling quite abandoned, for the mother-daughter relationship had always been marred by a subtle mutuality of distrust and caution that repeatedly manifested itself in protective rejection. Kathy, in effect, held her own happiness and health as hostage to the continued presence and attention of her father. She would suffer repeated attacks of respiratory disorders, coughing and wheezing in what appeared to be asthmatic attacks. These could only be allayed by the presence of the father, and he was constantly receiving emergency demands from Kathy or her mother to be helpful.

We have seen the distortions of self and relationships to which children and their parents may be driven in their efforts to reestablish under themselves a foundation of security that will permit continued growth and self-realization. The processes through which hostaging may be attempted are inevitably those of utilizing another person in a manipulating manner to achieve one's own freedom from fear and anxiety. Ultimately, however, although we are all creatures of social interrelationships whose self-maturity must involve experiencing ourselves and our needs with and through others, this freedom can be gained only through one's own self-awareness and development.

BENJAMIN SCHLESINGER, Ph. D.,
AND EUGENE STASIUK, M.S.W.

Children of Divorced Parents in Second Marriages

Just how do remarried parents view their children's adjustment to the new family situation? Excerpts from tape-recorded interviews with parents who bring children into a second marriage, as well as those whose mates bring children into the marriage, reveal a number of unexpected problems as well as those commonly anticipated.

This chapter extensively investigates the reality of interpersonal relationships in a remarriage and provides the reader with a number of insights, as the parents view reactions of their children and stepchildren. Also valuable are the suggestions for handling situations in a remarriage, which are made by the respondents interviewed by Dr. Schlesinger and Mr. Stasiuk during their study of almost a hundred couples.

INTRODUCTION

The following material comes from a study on remarriage which was completed in 1969 at the University of Toronto School of Social Work. The study was conceived and directed by Professor Benjamin Schlesinger, who acted as consultant throughout the project, and as editor of the final document. This is the first study of remarriage in Canada and the second in North America. (In 1956, Dr. Bernard completed a study on remarriage in the United States which was published in book form as *Remarriage*, Dryden Press, New York.)

In this study, we define second marriage as a marriage in which one or both partners have been married before, and the first marriage has been dissolved due to divorce or death. We interviewed ninety-six couples; husbands and wives were seen separately by our research team consisting of Judith Bamiling, Edyth Jacobson, Jewell Lanterman, Alex Macrae, Brenden Montgomery, Dee Osachoff, Elizabeth Smith, and Eugene Stasiuk. The couples came predominantly from the Metropolitan Toronto area with some from the province of Ontario within a one-hundred-mile radius of Toronto.

The subjects had brought into the second marriage 109 children, and eighty-nine children were born to the second union. These findings relate to children of divorced parents brought into the second marriage.

ADJUSTMENT

As the majority of the divorced males did not bring their own children into the remarriage, it is significant to note that 69 percent of them said that the children brought into the remarriage were exhibiting adjustment difficulty. The responses of the divorced females—who in all cases except one brought their own children into the remarriage—were almost equally distributed between the affirmative and negative as to whether the children had difficulty in adjusting to membership in the new family.

The respondents were asked to give an explanation as to why they felt the children did or did not find it difficult to adjust to being a member of the new family. Some of their responses may help to give an idea of typical answers.

A divorced male married to a widowed female with children,

and who now has one child of the new union, said: "The children had their set ways and I had to observe how they treated their mother, and learn how to approach them without hurting their feelings."

A divorced female with two children, married to a divorced man with one child, and then having one child of the present union, reported: "It is more difficult for some than others. It is hard for an only child to share a new family. It is hard for a child to change positions in the family system. It depends on the child's relationship with his natural parent."

A divorced female, married to a single man, felt adjustment for her fourteen-year-old son was easy because, "my husband treated my son like an uncle because my boy already had a father."

As indicated by the above quotations, many parents recognized there were difficulties in adjustment that their children had to make in areas of sharing the previous parent, trusting and accepting the new parent's personality and ways, and fitting into the new family system with siblings. However, a gradual adjustment period was indicated as being the usual pattern, with this adjustment or "getting to know each other" starting very often in the courtship. Frankness and honesty in discussion with the children of areas of concern was given a high value. Many respondents realized there were differences between the former and the new parent that took time to adjust to, so that competition of stepparent with former parent was not deemed wise.

COMPARISONS

From responses given by both the natural and the new parent it would seem that approximately 70 percent of the respondents said that children do not compare their former parent to the new parent. Significantly, the divorced females, however, in contrast to the overall opinion, thought comparison by children of former parent to new parent was more common.

A divorced male and a divorced female in a remarriage to which they both brought children said: "I suppose they do [make comparisons] at times, but I know they care for me and are happy. This is all that matters."

A divorced female married to a divorced man who didn't bring his own children to the remarriage said: "There is a marked difference in personalities between the former father and the present father. The children cannot fail to notice the difference, and are confused at times when they want to remain loyal to their own father, but they appreciate what their new father is trying to do for them. The boy especially has trouble as the divorce was a traumatic experience for him at age nine."

A divorced female with one son, married to a divorced man with no children, said: "My son sees his own father two weeks each summer when he is wined and dined. The real father is younger and bends over backwards to impress his son. My present husband doesn't buy my son's affection as his own father does."

Many respondents mentioned that there was no open comparison of the previous and present parent. Many children were too young to remember their natural father or, if they did, they remembered the fights their parents had had, and that their absent parent made "mommy cry." Generally, in these cases, the comparisons were in the new parent's favor, as the child saw the new father making the mother happier.

CONTACT WITH PARENT

With regard to whether or not children maintain contact with their former parent, it is self-evident that only the responses of the divorced persons bringing children into the second marriage were tabulated. Sixty-one percent of all divorced persons who brought children into the remarriage stated that their children maintain some contact with their former parent, whether it be through actual visiting, or through telephone conversations, and/or correspondence.

One divorced female said: "The children are allowed to see their father whenever he wishes to see them, but visits with him and his wife seem to be becoming more unsatisfactory, as the children are getting older and are starting teen-age lives of their own. They are developing their own lines of thought, and now they seem to sometimes find visits with their father an inconvenience rather than a pleasure."

Another divorced mother said: "The children see their father twice a year, but would do it less often if he didn't raise such a fuss."

One divorced male said: "I can't stop the children from seeing their mother. I take them out with their mother, and we buy them things, but my ex-wife's values are confused and competitive."

In general it seemed that whenever contact with the former spouse exists, the contact is dependent on both the children and parents being mutually agreeable to the visit. In many cases, however, geographical distance prevents contact from being too frequent, as it is not uncommon for divorced parties to move some distance apart after the divorce. Thus, contact varies from a weekly or monthly basis in a few cases, to a more general trend toward contact only on special occasions. It was also observed that a number of respondents reported that contact was more frequent in the beginning of the second marriage, and gradually became less with the lapse of time.

CONTACT WITH FAMILY

It seemed that there is a general trend to encourage children to maintain contact with the former parent's family.

One divorced female reported: "My former in-laws are wonderful and understanding people and have also accepted my husband and his daughter."

Another divorced female stated: "The children visit their father's sister and mother and enjoy this family contact more than the contact with their father and his wife."

As contributing factors to the maintenance of contact with the former parent's family and the extent to which contact is upheld, an overall review of the explanations revealed such recurrent themes as geographical distance, acceptance of dissolution of marriage and remarriage by relatives, and agreement of children.

PROBLEMS FACED WITH CHILDREN

The three most difficult problems parents faced with children in remarriage were the following:

    a. Disciplining the children.

    b. Adjusting to the habits and personalities of the children.

    c. Gaining the acceptance of the children.

The divorced males cited the following problem areas:

    a. Cooperation of their children toward new parent.

b. Adjustment to increased activity in the home (especially where teen-agers were involved).
c. Increase in cost.
d. Discipline.
e. Extent of their involvement with the children.
f. Amount of affection to be shown toward stepchildren.
g. Jealousy toward stepchildren.
h. Emotional acceptance of children.
i. Manipulation by female children.
j. Winning their status gradually.
k. Acceptance of children's fixed habits.

The divorced females acknowledged the following difficulties:

a. Cooperation with housework.
b. Lack of respect on children's part for the value of money.
c. Assuaging children's fears of breakup.
d. Discipline.
e. Avoidance of taking sides between children and spouse.
f. Dealing with children's upset after visiting natural father.
g. Negative community attitudes.
h. Rivalry due to divided attention between spouse and children.
i. Adjustment of new parent to children.
j. Interference by relatives (especially grandmothers).
k. Lack of privacy.
l. Fear of children getting on husband's nerves.
m. Fostering a more independent and less clinging attitude in children.
n. Open communication channels between children (especially teen-agers) and spouse.
o. Financial considérations.

FEELINGS OF PARENT TOWARD CHILDREN

A brief survey of the respondents' explanations might serve to identify the problems that arose to cause a reversal of positive feelings toward the children of the former marriage.

A divorced female said: "My daughter is in competition with me for the affection of my husband. I resent the child's time with my spouse, yet he feels he needs to give the child a more realistic image of a father."

A divorced man who did not bring own children to the second marriage said: "My son looks like his first father, and that bothers me. I have more anger toward my son because he balks more and is more disobedient."

Another divorced woman said: "It is more difficult to express my feelings toward my daughter because my husband thinks she's being coddled. He'd like to send the girl to boarding school and end the conflict."

A divorced male who has no children stated: "My son hurt me because after he turned sixteen he decided to go and live with his father."

Another stated: "I feel my daughter had been deprived of a happy home in my first marriage and it makes me feel guilty. Therefore, I protect her more now, and it's harder to say no to her than to the other kids."

On the other hand, a wide assortment of explanations was given for the growth of more positive feelings between parent and children of the former marriage. Some of these were:

DIVORCED MALES WHO BROUGHT IN OWN CHILDREN

—I feel more relaxed now and am more content to let the children come to me when and if they need me.

—We tried not to make any difference between the children. They are loved and treated the same.

DIVORCED FEMALES

—We are closer. I don't feel pressure.

—I feel less guilty about him, and can relax with him more easily because he is so happy.

—I always felt completely responsible alone for their welfare and upbringing, but now I do not feel alone in decisions that must be made. I have someone to turn to and share decisions with.

DIVORCED MALES WHO DID NOT BRING IN CHILDREN

The responses of the divorced males who had children of their first marriage but did not bring them into the remarriage were studied separately in answer to the question about whether or not their feelings to the children of the previous marriage had altered in any way since their remarriage.

The general trend seemed to indicate that the divorced males have difficulty in overcoming the loss of their children. They express a desire to know more about their children, and feel guilty about the lack of, or loss of, contact with their children. Many respondents still felt a high degree of attachment toward the children of their previous marriage as exemplified by the following responses:

—They are not near me, so I long to see them. I am forgetting about them, but wonder about their well-being. I know I love and miss them. I wish I had some real control over their futures, education, etc.

—I was amazed and hurt at how little my grown children were aware of how much of myself I thought I had put into their upbringing and was startled at the hold my wife had over them. They may come to realize this in time, but I am much more inclined to regard them as two young acquaintances rather than enjoy the warmth I had expected I would find.

—I still have a fatherly feeling toward him, but it diminishes when I am away from him.

—I missed them horribly. It was a definite physical hole. My remarriage didn't help it much, until a child was born to close the gap. I feel they don't need me as much as I think they do, although I still have some guilt feelings.

—My relationship with my daughter is better. The first marriage was not happy. Therefore, a barrier built up which affected my relationship with my daughter. I waited too long for a divorce because of the child.

THE STEPCHILD AND THE PARENT

Some of the reasons respondents gave for their change of feelings toward their stepchildren included the following:

DIVORCED MALES—FAVORABLE RESPONSES

—Once we got it all sorted out, it became better, especially with regard to the older children. I had to prove to them that I was all right. Both their first father and I sat down and explained the breakup of the first marriage.

—We understand each other much better. I can recognize their good characteristics more, and they are making reasonable efforts to correct those which I think are to their own detriment.

—There hasn't been any changes except I love them more than ever, because I never think of them ever belonging to anyone else.

—I feel a greater responsibility to his future.

DIVORCED MALES—UNFAVORABLE RESPONSES

—I feel annoyed due to her rebelliousness. Perhaps I cause it.

—I feel more at ease and more familiar with them now. It's a matter of pride. These children don't have the scholastic ability mine do. I compared them as one would a Cadillac to a Volkswagen. I'm beginning to realize this is only a part, however.

—I had difficulty accepting them emotionally. I didn't know how to treat them. It has to be a gradual change. Now they're starting to accept my word willingly, but it's still difficult.

DIVORCED FEMALES—FAVORABLE RESPONSES

—Just grow to love them more.

—My husband had given such a true picture of the children's characteristics that the new strain of the unexpected has disappeared.

—I now accept them as my own.

DIVORCED FEMALES—UNFAVORABLE RESPONSES

We do what we can. There's still a strangeness. We differ in personalities. The boy is untidy, rowdy, but stable.

—She's difficult to raise but I wanted to be her mother and raise her, and so I am.

ADVICE TO PARENTS

We asked our respondents, "What advice would you give parents of children in a remarriage?"

DIVORCED FEMALES

—Move slowly. Be very sure of yourself in the new marriage. Kids can sense it if there is uncertainty. You must feel it is completely right.

—Husband and wife should agree on their ideas of child-rearing and accept each other's ideas of discipline. If you don't know each other's ideas of child-rearing, then you might as well forget it.

—Make sure children will be accepted by your spouse, as it is hard for children to accept a stepparent.

DIVORCED MALES

—Some men take very well to a new family. If not, you'd better be aware of the problems involved—more obligations, restricted freedom, etc. You can ruin all the people involved.

—Know your wife's attitude toward your own children even if you do not have custody of them, and know her attitudes as to how she would expect her children to be treated in the new marriage. Both spouses should have an idea about the attitude of the children to the new spouse.

—You have to decide to marry wife and children.

DIVORCED-DIVORCED PAIR

—Treat them all the same. Show no favoritism. Love one as much as the others.

—Always remember children are human beings, too. Love them above all. Sit down and talk the problems out and try to understand their point of view, for even young people know what they desire. Be interested in what they do.

—The benefits to both sets of children arising from the establishment of a proper home instead of two broken homes should be made evident to them.

—Include the children often in activities so they will not feel they have been replaced.

—Prior to getting married both parents of the new marriage should outline to children what is what. The woman must clue in her husband as to what she's been doing so a new family unit can be formed. Explain to the children as much as they can understand about the roles of the new parent. Don't talk to the children about things that should be discussed between a man and wife only.

—Don't show favoritism to your own children. Otherwise it won't be a happy marriage. I didn't realize it until later, but one girl resented me for showing favoritism to the other.

—It's important to give them love without insisting that they identify you as their parent. Accept their clash of loyalties and love them all fairly.

—Let children discuss their feelings and work out any problems they may have. They should maintain contact with the previous parent because he is an important part of their lives, and any rejection would be harmful.

—Let the real parent do the major disciplining instead of the new parent at first, because children accept discipline of their own parent easier, and they might tend to feel rejected by the new parent if he does the disciplining.

INVOLVEMENT OF CHILDREN OF FIRST MARRIAGE

Some general comments respondents gave may be helpful in assessing the extent of involvement parents have with children of the first marriage.

—Encourage them to maintain former interests, and carry on as usual.

—We do everything together now, but if he were older, he'd have a life more of his own.

—Everything is done as a family unit. We help the children with their school work, but not on a regular basis, just when they need it.

—I take the children out occasionally alone to a movie or supper, or work with them in the garden. When I'm alone with only one of them, it makes it easier to discuss personal problems.

SEX DIFFERENCES IN CHILDREN

We wondered whether there were any special problems in a remarriage which parents encountered with boys as opposed to girls. In general, most respondents did not differentiate, as they felt the majority of problems for children in a remarriage, regardless of sex, required a similar approach. However, there was a significant number of respondents who made comments pertaining to raising boys or girls in a remarriage.

NEW FEMALE PARENTS OF BOYS

—The new spouse must be introduced as requiring respect and as being a source of authority. I think this gives more security and leadership than the picture of a friend. My stepsons were asked to call me mother.

—Ask the old parent to have patience while you, as a new parent, learn. You must take responsibility instead of waiting for the old parent to make you. The old parent must give you support.

—Try to have the children realize before you remarry that you love the new husband very much and hope they will get to love you, too. Try to be patient and understanding. They might not appreciate that it is for their good also. We are going into this as a family. We took a vote and verdict was unanimous to accept the new parent.

NEW MALE PARENTS OF BOYS

—Explain fully what is happening to them. Don't insist fully that they accept you as daddy. It will come unostentatiously later. Don't push it.

—Accept the boys and do all the activities you can with them. Accept their responsibilities, *i.e.*, if they want a paper route, discuss it with them. Be consistent. Praise them a lot. Be lenient by giving them a little leeway, but not too much. Adjust your habits as well as asking them to adjust theirs, *e.g.*, now I pick up my clothes.

—Recognize that this is a new situation. Try very hard to understand the other person's point of view.

NATURAL FEMALE PARENTS OF BOYS

—If he has regular contact with his own father, the new father should act in an adult male-friend pattern.

—Foster a relationship between your boy and the man you're planning to marry before you marry.

—Boys especially, I think, want the presence of a father, and you must let the man rule where boys are concerned, so the boys see it is a permanent, steady influence.

—The stepfather has to be tolerant. Boys expect a far greater relationship from him, but because of the age difference, the expectations for the stepfather to be a grown-up playmate is difficult. The stepfather must make it clear from the beginning who he is, and then adjust to being a stepfather.

—I believe the husband should tell boys about sex. The husband should be the disciplining force. . . . The husband should adopt his stepson as soon as possible. I think it should be a law; otherwise it causes needless aggravation. I was called by the school authorities to explain to my son's school companion, because my son had retained his natural father's name.

NEW FEMALE PARENTS OF GIRLS

—The new parent must give recognition to the first mother. Don't tear apart or criticize the memory of the first mother. Make her feel free to talk about the first mother. If there's conflict, point out to the girl that everybody is different. Keep communication as open as possible.

—The parent shouldn't expect his new partner to assume the mother role immediately just because you are married. You have to grow into it and live with the child. If there are children of the new union, they should not be treated differently.

NEW MALE PARENTS OF GIRLS

—Don't dwell on fact that they came from a previous marriage.

—Treat them as if they were your own to the best of your ability. Participate with them in activities. Hear out their problems.

—Both parents should get together and stand firm on all matters. If my child asks me for something special that I think her mom should know about, I say that if it's O.K. with her mom, it's O.K. with me. So we never have the daughter playing me off against her mom or vice versa.

—It's a question of people coming to form relationships in a natural way, and working as a team.

RESEMBLANCE TO FORMER PARENT

As far as the natural parent was concerned, there were few who stated that the similarity in physical appearance of their children to their former spouse caused any problem. Their responses included the following:

—It worries me because I see so much of his father there. I wonder if he'll do the same things his father did.

—My daughter's mannerisms of sluggishness and forgetfulness are like her father's. This bugs me.

—This mystifies me. My son's facial features and personal attitudes are more acutely like his father's immediately after visiting his father. This upsets me more than the facial resemblance. I know my son's father uses him more or less to continue a relationship with me and to peek into my present life, even though in the past he did not want me, nor marriage, nor a family. Frankly I fear this man and what he can do to our son, not from any guilt on my part, but from the conditioning of the marriage with him.

—To a certain degree when I see my son looking like his father, I hope he will not develop what I considered harmful personality traits, and find I try to steer him away from actions that seem familiar. I don't know if this is right or wrong.

ADOPTION IN REMARRIAGE

In answer to whether or not the new parent adopted the children of the first marriage, an astounding 63 percent in our sample replied that they had not adopted the children from their spouse's previous marriage. Seventy-five percent of divorced males had not filed for adoption, and 63 percent of the divorced females had not done so.

Some of the reasons which divorced male respondents gave for not adopting were the following:

—The son is the only male in his generation to carry on the family name. His grandmother thinks this is more important then anything else, and pressures her son not to allow adoption.

—Our children are girls. We felt that when they get married they will change their names anyway.

—Because the former husband would have caused too much trouble legally, I haven't adopted the girls. He has a bad temper. Our lawyer wrote to him, but he refused. The girls adopted my name, not legally, but plan to do so on their own when they are of age.

—Because of her inheritance, I haven't adopted her. It's not fair to the kid, as money is there for her.

—I have not adopted the children yet. They go under my name, but it costs $125 for each adoption. I hope to do so eventually.

—The boy does not appear to desire adoption. He still is in close contact with his father, who would be opposed. Therefore, it has never been considered.

Although in a large percentage of the cases the new parent did not legally adopt the children brought into the remarriage, there was a substantial percentage who had overcome the difficulties described in the foregoing responses—problems of inheritance, disagreement of ex-spouse, financial expense, negligence, or ignorance. Primarily, however, what seemed to be a recurring motivational factor for seeking to adopt children is the emotional readiness of both parents and children to accept adoption.

In many cases, the children actually asked to be adopted, and in effect psychologically forced their parents to recognize and understand their needs to be adopted. In essence, some of these needs as spelled out by the respondents were: as follows: "It makes them feel good, they're wanted"; "Two surnames in the family makes it hard on children because they always have to explain"; "Adoption helped to unjumble our family. Now the children call each other brother and sister without explanation"; "It's very important to the children. It means they've meant enough to you for you to go out of your way"; "For practical reasons adoption assures that the new spouse receives the legally constituted portion of estate, as well as the children."

It seemed that there were variations in the lapse of time between the remarriage and the application for adoption of the children. Some respondents made immediate application and were able to effect legal adoption within a period of months; others did not apply until some years had elapsed. Parents who did adopt mentioned that they had discussed adoption with the children in terms of benefits and procedures. In some cases, discussions lasted over a period of time, allowing for individual expression of opinion. After adoption had been finalized, several respondents used this date to celebrate the occasion annually by going out for a family dinner. In the words of one respondent, "We saw no alternative but to adopt. After considerable legal expense we found out that the whole thing could have been done by the Children's Aid Society free of charge. Whatever the cost, it was worth it."

CUSTODY OF CHILDREN

Our respondents were asked if they would care to explain the reasons that custody of the children of the first marriage had been awarded to them or to their spouse. The following explanations are samples of what the divorced males and females said:

DIVORCED MALES

—When the separation took place the children were young and I could not care for them.

—Custody was awarded by the court to me as my first wife was promiscuous and committed to a hospital.

—It was better for them with their mother. She is a good mother. There's no friction now, and the kids get along well.

—I had to take the blame for adultery so I couldn't have the child.

—I didn't have the heart to take the child away from his mother. Both my first wife and her new husband wanted the boy.

—It was mutually agreed on after my daughter was consulted and chose to remain with her mother.

—We squabbled. I signed the custody order only after I got visiting privileges.

DIVORCED FEMALES

—My previous husband was guilty of adultery, so the court awarded me custody of the children.

—For one thing, I would not have separated without custody, and my previous husband was not in a position to look after two girls.

—I have custody of one child and my ex-husband has custody of the other two. I was sick with nerves at the time and felt I couldn't handle all three kids. My ex-husband took the first and third child because there was less fighting between them.

—My first spouse never wanted custody. He had trouble enough in keeping himself. He wasn't stable enough to raise him.

—According to our agreement, college education was to be provided for both children by the father, with some child support continuing until my son reached twenty-one, as long as he was still a student.

—I lost custody because of medical reasons, although I got visitation rights. However, I don't see my daughter now.

CONCLUSIONS

Many respondents felt that happiness was achieved by the children in a remarriage. Happiness was variously defined as emotional and financial security; regaining self-confidence and pride; finding more complete guidance, love, and warmth; broadening and understanding; relief from anxiety over the parent's unsettled emotions and conflicts; and a reduction in pressure for the children who felt a responsibility for the parent.

The reestablishment of a family life through remarriage was considered a basic need for children, as evident from such descriptive phrases as the following: "Family life establishes stability in the home"; "increases involvement and sharing with family members"; "broadens relationships with parents, siblings, and relatives"; "eliminates the stigma of being 'different' "; "fosters a resumption of normal household duties and roles."

Dual parenthood was considered by our respondents of both sexes as a very important source of satisfaction. Our respondents also felt that two parents could offer children more love and understanding; a greater participation in interests and activities; more scope for character building; an appropriately balanced degree of discipline; and an extended social relationship with the new parent.

SALLY-ANNE MILGRIM, Ph. D.

The Adolescent in Relation to His Separated yet Inseparable Parents

Much of the material presented in this book was derived from the protagonists in a second-marriage relationship, yet many of the decisions concerning their children were derived from contacts with social agencies designed to protect the interests of the family as an institution. How do professionals in medicine, the law, the courts, and the community view the children of disrupted marriages?

Dr. Milgrim provides a taped record of the thoughts of Dr. Nathan Ackerman, Judge Gilbert Ramirez, Mrs. Harriet Pilpel, and Dr. Olivia Edwards, whose daily responsibilities within their particular area of competence frequently confront them with decisions to be made on behalf of the children of separation and divorce. The sum of their concern for the welfare of the children who come before them provides the reader with insight into the multiplexity of problems, as well as the sympathy and tenderness often hidden behind the official title.

Warring adults do not make effective parents. Yet, the adolescent who is awarded by the court to one parent or the other as the result of a divorce decree or separation agreement begins a new phase of his life with a parent who is fresh home from the battlefield. Though the "hurly-burly's done, and the battle's lost and won," it takes time, sometimes forever, for the husband and wife to realize that the war is over between them as sexual partners. Furthermore, as parents they may never have been aware that their adolescent child has been right up front fighting alongside them. Unless the spouse who gains custody of the adolescent expects to carry off an emotional cripple from the battlefield, he had better stop warring as a parent.

This is one of the major conclusions drawn from four interviews held in New York with Dr. Nathan Ackerman, psychiatrist and Director of the Family Institute in Manhattan; Judge Gilbert Ramirez of the Family Court in Brooklyn; Mrs. Harriet Pilpel, Counsel to Planned Parenthood-World Population, and Consultant to the Special Committee on Divorce and Marriage Law of the National Conference of Commissioners on Uniform State Laws; and Dr. Olivia Edwards, Chief of Community and Group Projects at the Northside Center for Child Development in New York City.

The following comments (with minor adaptations from the spoken to the printed word) have been extracted from the tapes of these individual interviews. The four people were simply asked to speak with the interviewer on whatever they felt would be most helpful to the parent who had custody of the adolescent. No questions were prepared beforehand so that each person interviewed was free to speak on whatever he knew best and on whatever he felt most qualified. Questions or comments on the part of the interviewer which arose from the discussions are printed in italics.

DR. NATHAN ACKERMAN

The whole problem hinges on the simple human principle that the husband and the wife can be separated or divorced, but the parental couple cannot. They remain a pair of parents, biological in sense, forever. With respect to the offspring, the issue revolves around the emotional and social capacity of the father and mother to remain responsible, effective parents, even though the sexual union has been dissolved. How that works out depends on the whole evolution of the relationship. Unfortunately, many people dissolve the sexual union and in so doing are incapacitated in terms of being able to maintain a continuity of the parental partnership for their offspring.

The teen-ager in particular catches the brunt of the disturbance of the husband-wife relationship. He is first laden, and I mean laden, with an excessive emotional task of holding his two parents together and preventing the divorce, and in that position, he is expected to be the healer of the marriage. Again and again, one sees situations where a teen-ager first carries the burden of trying to hold his parents' marriage together, and when that fails, there is a burst of feeling of vengeance, because his own survival and his own security are at stake in the continuity of the marital relationship. He first carries the burden in the role of healer or preserver of the marriage, and then he turns into a destroyer of the marriage.

He feels a certain guilt then?

No, whether he feels a burden of guilt or not depends on how he has responded to the imposition of the burden to hold his mother and father together as a marital pair. And it is also influenced by the whole history of his life development in terms of whether he has been caught in an oedipal triangle. He may be overattached to his mother and unconsciously want his father out, even while he consciously rejects that role. He covers up his uneasiness about it, and then tries to hold his parents together as a married couple. Now, you know one talks in a vacuum without being specific about a given family.

It's very difficult.

And there are all kinds of variations on the theme, depending upon the whole developmental history of the family, the life cycle of that family, whether the teen-ager is an only child or has a number of siblings, etc. Also it is influenced by the role of the parents' parents. They, too, if they still live, become involved in the adjudication of the marital conflict and play a part in either holding the husband and wife together or breaking them apart. So three generations are involved. Now, insofar as the teen-ager is pushed into the position of the parents leaning on him to hold the marriage together, he is pinch-hitting for the influence of the grandparents. That implies a degree of reversal of the customary roles of the generations: the troubled parents become children in the emotional sense, and the teen-ager becomes a protective parent who is symbolically propelled into a parental position for the parent.

. . . A great deal depends on how the teen-ager has been emotionally exploited to be an ally of one parent against the other. I've seen people divorced where there's no letup in the war between the man and the woman at all. A vicious battle becomes perpetuated around the will of winning the alliance of the teen-age offspring from the other parent, with all kinds of manipulations to poison the mind of the teen-ager against one or the other parent. A lot of brainwashing is involved. In the worst cases, the exploitation of the teen-ager gets linked up with a perpetual war about how the monies of the family are going to be divided.

Shouldn't that be settled at the time of the divorce?

It's never all settled. Almost never. You can make any provisions you like in terms of alimony, but that still leaves the door wide open if there is a disposition in that direction for an unending war about particular expenditures: education, health, special schooling, summer camps. As long as there is a need to perpetuate the war, these people can always find a peg to hang their hat on. That's why in some divorce papers there are provisions for arbitration of certain disputes with a professional person. Sometimes it's a single individual, a psychiatrist; sometimes it's a committee. There is always the necessity in life for communication between the father and the mother about this or that aspect of their mutual teen-ager's future.

Do you recommend that arbitration be resorted to?

On principle, it is better if they can preserve the capacity for friendship, for cooperation, for effective dealing with their differences, without a third party. That is ideal. Even though they break up as husband and wife, they should preserve a certain allegiance as mother and father, and at that level talk effectively with one another about schooling, health, the dentist, or whatever. For example, the choice of college is often a place where a pair of divorced parents get into great difficulty with one another, or the sexual life of the offspring, or an engagement, or a marriage.

. . . I'm not happy with this discussion. It's in a vacuum, because it's not tied to particular cases, and families are extremely diverse.

Yet you seem to have made the generalization that although couples split sexually, they cannot split as parents.

Well, the problem is influenced by our cultural traditions. We're in a culture where a monogamous family is the dominant pattern, at least in theory, and the sexual union and the parental union are joined. There's a difference, however, between the formal aspect of the cultural standard and the personal informal realities. That's the hypocrisy of our culture, if you want to put it that way. But in a larger historical setting, the thing that mattered was parents and children, not fidelity in the sexual union. The only reason for marriage, which is a social invention, was binding the parents to a commitment to the children. Historically, there was no essential bond between marriage and sex. There was marriage with sex, marriage without sex, sex without marriage. The thing that has been important for the continuity of society has been the responsible relations of parents and children.

I think it is unfortunate in our culture where there is a shift in the sexual mores, where in the formal sense the sexual union and the parental union should be one, in fact they are not one. There is no real clarity of tradition; there is no clarity in the law; there is no clarity in the transmission of values from generation to generation about the parent-child relations. There is confusion, almost chaos, in our culture about the commitment of parents to children. There is also confusion and chaos about the commitment of children to parents, because that's a two way thing. Here we have a condition where there is a shift in the sexual mores and rapid changes in the divorce laws.

Across the country, there is one divorce for every four marriages, but in California, it's one to one. There are as many divorces as there are marriages. In California the laws have changed. You can have a divorce by simply saying you are not compatible. Now, California is a peculiar state in many respects, but the change in the laws of California is a harbinger of what may happen across the country in the different states. But, in a way that's a symptom of the extraordinary shift in human-relations patterns, not just husband-wife relations, but all human relations, particularly a transformation in the pattern of family, the institutional family across three generations.

In respect to marriage, divorce, and the care of the offspring, what is relevant is something that I've observed for many years. I've never seen a family where the divorce between the husband and wife is not parallel with manifestations of divorce between the parents and grandparents, and parents and children. This means that in the literal sense divorce of the husband and wife union is a symptom of alienation and estrangement of family relations across three generations.

Relevant to this is a phenomenon called "family anomie" . . . which is reflected in a lack of consensus on values, a disturbance in identity relations, and a pervasive sense of powerlessness. That's number one. Number two is chronic immaturity, the inability to assume effective responsibility and an impaired potential for viable family growth. Number three is discontinuity and incongruity in the relation between family and society. This is a "disease" of our time. You know the issue is not so much the literal aspects of divorce: the effect on the husband and wife, the father and mother, and the effect on the teen-ager; but in a much broader sense, it is a question of what happens as a result of the trend toward family breakdown and decay in our changing society. This trend toward family disorganization is not just limited to a small percentage of the community. It affects certain families more than others, certain families earlier than others, but it is a very widespread social trend influenced by the chaos of the times, a cutting-off of tradition and the inability to be guided by the past, the inability to predict the future, and the lack of guidelines in the present.

How do you attempt to help parents and teen-agers when there is a breakdown in family relations?

If you are going to be effective, you are going to have to deal with all the elements of the behavior system, regardless of the rupture of the sexual unit. If you are going to be effective, you are going to have to sit down with the teen-ager and the mother and the father, and you may have to include grandparents, and you may have to deal at different levels with multiple family constellations, if the mother and father are remarried. One can't cope with the experiences of a teen-ager who is the product of a ruptured marital union in isolation; so you have to sit face to face with that teen-ager and his mother and his father at the same time.

JUDGE GILBERT RAMIREZ

When a case comes before me involving an adolescent, he is already in trouble, either on a delinquency petition with society or on a PINS (Persons in Need of Supervision) petition with the parent, or on a neglect petition, meaning that the parent has been allegedly guilty of neglecting the child. My own experience has been that all three petitions amount to virtually the same thing. It's usually a result of the parent's neglect. We find that the child has been disobedient and sometimes so inordinately unruly that he becomes a delinquent and strikes out at society. Now I find that the major problem is with the parent who has custody and thinks that because he has it, he has the title and control over the child against the other parent. The mother uses that child as a weapon against the father. I say the mother because in the vast majority of cases, she is awarded custody. Sometimes the father is awarded custody in those cases where the mother relinquishes it or the court finds that she is mentally, morally, or physically unable to care for the child. When the woman has custody, we find that she feels the child is a possession of hers along with the personal property in the house. And there are various problems: she may remarry, begin to develop a family from the second marriage, or she may have to go out and earn a living. She may find that she cannot be with the child most of the time, or she's in a running battle with her former husband. This may create all kinds of guilt feelings on the part of the child if he shows any emotion for his father. The mother very frequently feels this is a betrayal. All too often we find that instead of the woman offering any help, emotional support, or guidance to the child, she begins to use him as a support, and whenever the child cannot give that emotional support, she turns on him. We have the case where the child gets into trouble in school. Instead of the mother reacting normally and quietly and patiently to that problem, she turns on him because she feels that by his acting out in school, he has betrayed her, somehow.

. . . Sometimes the mother will try to be a substitute for the father, while still playing the role of the mother, and that's almost beyond the ability of any single parent to do. Sometimes she does this because she wants to oust the father from the mind of the child. Sometimes she does it because she has guilt feelings. She has deprived the child of a father; therefore, she must now be a father substitute for the child as well as the mother. This is very, very hard on the girls as well as the boys. Obviously, it's very hard on the boys, because the mother seeks to control the boy's life to the point that he must eventually rebel.

She can't be the father. What can she do by way of substitution?

Frankly, what I can suggest is guidance with a professional. I don't consider myself a professional in that field. I'm quick to give advice as I see the problem. I know the mother listens to me simply because she knows that I can change the pattern of visitation, and change by law the relationship between the mother and child, by granting the father greater rights and limiting the rights of the mother. Judges view the child not as a possession of any one parent, but as a ward of the court, and no parent has title or deed to the child.

Doesn't the adolescent have certain rights? Can't he say, "I don't want to be with this parent?"

Yes, the child has the right to come forward. In fact it is fairly recent that all our statutes indicate that the purpose of custody and visitation is to do things that are in the best interest of the child. The child indicates a preference that must be given some weight, although it doesn't necessarily mean that he is in a position to make that kind of a decision, or that the court will be absolutely controlled by what he has to offer. I personally give the child a great deal of opportunity to express himself.

The mother then who has custody is not only afraid of the judge who can change the situation but also of the child who might say, "Well, you're not treating me just the way I want to be treated, and therefore, I'll leave." She fears you and she fears the child. She's just loaded with fears. What about the mother going to see a psychiatrist together with the father?

It's difficult when they're divorced, and they want nothing to do with each other. They hate each other. There is an incredible anger there. There's a hatred, and one can't speak about the one to the other without getting that person to virtually explode. It is a continuing war to the death. I see so many of these situations, because it is in the nature of things in our court. We feel that it is essential to the child to be well balanced in his relationship to both parents, not to favor one over the other, but rather to have a working relationship. Any feeling of love for one parent and hatred for the other only results in guilt feelings for the child. It leaves an ugly scar on the child's emotional being and a vacuum that can only result in incalculable harm to him in later years. When the mother insists that the child hate his father, instead of developing a normal human being, she is developing an emotional cripple.

Would you recommend that before anything be determined that both parents see a psychiatrist?

Yes. I think that the most important single individual in these cases is a psychiatrist. The ideal thing would be to have a group headed by a psychiatrist intervene in all these cases and have this group interview the mother, speak with the father, examine the child, and speak with anybody else connected with this picture. The group, consisting of the psychiatrist and perhaps a social worker or people in other related fields, should submit to the court a comprehensive report with recommendations as to custody and plan of visitation.

What happened to the ruling in New York State that parents were to seek help prior to getting a divorce?

That's on paper

Why can't it be enforced?

It can, but unfortunately there is a staff of only a few people in each county, due to lack of adequate financing; and there are thousands of people applying for divorce every year. There are only a handful of people in the Conciliation Bureau.

It should never have been called that.

What's in a name?

Well, I don't think it's just the name, but the idea behind it. The idea that parents should submit themselves to the possibility of conciliation at a time when they are really at war is repulsive to them. If instead they viewed the psychiatrist not as a conciliatory measure but as a supportive one, they might be more willing to see him. Even though they very definitely intend to split, and as a matter of fact, specifically because they intend to split, they should have the support, especially for the children.

Yes, good! But, that's a new concept . . .

Seeing a psychiatrist for supportive measures at this time was not intended by the bill?

No, all that was intended was to bring the parties together with a view to possible reconciliation.

That's unfortunate, because if we think of the two people about to be divorced remaining as parents after the divorce, they really need that support for the sake of the children.

That is an entirely novel concept to the law. Even on conciliation, which traditionally has been the thing that has always come up in discussions of legislation relative to "quick divorces," there should be an opportunity to let off steam prior to obtaining a final decree. The conciliation service can only function if it is staffed by well-trained professionals. The fact is that our present conciliation service is only available to the small number of litigants who formally express their desire to avail themselves of this service. If one or the other says "hopelessly incompatible," that's the end of it. Nothing beyond conciliation was ever contemplated. Now, I agree with you; I think that the question of proper parenthood and guidance is of the utmost importance, regardless of the outcome of the divorce action.

What further advice would you give the mother who has custody of the adolescent?

She has custody of the child, and no one is going to take him from her; but there are certain responsibilities that attach to custody. If the child is an adolescent, he has a mind of his own, and she may not suppress him. The child should make his own decision regarding a vocation. All the parent can do is guide him, but not impose a vocation upon him. The husband has a right to visitation. She cannot take that right away from him, and it's the best thing that can happen to the child. Let the father continue to be interested in him. If the woman makes it difficult for the man, he may eventually stop visiting the child; and it will be the child's loss, because the time will come when the father will show as little interest in the child as he shows for the child's mother. He will be as indifferent to the child as he is hostile to the mother, and he will lose nothing. He just gets rid of something he didn't need in the first place. To the mother who says, "I worry when my child is with his father," I say, "Why don't you take a couple of aspirins."

To the father I say, "You have the right to visit with your child, but the right to bring up the child is the mother's. When you're with him, don't talk about the mother. Don't tell him to do anything that would irritate his mother. Don't tell him to wear white shoes when she says black, because remember, after all is said and done, it's the mother's responsibility to bring up the child. Much as you'd like to be able to bring him up, the court has granted custody to her, so satisfy yourself with the fact that you're going to have the child only once or twice a week, and do the best you can for him during those hours. Don't convert that child into a rebel against his mother, because you're only going to hurt the child in the long run, and develop a disturbed human being."

MRS. HARRIET PILPEL

When we are talking about adolescents, we're talking about people who are realistically going to make up their own minds. Matters of custody are usually determined, certainly in middle- and upper income groups, by a separation agreement between the parents, and that separation agreement is normally made the basis for a subsequent divorce decree. Now I would say upwards of 90 percent, maybe 95 percent, of custody matters in dissolving marriages are determined that way. They are bitterly fought through, usually with both parties having attorneys, but by the time they have finished, the court really has nothing to say about it, and theoretically the adolescent has nothing to say about it. The mother and father have made this disposition. In the final analysis, however, you cannot make an adolescent live with anybody he doesn't want to live with. I have had the experience of the mother and father battling back and forth over custody, only to have the adolescent in effect thumb his nose at the whole situation and announce, "I am going to live with my mother," or, "I'm going to live with my father," or in some cases, "I am going to live with my grandmother," or somebody else. Remember, adolescents have rights, both realistically in the terms that I just mentioned and legally. More and more, it is being recognized that they do have rights. Therefore, I think it is important that they be regarded as persons and be consulted, rather than be disposed of as if they were simply another item along with the other things on the check list for a separation agreement.

As to the advice I would have the parent with whom the adolescent is living . . . If the parent attempts to alienate the adolescent from the other parent, the chances are that that parent will lose the adolescent altogether. As a parent myself, I'm aware that during adolescence, children tend to resent whoever is exerting any control over them. If they come from a united family, they resent both their parents. If they come from a family where there is just a mother or just a father, they will resent the person in charge. If that person attempts to show that the other parent, the one who is not in charge, is no good at all, the natural resentment against the parent they are living with will simply boil over, and they will move over to the other parent. Therefore, it has always been my feeling that the parent who has custody should do everything humanly possible to maintain a warm and friendly relationship between the child and the other parent, regardless of what the feeling is between the two parents.

If the mother has custody of the child, does she have to pick up where the father left off in any way?

Well, what I'm trying to say is that the father should not have left off. There are women who have never assumed any responsibility for the financial management of the household, and they are suddenly the ones who are going to get money with which to pay the bills, and they have to make many decisions of a kind they never had to make before. In that position they become a more functioning member of the family group, and may inspire more confidence on the part of their adolescent children. I would think the best thing for them to do in such circumstances would be to treat the children as much as possible as participants and partners. My own feeling is that kids from about ten or eleven on are capable of a great deal more intelligent decision-making and consideration than they are usually given credit for.

. . . I suspect that many adolescents probably feel somehow partially responsible for the separation of their parents, even if in fact —and as usually is the case—they have no responsibility for it.

Do you make any recommendations to clients regarding help for their adolescents?

I don't consider that it is the function of a lawyer who is not a trained psychologist to do any counseling other than that incident to making an agreement setting forth a decent framework for the parties to live within. Wherever possible I do get my clients to go to marriage counselors, or psychologists, or psychiatrists, if not for the purpose of an amicable—or as amicable as possible—separation. In the case of the woman particularly, counseling is often very badly needed. If the husband is precipitating the separation, the woman is likely to be suffering from lack of self-esteem. She's also likely to be terribly frightened. In such circumstances, expert psychological counseling of some kind is extremely helpful, not necessarily to keep the marriage together, but to enable the woman to go on functioning and not feel like a social reject. I've seen a number of men also who feel that somehow the breakup of the marriage is their failure, that they have failed. They, too, often become very depressed, and again a therapist or whatever you want to call a counselor can be very helpful. People need to find out that almost always the breakup of a marriage is the fault of both spouses, or neither, that they are both guiltless and both at fault (depending on how you look at it). They need to find out what their problems are—apart from their spouse's problems—if for no other reason than to avoid making the same mistake in choice or action in their next marriage.

What about the law in New York State providing for such help?

In New York State there is a so-called compulsory conciliation procedure, but it has not worked well, partly because there just aren't enough qualified people to give the help needed. Expert counseling can help, and intensified training of more and better marriage counselors would go a long way to preventing divorce or, where it can't be prevented, to making it a more civilized process, not only for parents but also for children whose frequent need for counseling should also be recognized.

DR. OLIVIA EDWARDS

Today parents are very much aware that they should not allow their own differences to be imposed upon the child, but it is sometimes quite difficult not to allow one's bad experiences with the other mate to rub off. I think that even though a mother has convinced herself that she will say nothing detrimental about the father to the child or in front of the child, her very attitude may come out in the expression on her face when she talks about the father. Now, if she feels that bitter or that hurt, it may be too difficult to hide, and perhaps she should express this openly. Particularly if the child is a fairly intelligent adolescent, she can quite openly say that she has been very hurt, because the child knows it anyway if he has lived with both parents. She can say, however, that she does not expect the child to take sides and ally himself one way or the other.

Certain problems come up around how the father may influence the child. I've had cases in which the mother has complained that the father or the father's people (if they take the child) would say detrimental things about her to the child. I think the mother may feel fairly secure if most of these things which the father is saying are not true. She can help the child to understand that much of this stems from the father's feelings because of any hurt he may have experienced. I think the mother should be aware that in any relationship, no matter how badly she feels she has been treated or even 100 percent mistreated, she can always examine her own behavior to see what she has done to add to the situation. In all fairness the child should be made aware of this.

What would you advise the parent who is afraid of the father's influence during visits?

The first thing she has to realize is that she is probably not losing her child, because she has reared him. Perhaps it would be better if she would talk it over with somebody who can help her, but if not, she should try to communicate with herself to find out why she is feeling so insecure about this child. Why does she feel that he can be won completely away from her? If she has done everything possible for this child, it is not realistic to feel that he will go all the way over. She has to understand that the child will want to share in some of the father's activities. She has to be willing to allow him to do this and to know that she is not the sole parent. I think that too often when mothers have custody of the child, they begin to block out the father, as though the child had only one parent. She has to face up to the fact that he has two parents. Often mothers feel that they have borne the burden of child-rearing and should therefore reap all the benefits, but this child is the product of two people.

. . . If a child runs away from home to live with his father, there's something radically wrong from the beginning between the mother and the child, and therefore, perhaps, it would be better if the child had the opportunity to try living with the father, especially if the child is an older adolescent.

I should imagine the parent would be advised to keep the door open so that the child could easily return.

Yes, yes. I think that the child certainly should not be made to feel that once he has made this decision, this is it. The parents themselves, if they are reasonable people, might talk this over, and I would think the mother might try to get the father to influence the child not to leave home altogether. I think this gets into the question of the child playing one parent against the other. Some adolescents will try going from home to home and moving about from place to place. It is not only good for the parents, but it's very good for the adolescent to let him know where his home is. He has a place, and this is his place; and I think firmness is required here, that both parents will be quite firm about it. "Your home is here with mother, and you can visit father." Even if the father doesn't agree, I think the mother has to evaluate this. She knows her child.

Even though custody and visitation privileges have been settled in a separation agreement, you can't really say to the adolescent, "You have to live up to the contract," because the adolescent hasn't signed a contract. It's a contract between the parents.

Right. It's a contract between the parents and for the benefit of the younger children; but once the child becomes an adolescent, he is able to make his own decisions, to a point. When a child hits fourteen or fifteen, a mature, intelligent child who hasn't been traumatized should be able to make a decision, and more often that decision would be to stay with the mother. If, however, the mother is no longer in control of the child, the child is no longer going to school and is getting into trouble outside and fighting a lot, she may well allow the older adolescent to try life with the father.

But what if the child is doing well in his environment?

Then it is pure manipulation, or a testing out. A child wants to find out, "Does she really want me? How far can I go? Can I rebel?" In this case the mother needs to be quite firm: "You may visit, but this is your home."

Sometimes when the children do decide to leave, it may be a reflection of the mother's unconscious wish.

Yes, she wants to get rid of the responsibility.

The child acts out the mother's wish. So that even though she may protest, it's like placing children when the court will finally say, "We will place the child." Then it absolves the mother of guilt. You see someone else has said, "You must place the child"; I didn't do it. But all the time some parents have wanted to place the child, but couldn't say it, because of the guilt attached to it. This is why it is so hard to generalize, and I think that when the problem becomes a real tough one, the parents should seek professional help.

. . . When the parent gains custody of the adolescent, it is like giving the child twice to the parent, once when he is born and the second time when the court gives him to the parent. But the parent does not own him. The child is still an individual with his own individual rights, and he should have a hand in important decisions. He should know what is going on in the minds of his parents, particularly the one who has custody of him. I think that if there is communication from the beginning, from the earliest years, on the level that the child is at, then this communication can develop as the child grows older, and things can be talked out. Too often in families I have seen that the child really does not know what is going on. He doesn't know what is going to happen to him from day to day or week to week or where he's going to be, what his parent may do. I think that parents don't realize how worried children get about this.

What would you say to the mother who finds it difficult to think of her child bringing any joy into the father's life?

This results from the idea that this man needs to be punished a little more. Actually the mother may find it less punitive for herself if she lets go. Sometimes when you let go, you hold on, you keep. But if you fight too hard to keep something, you lose; so it may be a technique to keep what you have.

. . . It is extremely important for a mother to realize that she needs a life of her own, apart from her life with the children. She should try to develop outside interests so that this is her life, too. She can use this as support, and she doesn't have to rely on her children to supply all her needs, because this is very bad for the children. It's a definite burden on the children, and will cause her to cling to them, to the point that it is unbearable for them.

• • •

It was ethically impossible for the four people interviewed to divulge the specific details of individual cases which they handled, and hence their concern regarding the generalizations which they were forced to make. In spite of the difficulty in making these generalizations, it seems fair to conclude that there are still words of wisdom applicable to every divorced or separated couple with a child of adolescent age. The main advice appears to be that although separated as a couple, every effort must be made, including the possible use of supportive counseling when necessary, to remain united as parents in the attempt to assist the adolescent child to achieve an emotionally healthy and productive adulthood.

IRVING L. GOLOMB, LL. B.

The Scope of Legal Responsibility

In this chapter, Irving L. Golomb, a New York attorney with many years' experience in marriage law, addresses himself to a wide range of practical and legal issues. What emerges from his examination of these complex areas is a clear picture of the rights of divorced and separated parents toward their children and, equally important, the limited rights and privileges afforded by the law to their offspring.

It is interesting to note some of the changing conceptions of law, and it is surprising how relatively few rights are provided to children of separation and divorce even under the liberal interpretation given to current statutes. Mr Golomb's contribution points in the direction of a need for a thorough and apparently long overdue legal review of the entire complex area.

The argument is often heard, in these days of heated controversy over abortion law reform, that every child, even while a fetus in its mother's womb, has a right to be born. But what are his rights once born? And what, after separation or divorce, are the rights of his parents? The last question is the subject of this chapter.

Research on and the evaluation of the legal rights of children of broken marriages produce disappointingly negative results. English Common Law recognizes legal rights only in those who, by attaining the magic age of twenty-one, become transformed—infants the moment before, legal adults the instant after. Our law, evolving from this source, has not moved far. Scattered instances of legal reform have outlawed child labor, removed the stigma of illegitimacy from children of annulled marriages, and set up procedures for enforcing support of children by irresponsible parents.

Yet, while total disinheritance of one spouse by the other is generally prohibited, parents inclined to disinherit their children are free to do so. True, the minor inherits if his parent has made no will. But he has no redress when the parent's will ignores him. Considering the frequency with which estrangement of parent and child follows—if it has not already preceded—the removal of a parent, this is a strange discrepancy in the law. The nonblameworthy estranged spouse may inherit. The at least equally blameless child has no comparable right.

In matters of custody and visitation, the law offers a parent a variety of remedies. These include habeas corpus and modification of existing custody or visitation arrangements by court order. It is a sad reflection on the state of family law that the habeas corpus remedy originated not with the effort to bolster the rights of children, but as a procedure for challenging unlawful arrest and detention. In time, it expanded, became transplanted, and took root in the field of parental custody, for which there had not previously been any available relief.

The child has never had, nor does he today have, any rights comparable to those of his parents in such matters. The law affords him no right to petition that he be retained, maintained, or visited by either parent. He may be the pawn in their struggle. They may contend over him or ignore him. The child, however, lacks the right to seek the protective custody of either parent, and he can bring no proceeding to enforce that nonexistent right. When he has been the victim of physical neglect, appropriate proceedings may be instituted by agencies, such as the Society for the Prevention of Cruelty to Children, against the erring parent; but the child is himself powerless to act.

Separation and property settlement agreements entered into between parents customarily give custody to one parent and visitation rights to the other. Language is frequently encountered in such agreements to the effect that the failure of a parent to exercise rights of visitation shall not be deemed a waiver of future rights of visitation. The effect of such a clause may be to allow a long-absent parent, or at least a sporadically visiting or irresponsible one, to leave abruptly and arbitrarily, later to return at will to insist on his rights of visitation with a child long alienated. The custodial parent, believing in good faith that she is protecting the child by denying visitation in such circumstances, may find that she has legally justified a refusal to pay support moneys for the child.

Significantly, the child has no right to enforce visitation or custody provisions of an agreement between his parents. In other areas of the law, contracts made for the benefit of a third person—who is not a contracting party but to whom there is a duty or obligation owing by the promising person—may be enforced by that third person. This doctrine seems never to be applied to the visitation and custody situation.

In contested litigation over matters of custody, courts in recent years have begun to pay more heed to the parental preferences of children, particularly adolescent children. It is being increasingly recognized that it is exceedingly impractical for courts to disregard the preferences and desires of children for or against either parent. Unwilling children, awarded to a suing parent, have too often been the subject of repeated litigation that comes from the failure of the victorious litigant to enforce, on the home front, his court-won victory. The courts recognize ever more pragmatically the impossibility of attempting to police and enforce an award of adolescents to parents they reject. By yielding to a youngster the power of selection and, implicitly, rejection, the courts may in part be conceding the inevitable and in part fortifying the adolescent's need to protest, his urge to rebellion, and his objection to authority.

If, in fact, such yielding to the seemingly inevitable has not been too clearly articulated in court decisions, it is still an empirical experience in the life of many a minor, suddenly made conscious in the midst of a court battle of his power of choice of one as against another parent. Whether or not this is socially desirable, it remains an area in which the child may be heard and his rights respected.

With the sudden recognition of his power, buttressed by court decisions granting him the right of free choice of parent, the youngster may be expected to exercise wholeheartedly and energetically. Thus, in one case, the father won the custody of an adolescent daughter over the objections of a fanatically religious mother. The latter had good cause thereafter to become concerned with the loose moral fiber of the daughter's life with her extremely permissive father. The daughter was, however, having too good a time to ever wish to return to her mother's strictures. In the absence of showing full-blown promiscuity or addiction to narcotics, the daughter was bound to remain with the father. Correspondingly, the mother was ever more relegated to frustrated failures in her efforts to achieve even a working relationship with the child, let alone custody.

In the writer's experience, the tendency seems rather pronounced for the "Americanized" custodial father to be much more lax in the disciplining of a daughter than a custodial mother would be. For good or evil, this permissiveness seems to be preferred by most children. In the absence of severely damaging circumstances, the courts more and more recognize and enforce such preferences.

In cases in which one parent may have suffered severe mental or emotional illness and may therefore have been necessarily separated from the child for the period of time during institutionalization or recovery, it frequently happens that the other parent successfully entices the child away from the sick parent. Upon recovery, the latter may find that substantially all relationship has been eroded. The child may have been so terrified, albeit exaggeratedly or even without cause, at the behavior of the institutionalized parent, or even the fact of institutionalization, or by reason of its implications for him, as to seek to obliterate all such memories by avoiding contact with that parent. Courts historically are shaken and frightened by the incidence of even transitory mental illness. They require great reassurance and substantial proof of recovery as a precondition to considering the award of custody to a parent who has suffered a breakdown. Adding to this the ever increasing respect given to the preferences of the adolescent child, there is imposed a terrible punishment upon the formerly ill parent, who, upon recovery, is often prevented from reestablishing any relationship with his or her offspring.

Moreover, permanent custody agreements, entered into by a parent at a time of severe mental illnsss and impaired understanding, have a nasty tendency to remain permanent, even though the conditions under which custody was surrendered have ceased to exist.

A wife who is dependent for her maintenance upon her separated or divorced husband while she attempts to recover from such illness is not prone to take legal steps to nullify the separation agreement. By doing so, she would be simultaneously repudiating the provisions both for *her* support and for the husband's custody, while seeking custody of a child she is herself unable to support. On the other hand, if she waits some years for full recovery and attempts to set the agreement aside, the argument must be anticipated that she has long such ratified the agreement by accepting its benefits, and she cannot therefore assert that the agreement was unconscionable and voidable for duress, undue influence, or former lack of mental capacity.

In matters of emotional neglect, the child has far less redress available than when physically neglected. There is simply nothing a child can do when a parent has ceased to call, write, communicate, or talk to him. Many a visiting parent shields himself from emotional contact with a child by spending his visiting time at movies, restaurants, museums, or in other formal entertainments which lend themselves as a cover for emotional neglect. These pastimes allow the visiting hours to tick off while visitation takes on a passivity that obscures and, by rote repetition, chokes off any meaningful parent-child relationship. The child is without power to call for help in the courts when he is losing such a parent.

The pressured child, caught between the crossfire of the custodial parent who utilizes him as an instrument to play out past antagonisms and resentments against the other parent, sometimes performs surprisingly. In one case, a fourteen-year-old daughter, in her mother's custody, repeatedly assured her father of her desire to spend her vacation with him and his new wife in Europe. On the strength of her assurances and a provision in the separation agreement giving him one month's vacation rights each summer, he went to the expense of purchasing transportation and making reservations. Upon learning that the mother had made camp plans for the girl instead, he was urged by the daughter to bring a court proceeding in order to insure her right to the European trip. He thereupon commenced a not inexpensive court proceeding, hoping to obtain an order permitting the voyage. A pretrial conference in the judge's chambers disclosed a strange twist. The girl suddenly asserted, in full pendular swing, that she preferred summer camp to the glamorous Greek Isles, all to the astonishment of an incredulous father. It may well be that the child was influenced to this view by a domineering mother. In any event, in such matters as vacation time visitation, the courts are prone to pay great heed to the preferences of adolescent children. In this test of the power of the child to utilize the court as a means of manipulating one parent against the other, the child came off with a new-found sense of her power and rights, although in the process she may have permanently rejected and alienated her now disenchanted father. The court did not, and ordinarily does not, investigate the psychological reasons for the child's dual behavior. If the reasons reflected her own inner weaknesses, which lent her alternatingly to excessive control by one or another parent in the pendular battle between them, they were outside the court's scope, and her problems would remain untouched.

The implicit right of the child to be cared for during his infancy, even when his parents have been divorced, has given rise to a presumption that the mother is the parent best suited to protect and nourish him. Only in contested litigation over custody are the courts prone to examine this premise and explore the possibility that the father may be the preferred custodial parent. Substantial evidence of neglect and maltreatment is often insufficient to prevent the award of custody to the mother. Even in cases of actual abandonment over a number of years without contact, the return of the mother to the scene seems immediately to reactivate a presumption in her favor.

A word should also be said about the child of no marriage who can therefore never be the victim of divorce but who generally has no rights whatever to a father relationship except insofar as his mother may succeed in effecting child support from the father through court action. The out-of-wedlock father and his child are not otherwise generally recognized as father and child. Each is correspondingly without rights although there are beginnings of change in the law which indicate the possibility of a less rigid approach and a more realistic recognition that there is something more than money between such a father and his child.

Aside from the other questions involved, tugs of war of long duration between parents, each attempting to capture the child, may come to be more destructive to the child than might have been any decision in favor of either parent at an early stage of the proceedings. What is clearly indicated is a need for intensive study of the emotional problems of parent-child relationship so that they can be handled expeditiously and without hostility and ferment.

HELEN D. WARGOTZ, M.S.

The Adjustment of Children Raised by Separated or Divorced Fathers

As a social worker concentrating upon the problems exhibited by adolescents, particularly those problems common to young people raised by fathers in a motherless household, Mrs. Wargotz brings to her discussion a wealth of practical experience. Fathers faced with children torn between them and the mothers —often inaccessible, yet living—will find in this chapter much that is probably familiar. Some may find it of assistance in better understanding their own child's reaction and in encouraging a search for assistance in coping with their problems.

In reviewing the family lives of fifteen separated or divorced fathers who raised twenty-six children in motherless homes, I discovered a wide spectrum of human experience. This material comes from the second part of an ongoing study started in 1966 that grew out of my experiences in offering a program of guidance in a motherless home as the director of a service for guidance to teen-agers. The study examined the effects of a mother's absence on the personal, social, scholastic, and interfamilial adjustments of children.

There are sixteen males and ten females in the study, five of them only children. The fathers occupations cover a wide range from blue collar to white collar. When interviewed, thirteen fathers had been divorced and two separated.

The fathers all need to wear two hats—that of the wage earner, the other of the homemaker. A frequent saying has been "To find a good housekeeper, there's the rub!"

In spite of many difficult experiences with their mothers, some children look forward to visiting them. In the children included in the study, there are many evidences of difficulties, which range, in the case of the boys, from bed-wetting to temper tantrums. Among the ten girls, there is a comparable range of emotional reactions to stress.

The mothers of the twenty-six children show a wide range of emotional problems in living. Some are alcoholic or addicted to drugs, several have had to be hospitalized for severe emotional disorders. One indication from the study is the need to know a great deal more in depth about the emotional problems of both the fathers and the mothers, and of the circumstances that led to family disruption. Some of this inquiry has been undertaken but is not reported upon here.

It is interesting to note that in fourteen of the fifteen families in the study, one or more family members—either mothers, fathers, or children—has been seen professionally for their difficulties in living. It seems clear that the fathers in the study, because of their responsibility for the children after separation or divorce, manifest a greater need than the average father to show that they can do an adequate job of child-rearing. One consequence of this is that they tend to overlook danger signals in their children of impending emotional distress.

Not only visiting with mothers and siblings but also visiting with relatives may contribute to the enhancement of a child's positive feelings about his roots and about himself as a person. We know that children look elsewhere for emotional nourishment when it is not forthcoming from the home situation, and this seems to be particularly true in a motherless home. From the study it is clear that in many cases children in motherless homes reach out to, confide in, and frequently feel loved by a full-time housekeeper when one is present in the home. Often the same tendencies are expressed toward baby sitters and friends of the family who come to visit.

The study indicates, among other things, that the father's attitude toward his separated or former wife has much bearing on his or his children's feelings about discussing the absent mother. The fathers studied show a wide range of attitudes, both positive and negative. Only six of the fathers fail to disclose bitterness.

The following suggestions to fathers in a motherless home arise from this study and from my experience in working in a teen-age guidance center:

1. Fathers who assume responsibility for taking care of their children should consult a professional, such as a psychiatrist, psychologist, or social worker, within three months after assuming such responsibility.

2. Professionals who are consulted should have at least ten years of experience in working with children and families on an individual or family basis.

3. In instances in which separated mothers are emotionally troubled to the point where they require ongoing psychotherapy or hospitalization, it is wise to have regular emotional checkups for both the children and the family over a period of years. This is especially important at significant developmental milestones—puberty, adolescence, young adulthood—and when new school adjustments are being faced.

4. In his consideration of a homemaker, a father should seek to select a reliable and motherly woman, preferably on a full-time basis for preschool children. If the father can afford it, such a housekeeper should be retained during the period when the children are growing up to afford them a stable relationship with another adult.

5. Fathers should consider having dinner at home almost every evening. Ongoing communications can be best maintained around the dinner table.

6. Home life should continue normally, with opportunities for the children's friends to visit even when the father is absent. In this case, another adult should be present. Sunday should be a family day, providing open house for relatives and friends.

7. Through participation in community activities, as many contacts as possible should be fostered by the father and should include, wherever possible, the children.

8. Especially for young children, female teen-agers or college students preparing for nursery school work or teaching should be used as baby sitters. These young woman can help bridge the generation gap and bring about good rapport with the children.

9. Fathers may profit from a greater awareness of the developmental expectation of their children. A course may be helpful; increased information may help alert them to emotional danger signals.

Finally, only when a father has attained a genuine understanding of himself and his former wife will his anger dissipate. Sometimes it requires professional help, as well as much effort on his own part, to achieve this.

INTERVIEWS BY THE EDITORS

Parents Speak of Their Problems and Responsibilities

*In the three interviews that follow, the reader has an oppor-
tunity to listen in on discussions with parents as they consider their problems and responsibilities toward their children.
The first interview consists of a discussion with middle-class
mothers, the second is concerned with how middle-class fathers
view their responsibilities, and the third discussion involves a
consideration of some of the special problems confronting
mothers from economically deprived environments. All of the
interviews were taped in the New York City area.*

*It seems clear to the editors, after reviewing our discussions
with these parents, that there are widely different conceptions
of the role of the divorced or separated parent vis à vis his
children. In the main, the parent's conception is reflective of his
own personality, personal needs, and fulfilments, as well as the
influence of his socioeconomic background and the special
problems that it may present.*

INTERVIEWS WITH MIDDLE-CLASS MOTHERS

The material that follows is an interview conducted in New York City with middle-class mothers. Because of the composition of the group, the interview strikingly highlights experiences of mothers who have become heads of the household and who come both from an urban area and several suburban areas in the Northeast.

The women, often times struggling to function both as mothers and fathers, speak eloquently and to the point about their problems. The reader will encounter problems of the alcoholic father, the manipulative husband, and the indulgent parent seeking to purchase friendship and love from children whom he has left behind.

INTERVIEWER: What problems have you confronted?

HELEN: Well, the problem is my husband, who is an alcoholic. The children and I lived with this for twelve years before I finally took the step to get a divorce. It was a matter of my children having to deal with very ambivalent feelings that they themselves did not understand. When I did tell them that I was going to seek a divorce, my daughter took it well—she's the younger one—and my son just went off in all directions. For the first time in his life, he disliked me intensely, because he felt I had thrown his father out of the house. At the same time, he had both love and hate feelings for his father, and this is what he was trying to cope with. There are other ramifications like drug abuse and that sort of thing, which I feel my husband was directly responsible for.

INTERVIEWER: How old was your son at this time?

HELEN: Nineteen. He ran away and lasted four weeks in California, then back he came. But he seems to be shaping up very well now. He's still got a way to go, but there has been great improvement. It's very difficult to know exactly how to handle each situation as it occurs. For example, I'm very fond of animals. I had a dog, but my son insisted that I was very cruel to have a dog because there were cats in the house. I felt that it was his way of telling me that he felt I was cruel, that he didn't really mean the dog. At any rate, I went along with him and got rid of the dog. When he came back from California after having run away, he bought me a cat, which I felt was to compensate, although nothing was ever said.

I feel that the basic problem here is how to explain ambivalent feelings to a teen-ager.

INTERVIEWER: Is there someone else who wants to contribute something based on personal experience on this point?

ADELAIDE: This concerns my teen-age daughter who had a weight problem which, I think, was due to the fact that there was so much bickering in the home. She ate continually. Then, when she got slimmer, she felt that the world was her oyster and that she could conquer everything. However, the bickering continued. Not being able to relate to her father, or feeling rejected by her father, she became entangled with a boy. She went through the usual thing, and we went through a period which wasn't very pleasant.

Now we're divorced, and my nineteen year old feels total rejection, not only by her father, but by the whole world. I don't know how to deal with this situation. She's getting psychiatric help at present—I feel there must be something that can be done for a sensitive, intelligent youngster. Although she's nineteen now, she had her problem when she was seventeen, and it all started with a case of obesity brought on, I think, by the bickering between my husband and me. Now, I'm having difficulty disciplining her. I really don't know what to do.

INTERVIEWER: Is there someone who wants to talk to Adelaide's point? Can anyone contribute something from her own experience?

RITA: My name is Rita, and my husband also was an alcoholic. My son is thirteen. I find it very difficult to discipline him because at this point he's bigger than I am. He's very proud of this fact, but he, too, is very confused by the situation. However, I think he understands that his father is ill. Before we separated, I had covered up the drinking. My son doesn't understand the illness entirely, but my husband and I did have a reconciliation. After his father came home, I no longer covered up the drinking. We hoped that he would stop. My husband had said he would stop and didn't. So I think my son is able to deal with the drinking problem somewhat, but I still find him a difficult child to discipline. I hope that I won't run into any of Helen's problems.

GAIL: May I just ask, was your son close to his father before he became a drinker?

RITA: I don't think he was that close to him.

GAIL: My son adored his father before.

RITA: I think his father was a little bit distant with him.

GAIL: I have the feeling of rejection on his part. I find that this is quite a problem thing with children. They turn to outside sources of affection, or what they think is affection, because there's a lack of a relationship at home. I know I can see it in this way.

HELEN: Do you think your daughter blames you for some of the problems that happened?

RITA: Well, of course, now she blames me because of the separation, but I've asked her to go back to her father for a while just to see if she would prefer staying with him. I don't know.

GAIL: I think my son—I don't know whether Helen found this— maybe at times blames me for not being able to control his father's illness.

LYNN: Well, he's young enough to feel that way. It's hard for children to realize until they get much older.

GAIL: I just keep clinging to the thought that maybe later on he'll understand. I hope that we can keep on an even enough keel so that when he can look at things from a little bit more mature standpoint, maybe he will be able to understand and look at life well enough to be able to adjust.

INTERVIEWER: May I ask, have you run into any problems with respect to attitudes in the neighborhood that might have an effect upon your disciplining or handling your children? What's been your experience in this regard?

ADELAIDE: My daughter's father was a rather strict disciplinarian as far as he went. All her friends were able to stay out late and do whatever they wanted. She was supposed to get home at twelve. After all, she was a young girl, but she resented the fact that she had to be home at a certain time when all her friends were able to stay out as late as they wanted and probably disappear for two or three days over the weekend.

INTERVIEWER: Has anyone else had any experience with respect to attitudes of neighbors?

RUTH: Neighbors frown on divorce, naturally, and the child is just not accepted in society, as a rule. I'm from a small town, so I know. My daughter has suffered because I was divorced. In a small town, it's maybe one out of fifty who are divorced, so the child naturally feels different from everybody else. Everybody goes home to his mother and father, and my daughter only has her mother to go home to—she can see her father on Sundays— and it's difficult. The neighbors get quite belligerent, but there's an attitude they take toward divorce that the children can't accept.

INTERVIEWER: Can you tell us in what way your daughter feels different?

RUTH: Well, she doesn't feel different now. She's twenty-two now and she doesn't feel different. But when she was nine or ten years old, she felt different, because everybody went out with his parents. Yeah, teens are very difficult, and she felt different from everybody else. Everybody had a mother and father, but she didn't. They get over that. When they get to be twenty-one years old, they get over that.

HELEN: My daughter, Jody, whom I consider a very well-adjusted child, was very anxious for me to get a divorce. At the time she was seventeen or eighteen, and she was going with a young boy in the neighborhood. It just so happened that the boys' parents had picked out a young girl for their son. Naturally, Jody was not considered a very good prospect. When she went to their home with their son, it was very obvious, and my daughter picked it up immediately. Fortunately she was the kind of kid who understood. In other words, she was the complete opposite of her brother. My son would have run like a bat out of hell, but my daughter—I wouldn't say that deep down there wasn't some sort of pain, but she coped with the situation very well.

INTERVIEWER: Some of you have children who are older. Do you find that there's a change in the kind of problems that you confront? Is there someone who wants to address herself to that?

TERRI: You know, you're all women alone like myself. You say you have teen-age daughters, but have you tried to have them feel like you need them? I mean, have you tried that? It's terrific. You need them. Really. My birthday came up—I was forty-two years old —and my daughter came home for the weekend. She took me out to dinner and to a movie, and I sent her a bread-and-butter letter to college, thanking her for such a lovely time. I treated her as a friend, but you see we don't have any secrets. I really tell her everything, and I mean everything. We stay up all night talking—you know, about boy friends and men, and things like this. I tell you I don't have a problem with my daughter. Through the years she's always told me, "Mom, you're different, you know, you're different," but now I'm beginning to realize what this difference is.

I've listened to so many people—women like myself who are

alone—and I ask myself why they don't get close to their girls. You know what I mean—tell all, and you tell her, too.

LOIS: I have younger children, so I'm sort of out of this, but I don't want to feel that my daughter is a buddy with me. I don't want her to take responsibility for my problems. I have a mentally ill son who's eight, and it's very hard for my daughter. Some of the neighbors reject my son because he can't function and also because there's no father to come down and protect him. I also have a younger child —my baby's two and a half, a year and a half when his father left. It has been very very difficult because the nonfunctioning child just doesn't understand that Daddy isn't around. Of course, they see their father on the weekend. I live a single life on the weekend, and I live with the children during the week. When there's any problem, my son thinks his father can help him. There's no way of explaining that his father is not providing the money so that we could get along without so much strife. His father makes it seem that he just loves my son so much—he's always dripping with attention when he's visiting —but yet when the boy is not with him, you know, it doesn't matter.

INTERVIEWER: May I ask, is this matter of visitation of your former spouse a problem that you run into characteristically? Will someone address herself to that?

RITA: Yes, it is a problem in my case because his father, I guess because of his illness, can make things very difficult. As a matter of fact, I think I'm going to have to refuse to allow my son to go out with him because the last time his father did get drunk. I just can't allow him to take my son out under those circumstances. Also he decided to get a car, and I just had to tell my son that he's not permitted to get in a car with his father. It's a very hard thing to explain to my son and have him understand. There are times when he doesn't want to speak to my husband when he calls on the telephone, so under these circumstances there is a strain there. I think at times it would be almost better if my son didn't see him.

INTERVIEWER: Does anyone else want to address herself to this?

HELEN: My experience has been identical. When my husband does remember to call, he repeats the same thing over and over again, and as old as my children are, it frightens them. They don't understand it. I hear my daughter say, "But you just asked me that, Daddy," so what are you supposed to do? He took her out one evening, a big evening on the town, and then he took her to a bar. At the time she was going on seventeen, so it is quite a problem.

INTERVIEWER: Do you ladies want to address yourselves to this?

JEAN: I have a daughter and son, and my daughter, of course, wants nothing to do with her father because he never properly supported us and never assumed adult responsibilities in the home. I have no indication that the divorce has affected my daughter. She seems very happy, very wholesome, and is doing beautifully in school —everything is just perfect so far. I don't anticipate having any trouble.

INTERVIEWER: And how old is she?

JEAN: She's sixteen. My eighteen-year-old son is another matter though, since these days he's getting to be more and more like his father. My husband is an avid golfer. As a matter of fact, that was one of the problems of our marriage. He was golfing all the time instead of working. My son loves the sport, too, and he seems to find that he likes to be with his father a great deal. I am beginning to see signs of this hedonist trait cropping up in my son. He is beginning to like pleasure—like playing golf, rather than working—and of course an eighteen year old can get himself a job and like the idea of working. I think that it's detrimental to my son's welfare to be in the company of such a man. While there are people who gamble and who drink —and these are vices—I think there's a vice that is far worse. A man who gets away with not providing, with taking care of just himself and not assuming adult responsibilities, and who has no conscience about it and doesn't even want to pay the amount awarded to me by the court—that's the worst vice. Well, I have this problem. I think exposure to this man is going to become a major problem because he lives a life of almost complete irresponsibility. He's not living up to his potential.

INTERVIEWER: Does anyone else want to address herself to this problem?

LOIS: I have a very similar problem. I was married to a man who potentially can be a very good wage earner—he's a graphics designer, a very talented one, and he's been recognized. But he doesn't want to work at a steady job, so he free-lances. Free-lancing means that I can go two months without getting any money. I haven't been able to do anything legal because I haven't got the money to go to a lawyer, and I haven't had the guts to go to Family Court.

It's also a very hard situation not knowing whether to send children to visit him. He lives with a girl, and this is another complication because my daughter, who's four and a half and pretty bright, calls her Mommy. She comes home saying Mommy says this and Mommy says that. I've been able to handle it, I think, very well. I've told her that a person has only one mommy and one daddy, but she calls this other girl Mommy to get to me. So far I've managed to walk away from it.

It's very hard to know whether to expose children to another family unit. I do it only because I'm young and I want to go out and meet men, and I want to get remarried. I feel at the time when I am set and situated, I will prevent visitation because the little one has never really known his father, and I think my daughter could adjust to a limited visitation.

INTERVIEWS WITH MIDDLE-CLASS FATHERS

Fathers have largely been ignored when seeking impressions of how divorced parents perceive their children. Most studies on divorce have concentrated upon the parent in custody—almost exclusively the mother. It is not surprising, however, to find that fathers, too, feel anxious and guilty about the disruption of their homes. It seems from the record that fathers care deeply, and continue to do so after divorce and separation. Their major concern is to maintain a warm relationship with their children, and their disappointment at the often hostile reception by their children is obvious.

The following discussion is full of recommendations for fathers in similar circumstances—how to meet situations they have faced, and what to anticipate from their children in the period immediately preceeding the marital breakup.

LARRY: Now, what I'd like to know is, are you asking questions about our relationship with our own children, or children that we've acquired as a result of a second marriage and how they adjust to a marriage?

INTERVIEWER: All children—the children that you have and bring to the marriage with you, the children which your new wife brings into the marriage, and the children that you have with your second wife as well. We'd like to know what your relationship is now with your children. People have reported that their major problem is having children accept their new situation.

LARRY: My daughter is now twenty-three years old. At the time of my divorce from her mother, she was about eighteen years old. Her reaction was complete animosity. I attributed it to the fact that she believed very strongly that I had deserted, and not just merely legally divorced, my wife. But there was a time—a good period of time—when I didn't live with them prior to the divorce. After the divorce, for quite some time, I did not wish to visit either the mother or the children. When I did decide to show up, it was as if I were a stranger, and there was a bitterness on the part of my daughter. My son, who's about fourteen now, still has mixed emotions. I would say that I have an ally in him, but a very wary one at that. My daughter though just borders on hatred toward me.

GEORGE: Actually, I was divorced once and then I remarried the same woman; now I am separated and getting a divorce from the same woman. The attitude of the four children—particularly the younger ones, fifteen and thirteen years of age—is one of indifference taken to somewhat exceptional lengths. It's as if this is their way of saying to me that I should not have separated from their mother. I find it very difficult, for example, to get them to share activities with me. If I want to take them to a ball game, they're very reluctant to go. Of course, I think the situation is not as bad as it might have been if their mother and I had really been compatible. We had a very stormy marriage for many years, and I think that this is the reason that perhaps there's not as much animosity as there might otherwise have been. Going back to the earlier divorce, I felt that the girl was somewhat more strange than the boys. She seemed to react with more animosity than the boys. This was probably because she felt closer to me than the boys. I've only talked with her by telephone during the last eight months of separation, and she is still strange.

LEE: As far as I can detect, there's no noticeable difference in the attitude of my children toward me. I have one who's nineteen, one sixteen and one ten—all boys. I know that they, like anybody else would, tried to find someone on whom to place the blame for the situation in which they find themselves. I think they would say it's their mother's fault more than mine. This being the case, I suppose that it's understandable that their attitude toward me has not changed. I don't know what their attitude is toward their mother— I have no contact with her, although the children live with her.

INTERVIEWER: Do you have any advice for those contemplating divorce where children are concerned—anything that you think could help?

LEE: Well, I would say that if there's a contemplation of divorce, or separation, try to be as pleasant around the children as you can. Don't run each other down. This is something we did not do, and I expect this has helped in our situation. Particularly, I never tried to influence the children against her and I don't think she did against me.

GORDON: My situation is, I would imagine, somewhat different. I was married five years and we have a three-year-old son. One day I was there, and the next day I was gone. The only thing I can say is that if we had a bad marriage, we tried at least to have an amiable separation so as not to affect the child. We figured that at three years old, the child is very impressionable. As far as relationships go, the child is very much attached to me as well as to his mother. I see the child once a week; we go out and have a ball. The only problem that I have is when I leave. He's three years old and he calls for his father and he wants his father. He says he misses me, he doesn't want me to go away and he's happy when I come. My wife and I have tried to tell him that we love him—his mother loves him, his father loves him, everybody loves him—trying to give him the best security that we can under the circumstances.

INTERVIEWER: Is there anything else you can think of that would be of benefit to somebody entering into the same situation?

GORDON: I would say just the way we handled it. We tried not to bring our son into the conflict, not to have any stormy scenes with him around, hoping to shelter him and to cushion the shock as much as possible.

STAN: I have a daughter, thirteen. She lives in a residence school out of the city. I have a son who is ten, who also lives in a residence school out of the city, so my case is a little different than Gordon's. Before they went away to school, there was quite a strong emotional problem with the children. My son had a serious emotional problem —he couldn't attend public schools anymore because the divorce affected him that way. I think one of the difficulties between my wife and me at that time was that I did not think she had the ability to raise the children—I don't believe there was much communication between the children and her. The children were looking for a certain affection from their mother and she wasn't able to give it to them. Of course, this is my side, but this is the way I evaluate it as I see it in retrospect.

With my daughter, it took quite a while for me to adjust—it was not until she left the home and entered the residential school that we came to know each other. Because she wasn't influenced by her mother or the grandparents, she was just kind of on neutral ground in school with counselors and a social worker. I came to visit her and occasionally she visited me. Eventually she stayed with me over the weekend. Now we can communicate a little better, we can see each other and respond. She's come to know me a little more, gives me more affection, and talks to me about how she feels. I'm able to get more from her by talking to her on her level, and she gets more from me.

I think one of the reasons why broken marriages sometimes leave a bitter aftereffect is because of the way the divorce laws are set up in this state. They prejudice the man's situation right from the beginning, even though today there are grounds for divorce other than adultery. I think the case of alimony and support is a big area that has to be worked on. I think the laws are unfair in this area. When financial problems are resolved, a lot of emotional problems disappear with them. One of the biggest strains on the man's side is giving money, money that he often feels is unjust. I think there should be some equality in the law.

INTERVIEWER: How best can you prepare for a break in the best interests of the children?

STAN: Once you become aware that the marriage cannot function, you must not get involved with the wife emotionally or make the children aware that you're going to do something. You must be calm and collected, and you must evaluate the situation. Contact some legal advisor beforehand and let them be aware of what the situation is. Get advice early, way before you walk out of the house. If you have any problems, I'm certainly sure that there are groups in the area, groups who are working for better laws. I would say we divorced men are not for eliminating alimony because there are just causes for it—we're all for support—but it should be equalized to consider the man's ability to pay and still live himself.

PETER: I was always very close with my children. I have a girl twelve and a boy seven, who are living with my wife, and I would say in all honesty that our relationship is even closer now than it was before the divorce. I was listening to what Stan was saying about the legal aspect of divorce. My wife has the children more—how can I put it?—out of vengeance than an actual desire to have them. At the time of the divorce I was fairly strapped for money so I had to shop around for the cheapest lawyer I could get. As a matter of fact, I'm of the opinion that my daughter might even have the desire to come and stay with me, but again this gets into a legal tangle, you know.

INTERVIEWER: How often do you think you should see your children?

PETER: Well, that's the funny part of it. I feel kind of victimized by the whole thing, you know, because I didn't have the proper legal representation at the time. I see them on a Sunday—that's all the law allows me.

INTERVIEWER: Should a man who is going to get divorced or separated plan on seeing his children several times a week in order to help them adjust?

STAN: That's my opinion. There are differences of opinion, you know. Some people say, "Well, let the kids start their new life and just see them as little as possible." I don't agree with that. I feel my kids need me.

INTERVIEWER: Have you observed any problems that might have been prevented if you had properly prepared for this divorce or separation before you went through with it?

GORDON: As I said before, my kid is three, and to me a child of three years old is so impressionable that I tried to work out the divorce arrangements to his benefit. I suppose I felt that it wasn't his fault and he shouldn't be punished because of it. As for the legal aspect of the divorce, I went all out for him. My wife has my son and she has the house. It's all for him rather than for her. It turned out that she got everything, but at least I feel that the child is provided for, and at three I feel it's very important.

LEE: I don't know that it worked out quite well in our case. We prepared the children by sitting down with them and telling them that we didn't get along and that I was going to go live somewhere else. I don't recall now our mentioning how often I would be around to see them, but I was going to live close by. As it turned out, each of them generally spent a night a week with me in the beginning. I'm sure it was a lot harder for the younger boys to adjust to the new situation because it seemed more foreign. A week seems like a long time to a little boy ten years old.

STAN: I think the relationship between a child and the father should depend upon the father's ability to communicate with the child and the child's ability to comprehend. Now, of course, my son —the younger boy of ten—is quite bright and even though emotionally he's immature, he still has the capability of understanding and comprehending the things I have to say to him. I try to relate to him on his level. Now he's also away from the home so he's not subjected to getting ideas from his mother that Daddy's no good; and things like that. But there's no cut and dried situation in which you can say you should see the child once a week. See him two times a week, or maybe once every other week. I see my son once every other week, but I see him for a period of four to five hours. During this four or five hours I try not to get involved in going to a movie. I try to get involved in playing games with him, of doing things together, constructing things, asking questions, and his asking me questions.

Now, what I can get out of my son may take some fathers months. I've learned to develop the relationship. This you have to feel out. Let him ask questions constantly; this is how the child can respond to you and you to him.

I have to treat my daughter in a different way. It was hard to hold hands when she wouldn't let me hold her hands, but after a while I spoke to her, I tried to be on her level, I tried to understand her problems. Each situation is different, but I try to make a sincere effort to understand. And yet at the same time I don't go out of my way to be overly nice to her because I don't want her to feel that I'm catering to her. I have to treat her as an equal and she has to know that. She'll respect me more, and I know I'll respect her more.

INTERVIEWER: How should you introduce your child to somebody with whom you're going to have a personal relationship?

LARRY: I'd been going with a girl for two years. She was working in the same area that I was, and we arranged to have lunch together. I invited my boy to join us, and I prefaced this introduction by saying that I knew this girl and liked her very much. I wanted him to meet her, but there was no obligation on his part. "I just want you to go to lunch and meet her. Talk with her and have her talk with you." His reaction before the introduction was complete indifference—he was just interested in having lunch and going home. During the lunch I must say that he enjoyed this woman, took part in the conversation, and went away feeling that he had spent the hour we were together very enjoyably. The only mistake he made was that he told his mother. That built up that much more animosity between us.

MARTY: I would tend to be a little reluctant to introduce my kids to anyone I was going with casually. I think I would kind of hold off until I was going with someone with serious intentions—with the prospect of getting married again. For some reason, children, especially my children, assume that a woman that I was going with would, in a way, be their future mother. There was one situation where I came very close to getting married again. The kids more or less understood that this woman was going to be my wife and they liked her very much. When it didn't work out, they were very unhappy about it. I would want to spare them from that type of experience again.

INTERVIEWER: How did you introduce them?

MARTY: It was kind of a casual thing. This woman has three children of her own and we all went bowling together. It was a very relaxed afternoon. We had dinner together and they just got to know each other on a very friendly basis.

INTERVIEWER: How did the kids get along?

MARTY: Like kids do—without any trouble at all. Kids seem to find other kids, you know, they just fall in. There was no problem, no resentment.

LEE: This is a problem I've thought about to some extent. There have been a couple of women that I've introduced my boys to rather casually. As it turned out, it developed that I wasn't interested in either of them. I've discussed the possibility of my getting married again with my boys, and they seem to take a positive attitude. If this is something Dad wants, they'd be happy to have it. I don't know how much they've thought about it or about how much attention it would take away from them. I haven't discussed this aspect of it with them, but I wouldn't want to be negative about it.

INTERVIEWS WITH MOTHERS FROM DEPRIVED ENVIRONMENTS*

In these interviews, the women, deprived by social, economic, and cultural circumstances, speak in a most mature and insightful way of

*This discussion has been made possible through the cooperation of the Madeline Borg Child Guidance Center of The Jewish Board of Guardians. Marlene Golub, M.S.W., caseworker in charge of the Big Brother unit, organized the discussions.

their children and their emotional needs. They also speak of their desires for the children's future and the struggles they undergo to provide for the children in a world which is not very accommodating. What is most interesting is the mothers' careful support of the Big Brother movement, which attempts to supply fatherless boys with mature male images as supportive figures during their growing years.

These interviews are with four mothers whose children have been assigned "brothers" from the Jewish Big Brother movement. There is also a Catholic Big Brother movement that provides a similar service and has similar goals.

All the women interviewed were white. Flora's marriage to a black man terminated three and a half years ago. Her son Cass is nine years of age. The second woman, Florence, is the guardian of Richard, who is now thirteen years of age. His mother is Florence's grand-niece and is now a patient in a state mental hospital. After a divorce from Richard's father, she remarried; her son does occasionally see his stepfather but has never seen his paternal parent. The third woman, Nilda, is of Puerto Rican origin. Her son Diego, fifteen years of age, has been with the Big Brother movement for three years. A fourth woman, Silvia, has a son, James, eleven years of age, who sees his remarried father once a week.

The mothers' explicit request to the agency was for a Big Brother with whom the child could identify as a masculine figure. The caseworker actually found that the implicit request was for a sort of substitute marriage partner. Each of these women lives alone or with her own maternal parent. Each of these women has exhibited disturbances in relating to others on a mature level, with strong indications of dependency needs.

The Big Brothers or, as they will be labeled here, B.B.'s, are in general Jewish professional young men. Each came to the agency to ask for placement with a little brother with whom he could establish some relationship. Each was cautioned that he should not interfere with any child-rearing problems—for example, the mother could stress a certain time for the child to be returned home, or punish the child in her own manner, without interference by the B.B. Each was asked to ignore the mother's disciplinary techniques in his relations with her and her son. The B.B.'s, in these cases all medical students, have found the mothers more difficult to handle than their children, because of the women's needs for affection and attention. Essentially what has happened is that the child is being used to duplicate the relationship which had been established earlier by the mother and the child's natural father. Now repetition of this relationship is being duplicated by the mother, with some resentment of the B.B.'s refusal to act out the role of her former husband.

All of these mothers are in the low to low-middle socioeconomic group; they have supported themselves with or without the aid of welfare. Although some of the fathers do contribute a minimal amount to the support of their children, it is insignificant when compared to the total needs. There is always a struggle to ask the child to request payment of the alimony granted by the courts of their estranged father when he does see him. It is an even greater struggle to ask the mother to relinquish totally the right to ask the father for support and to carry the entire burden herself.

What has been found to be common among such mothers is their lack of confidence in taking responsibility for the development of their male child in a household without a father present. This becomes most apparent in the area of disciplining their sons. They anticipated that the B.B. would become the disciplinarian, and they are anxious to relinquish this role and its responsibility. However, the B.B.'s are unable to be the authoritarian figures whom the mothers would like to see them represent. Since the mothers feel themselves helpless and manipulated by outside forces, and yet are unable to displace this responsiblity onto the B.B., what happens is that both the B.B. and the mother psychologically vie with each other in this area—both trying to avoid taking responsibility for disciplining the boy.

The women in this group are of varying religious backgrounds. It is significant that they are very attached to their own mothers and were married shortly after graduating from high school—sometimes after having a relationship with a man, without thinking out their needs and roles. Impulsively they got married, and for a short time afterwards things seemed to be working out because there was no real need for either husband or wife to take any serious responsibilities. However, after the child came, someone had to care for it. The parents had never worked out their own personality problems and, as a result, the child exaggerated their personal difficulties. The child's coming resulted in the mother's evicting her irresponsible mate and going back to live with her mother with her male child. Sometimes the mother gives the caseworker the feeling that she would like to throw the male child in her mother's face and say, "This is what you really wanted of me. Here it is!" The grandmother's role is equally as important as that of the mother in the upbringing of the child. The natural father plays a rather passive role; he is there inconsistently if at all. The mother has been known to say to her male child, "Look, you are just like your father. You will never amount to anything. You never can do anything right and you are just a bum like him." As a consequence, quite often these children have difficulties concerning their male identity—hence the need for the Big Brother movement.

FLORENCE: The children in the B.B. movement need more time with their B.B. The boy looks forward to this contact all week. He says, "I would like it even every day." He is fond of his B.B.—a very nice man, I like him myself. (Comment by interviewers, "That is very encouraging." General laughter. Florence responded to the innuendo with, "He is married and has two children—I wish him a lot of luck." One of the other mothers also laughed and stated, "We all have such thoughts.")

FLORA: My son, Cass, is nine years of age. He has a wonderful relationship with his B.B. Because my son is young and therefore has a limited span of interest, I believe that he spends a sufficient amount of time with his B.B. He loves his B.B. I see a change in my child because of this relationship. There has been a definite improvement. For my child this man is perfect. For one thing his B.B. is compulsive, and when he says that he will be here at 9:21, my son can say with confidence at 9:20 that in one minute there will be a knock at the door. Howard, his B.B., is always there on the minute. For my son this is most important because he has to have someone who is consistent, on whom he can depend without question.

SILVIA: My son, James, who is eleven years old, sees his B.B. every other week. He is really crazy about his B.B. and looks forward to his visits. He prefers being with Mark to being with his real father.

INTERVIEWER: What qualities does he find in his B.B. which he misses in his father?

SILVIA: He feels that his B.B. has a real interest in him and that his father has none.

CASEWORKER: How does the B.B. discipline James?

SILVIA: I cannot tell. He does not assist me in disciplining my son and he once told me that he does not wish to become involved. He told me that he does not feel it right that he be involved as the middleman in the disciplining of James.

INTERVIEWER: Do you have problems of discipline? And which ones do you feel are due to the absence of a father in the home?

FLORENCE: First of all, he is a boy and prefers males to discuss things with and to do things with, although he has had me since birth. He never had anyone else. Until a year ago, when he was twelve, he was fine. Since that time, he has had a change of relationship with me. Now he has started to use his hands on me. If there was a father in the home this would not happen. He has no patience to remain at home. He makes trouble when I insist that he take a bath, change his clothes, comb his hair, clean his nails, and such things. If there was a man in the house, he would imitate his example. I cannot get him to do these things to maintain his health, and he uses foul language when I insist upon them.

He objects to much of what he hears about his mother—he does not hate her but is not fond of her. He feels that much of his situation is due to his mother having done something wrong. There is no knowledge of the whereabouts of his natural father. When James' mother gave birth, his father just disappeared. About four or five years ago he asked about his father and said, "Let's not kid ourselves, I had a father. What became of him and where is he?" He was too young and I was advised to tell him that his father went to Europe and that was the story.

INTERVIEWER: Do you believe that this story is advisable under the circumstances?

FLORENCE: Yes, it is. The boy's mother has since remarried and he now has a stepfather. He gets along too well with this man. If he never saw him at all it would be best. I objected to this man from the first day he came into the house, but my niece would not listen to me. He is unfit to be an example for the boy. This not because I am Jewish and my niece married outside of her faith, but this man does not work, does not keep up the house, stays away from the house for weeks and months at a time, and cares nothing for his own natural children. My "son" is attracted to him just because he is a man. He would be attracted to any man. This man discourages him from continuing in school and also antagonizes him against other races and people.

Another thing wrong is that Richard is satisfied with nothing but the best. When he went to the wrestling matches last week there were all sorts of prices and all kinds of seats. I felt that a young child like that with an allowance could get a fairly nice seat for $3.00. His eyes are good, his ears are good, there is no reason he should pay $6.00 for a seat like an old man who really cannot see. He objected to this and wanted the highest-priced ticket.

INTERVIEWER: Where does he get the money?

FLORENCE: I have to give him the money. I used to give him a lesser amount, but now I give him $3.00 per week because I realize he wants to go to the movies or buy himself something. I don't believe in not giving a child an allowance.

CASEWORKER: Do you feel strange about the B.B.'s lack of interaction with you?

FLORA: I think at the beginning that I did feel left out. The B.B. would just arrive and take Cass out for a walk. When he did this without speaking with me for a few minutes, I resented it. Now our relationship has changed. Sometimes the B.B. calls on the telephone when Cass is not at home and we talk about many things—himself, for example, his relationship with Cass, and his problems in medical school. I now feel that I have a relationship which is important to me as well as to my son. My son believes that his B.B. is now part of the family. Sometimes when the B.B. brings Cass home, Cass goes into his room and the B.B. and I have an opportunity to talk together. The illusion I imagine on Cass's part is that we are like a mother and father—although I am old enough to be the B.B.'s mother. My son feels safer because I do have a good relationship with his B.B., although children of nine years of age may be a little confused about a mother-father relationship.

INTERVIEWER: In the event a male friend calls on you, what is the observable reaction from your sons?

SILVIA: When the man arrived, I said, "I'm leaving," and my son went to look at television. He never mentioned this afterwards and made no comment about him whatsoever.

FLORA: Such a situation occurred a long time ago, and at the time Cass was much younger. He wanted to accept this man, but I did not. So it was only that one time. Recently, however, we had a hypothetical discussion about my meeting somebody and wanting to get married, and he said he wouldn't like the idea. He looked at me suspiciously and asked, "Do you have someone already?" Years ago he used to ask me constantly why I did not remarry and have a baby. Now apparently he thinks his B.B. is enough. I believe that at this point he would be against my remarrying because it would take my love away from him. Now he is afraid that if I could love someone else I would not love him.

INTERVIEWER: If you did meet a man, how much would your relationship with him be influenced by the attitude of your son toward your remarriage?

FLORENCE: Although I am a grandaunt, when my "son" was younger he used to urge me to meet a nice man and get married. "Look," he said, "I would have a daddy, and we could go out together and not have to stay at home." He is still envious when he sees friends get into an automobile with their fathers. He does not say this out loud but you can read it all over his face.

SILVIA: This is true. All of the boys feel this way. They are envious of a normal family life. They are particularly affected by things such as television stories of a family relationship which is warm and stable, where the children live in a comfortable home in the suburbs—their father is a doctor and a respected member of the community.

INTERVIEWER: If your children had three wishes about a father, what do you think they would wish for?

SILVIA: I think James would like somebody like his B.B. He is always bringing him into the conversation. For example, he says "I want to be like my B.B.—I like the girl friend he is going to marry, I like everything about him." The second wish is that he would like to see me remarried, because he is always talking about it. The third wish I believe is that he would like to get out of New York City, because he feels that if he did, he would not have to see his father again. This is because his father calls for him on Sunday about 12:30. He takes James back to his house, where my son gets along poorly with his stepsister, and promptly goes off to sleep. His father has no interest in him.

FLORA: If my son were wishing for a father, I do not know if he is clear in his own mind if he would wish for a white Jewish man or a black man like his own father. I think his feelings are like mine. I don't know myself, particularly about wanting to remarry. If somebody came along whom we both liked, we could probably be happy. I don't know. His wishes and mine are intertwined.

INTERVIEWER: What do you personally wish for?

FLORA: I wish only for someone who is strong—someone who will pay the bills, who will worry about the things I have been worrying about since I was sixteen. With two husbands I have been paying the bills and making out the checks. Now I want somebody strong, someone who will take over. The wanting and the wishing for a husband is all a fantasy now, because I am not ready for it yet, and I believe that is one reason why Cass is also not ready for a new father.

INTERVIEWER: How do the children get along with their grandparents?

FLORA: Well, my son had a particular problem because he is a black child. My mother came around first, and learned to have an affection for my son. Cass still remarks that my father holds back, but my father is like this with all his grandchildren.

CASEWORKER: Until the relationship with his B.B. I don't feel that Cass ever accepted any male. He was rejected by his father and by his grandfather. I think that generally the B.B. provides a male figure of acceptance and a stable image which the boys' natural fathers did not provide.

FLORENCE: The first wish of my "son" would be that I find a father for him to live with. The second would be that I were a little younger so that he would be with me longer.

INTERVIEWER: Would bringing Richard up have been easier for you if your "son" were a girl, rather than a male child?

FLORENCE: Yes. He misses a man in the house with whom he could identify and whose personality he could imitate. When he is with me, he has no strength to copy. Some girls, however, are more difficult than boys.

NILDA: I don't know what Diego would wish for. He has always told me, "Mommy, stay alone." He feels that he is the man in the house, and he is very jealous of other men. It does not cause me much trouble because when he goes out to dance, which he likes very much, he tells me to go out—but he does not say that I should go alone, however. He is very protective. He told me that when he gets married he will buy a house with two apartments—one for himself and the other for me.

INTERVIEWER: Has he, in your opinion, gained much from his association with his B.B.?

NILDA: Very much. He loves school and does well. All of this is the result of his being with his B.B. He studies very hard. He has attended the Big Brother camp and wishes to be a counselor there next year.

FLORENCE: The B.B. has been of immense help. Since I took the boy, he has been constantly with me—wherever I went he also went along. I had no one to take him. The B.B. has been of such great help that I cannot praise the movement too much. The trouble is that my "son" has learned to depend upon me too much. He knows that I will always be there when he goes out—he always says before leaving the house, "Ma, will you be here when I come back?"

FLORA: Cass is that way, too. I have always had to work, and I am out daily. If I have to be out for some time on a weekend, if he thinks I will not be home at all times, he will have a tantrum.

FLORENCE: They are always looking for security and afraid of losing it.

CASEWORKER: They are afraid of being alone. They have lost one parent and are clinging very tightly to the one they have left. They are fearful of becoming an orphan, in a sense.

Children's Perceptions
of Their Parents

Part Two

Through these tape-recorded interviews, the reader is afforded an opportunity of getting a glimpse into the notions that children have of their parents. Part II, therefore, offers a contrast to our earlier view of how parents see their children. Looking at the two views is instructive; it is apparent that in a number of respects the views of the parents and of the children are more divergent than convergent.

The first tape is a conversation with a group of children from broken homes who are finding a father relationship through the Big Brother movement, under the auspices of a large New York City social agency.

The second chapter presents a mixed group of adolescents from an economically well-to-do area in one of New York City's suburbs. These children are better able than the Big Brother group to discuss more vividly, though no less painlessly, their perceptions of a fatherless home and its influences upon their relationships with their mothers. They are chiefly concerned with their mothers' possible remarriages and their own altered prospects for the future, and also their continuing relationship with their remarried fathers.

Although the problems faced by the younger children appear to them to be different, an examination of the perceptions of the older group shows that as the children grow older, many of their earlier perceptions of their parents are retained, and many of the problems persist and remain unresolved in adolescence.

Children from Deprived Environments Speak of Their Problems*

This interview—with two of the children whose mothers discussed their views of what it meant for their boys to grow up fatherless in a deprived environment—tells us just how painful is the absence of a male image. In an innocent and honest revelation of the subterfuges undertaken to maintain the fiction that theirs is a normal household, the children reveal much of their envy of their friends. In the process, they also discuss the young men acting as their Big Brothers and the supportive role they play in their lives.

*This interview has been made possible through the cooperation of the Big Brother movement at the Madeline Borg Child Guidance Center, Jewish Board of Guardians, New York City. Marlene Golub, M.S.W., caseworker in charge of the Big Brother unit, was most helpful.

The children who participated in this discussion are the sons of two of the women who spoke of their experiences in the chapter, "Interviews with Mothers from Deprived Environments"; these are the nine-year-old son of Flora, Cass, whose father was a black man, the other is James, the eleven-year-old son of Silvia. The adolescent sons of the other women present at the interview would not cooperate.

INTERVIEWER: What do you think of the Big Brother movement? Would you recommend it to other boys who do not have fathers at home?

CASS: I think that if you have a lot of boys like me, you should keep it, because the Big Brother I have is real nice. He is smart and a lot of fun. I like smart people.

INTERVIEWER: Before you met him had you met anyone as smart as your B.B.?

CASS: No. I would also like to be as big as him. One thing I do not like about him is that he talks a lot—about things I do not know about.

CASEWORKER: You mean things with which you are not familiar?

CASS: That's it. I do not understand him all the time.

JAMES: I would ask a man who used terms I didn't understand what they meant, and if he didn't know I would consult a dictionary. I like my B.B. He teaches me about medicine, he is smart, and he is talkative. He is nice to be with.

INTERVIEWER: Does he remind you of someone you would like to have at home all the time?

JAMES: Yes, my father. I mean in a different way. I would like my father to be like him. That is, to be as smart and as nice to be with. When I am with my father, he is not understandable at all. When he yells and screams, you just cannot bear it. I understand the words he uses, which I don't like. He yells at his new wife, he hits her. This does not have anything to do with me, but I do not like it.

INTERVIEWER: What does the B.B. do that you would like to have your father do?

JAMES: He does let everyone say what he wishes, but he does not let anyone go without doing his share. He makes sure that everyone has his share of the conversation.

CASS: Well, I would like my father to be smart and to take me places such as those my B.B. takes me to. He takes me to his house and makes me feel good.

CASEWORKER: It seems that both of you are saying that you like your B.B.'s because they have a lot of patience with you.

JAMES: Can I say something interesting? When my father tells me to do something, he does not tell me why. He does not educate me whatsoever. When my B.B. tells me to do something, I don't even have to ask him why. He tells me why this is so important to do and why people should do this.

CASEWORKER: Has your B.B. ever disciplined you in any way? How would your B.B. go about telling you that your behavior was wrong?

CASS: I would do like he was my father and do what he wanted.

JAMES: I cannot recall if we have ever had a disagreement. However, if such a situation would arise, we'd hear each side's story and then we'd try to decide what was right. We'd come to a mutual agreement.

CASEWORKER: How does this differ from your experiences with your father?

JAMES: He just yells and screams. He does not care if I am right or wrong.

CASEWORKER: How about disagreements with your mother? How do you settle them?

JAMES: I try to convince her and then usually she does not see it my way.

CASS: With my mother, I first try to have her see it my way. If she does not, then I do what she wants. With my B.B., we first talk about the best way to do things. Whichever comes out best we do.

INTERVIEWER: If you boys had three wishes about a father in the house, what would you wish for?

CASS: I wish that my father would be in my house and would live at home. That he would be real nice, like my mother. That he would buy me a bicycle.

JAMES: Can I ask a question of Cass? I would like to know first what we are talking about. Cass, you have said that you would like your father to be like your mother—in what way are they different?

CASS: My father is a man with whom I cannot communicate with and whom I cannot understand.

JAMES: Do you think anything can be done? In my case, I think it is hopeless.

CASS: Well, I had three wishes.

JAMES: O.K. I would wish a complete college and medical education like my B.B. I would also wish that my father would be like my B.B. I would not want him home unless he would be like my B.B. I would also wish, as my third wish, that I would not have to see my father every Sunday.

INTERVIEWER: How does your mother talk about your father, Jimmy?

JAMES: My father thinks that I do not like him because my mother tells me bad things about him. As far as I see it, the bad things are true. My mother wants me to be prejudiced against my father. She does not like him and she wants more people on her side. It is like a battle.

INTERVIEWER: Are there any particular problems you have experienced because you do not have a father in the house? Would a father in the house at all times make a difference in your life?

CASS: If I had a father in the house at all times, it would not be as nice, because when you have something wrong, your mother knows how to talk better than a father.

JAMES: Since I do not have one, I cannot tell you. If I did have a good father at home, things would be different, because my mother would not always be yelling and then blame me. I have this theory that some people have a power drive. My mother is like that. She likes to show off that she has more power than children. Now if I had a father like my B.B., this would not happen. My own father only adds to it—he does the same things as my mother.

INTERVIEWER: One day you yourselves are going to be fathers. What do you think you would have to do to be considered good ones?

CASS: I would take my children to the park. I would take them wherever they would like to go. I would not be as strict as my father, who yelled a lot.

JAMES: I would give them an education they would never get in school. I would teach them how to get along with little children. I would not try to show off. Sometimes when I am with my mother, I say to myself, "I want to show off like her, I want to get my revenge." But I don't think that it is true now; just because she is wrong does not make me right. I would try to teach my children things without making them angry. I would not yell if they could not understand me.

INTERVIEWER: How about the other boys you know who do have

fathers at home—are there any problems in making friends with others because of your situation?

CASS: Not inside their homes, outside of them. For example, the building superintendent picks on me because he knows that I don't have a father at home. Big kids also pick on me. I don't do things to make them do it. If I had a father, this would not happen.

INTERVIEWER: What about the families of your friends, living in your own apartment house? Do they invite you in to play?

CASS: No. I don't know why.

INTERVIEWER: Is this because you do not have a father at home?

CASS: No. They don't even know that I don't have a father at home. I tell them I do have a father but not that he is not at home. I do feel guilty about not having a father at home, because if someone fights with me and I beat him up, he says, "I'll get my father after you." My mother cannot fight for me this way.

JAMES: I have a different gimmick. Cass covers up by not telling anyone that his father does not live with him. With adults, I meet them with a story about what's happening at home which makes them feel sorry for me—that my mother, for example, yells at me, and how bad things are because I have no father at home. This is not true, but it makes them feel sorry. This helps a lot, it relieves my guilt.

CASEWORKER: Do you feel guilty about your parents being divorced?

JAMES: Not really. It goes far back. Jerome, a classmate of mine whose mother is a psychologist, taught me all about analysis. He shows off all about it, like I do. He tells people that his father died in the war when he was young and that he did not know him. He says that he thought he was the cause of the divorce his parents had, and he felt guilty that his father was not at home. I don't know if I ever felt guilty. My friends never say anything bad about my not having my father at home. In that way they are my friends.

CASEWORKER: You seem to be selective about who your friends are so that you will not be hurt.

JAMES: That's true. I guess that if I had a father like my B.B., I would never be hurt. There is only one person who made a negative comment about my not having a father. This one is jealous because I am smarter than he is, and he tries to get the others on his side. He says, "You know, his (meaning mine) father does not live with him."

I let other people do the answering. But I would never answer him because I would not give him the satisfaction. I ignore such people because I know I cannot say anything about it.

INTERVIEWER: Your father has remarried and has a child with his new wife. How do you get along with her?

CASS: Well, she is a pest and blames everything on me. I cannot stand her.

INTERVIEWER: How do you get along with your father's new wife?

JAMES: Well, she is a drug addict.

INTERVIEWER: Is this true?

JAMES: It really is not true. My mother got me against my father, and my father is getting me against my mother, and I am in the middle and don't know where to go. I usually cling to my mother. I see what my father is doing—my mother is right, I guess, and my father usually is not. At one time my father told a relative on his side of the family that someone we know as a bad person "is just like my mother."

Interviews with Middle-Class Adolescents

If there are any doubts of how much children regret the breakup of their parents' marriage, and their own strong determination to keep their own children from such a trauma, the interview with this group eliminates them. Behind the brave talk and the careless language, these young people make plain their dependency upon a stable marital union, a relationship which no longer exists in their homes. Among their recommendations for preventing similar situations in the future are premarital unions, not yet acceptable to our culture, although they seem to make logical sense of a sometimes senseless relationship.

The group consisted of five teen-agers: Amy, Chris, Sue, Don, and Geri.

INTERVIEWER: I'd like you to say a few words about how you feel in a household with only one parent.

AMY: In a case like that, if something happens, you don't know which side to go to. If your father says something, you don't know if he's right, or if your mother is right. It goes back and forth, and you're stuck in the middle. I don't know which way to grab from. I don't know which way to absorb from.

INTERVIEWER: If you had three wishes concerning your home situation, what might they be?

GERI: I never really thought about it, but I'm glad in a way that my father isn't home because it wasn't good when he was. Now it's harder, because if I get into a fight with my mother, I'll call my father up. If I get in a fight with my father, which isn't very often, I'll go to my mother. So I guess number one, I would wish that my mother would remarry, because it would make her happy—and because my father did get remarried. Number two, well, I really wish they never would have started arguing like they did.

DON: Just my mother's left, so I wish maybe she could understand me more and try to let me have more say in what I want to do. I lost my father when I was seven, so that's really before I began to appreciate him.

INTERVIEWER: Has there been a difference in your home because you haven't had a father while your friends have had fathers?

DON: Just when I get in trouble. I get in more trouble, because my mother can't really do anything to me. What can she do to me when I do something wrong—if she can't punish me?

SUE: If I had three wishes, I guess one would be that I could be uninvolved in the problems and conflicts between my mother and father. When they're separated, of course, I'm in the middle. I wish that I didn't have to put my sympathies on either side, but you're kind of forced to. And I guess I wished my father would get remarried, and I kind of wish my mother wouldn't.

INTERVIEWER: It would be great if your father remarried, and your mother did not? Why?

SUE: Because I know I'd only end up giving the other guy a hard time. Because I'd resent another father trying to take my father's place. I would never respect him—well, I'd respect him for trying to be a new father, but I could never obey him if he gave me a command and I didn't want to do it. I'd be more apt to turn around and say, "Who are you to tell me what to do?"

INTERVIEWER: Have you found any social difficulties because you don't have a father in the home?

SUE: No, but I found some when he was in the house. When my father was living at home, there were more anxieties. I was worried about when they were going to start fighting and who would be there at the time. I had to kind of gear my schedule to the moods of my parents. I guess the only social difficulty I find now—which is kind of past since my father's left for a considerable length of time—is because my mother is quite cranky and moody.

INTERVIEWER: Do you have any difficulty with your sister because your father's not home?

SUE: Yes. My sister is my half sister. I never knew this until about five months ago. My father never got along with her. I was always the favored one—at least my father stuck up for me while my mother would always go to her side. My sister is twenty-two—she's old enough—but now when I get into a fight with her, everyone is more or less on her side now that my father's gone. It's me against everyone.

CHRIS: I'm glad my mother didn't remarry. I wouldn't take any crap from a stranger.

INTERVIEWER: What kind of father would you like to have?

CHRIS: At this point? None. I used to want one. When I was younger, I always wanted to hunt, and my father was never much for the outdoors.

INTERVIEWER: How do you get along with your mother?

CHRIS: That's a mess. Sometimes good, sometimes bad. I play my parents off against each other. If I have a hassle up here, I go down to my father and that kind of straightens it out. Sometimes he gives her a call—oh, it's beautiful.

INTERVIEWER: Do you find not having a father in the home is a benefit or a detriment? How do the other fellows look at you?

CHRIS: They treat me regular—as much as I could want. No, they don't treat me any different.

INTERVIEWER: How about you, Sue?

SUE: I guess the only way I can put it is that if I had a choice, I'd rather lose my father, because my social life is therefore much less restricted. Now that my father's gone, my mother tends to be a little bit more hesitant because she's not sure if my father'd approve. But my father was always lenient—he never really cared where I went. I was his good little girl.

INTERVIEWER: Did you want that—being trusted to that extent?

SUE: Yes. I really did. I came in once at two o'clock in the morning and my father just stood up and said, "Oh, you're home early." It was great—I didn't have to sit up for another hour giving explanations. I went through the whole thing the next morning with my mother and I had to explain why I got home late and everything. My mother's much more strict now. When my father was home she'd say, "Ask your father." My father would say, "Ask your mother." I could just leave the house and they'd both wonder who said yes—it was a lot easier.

AMY: My parents are both living with me. They're thinking of a divorce, but I don't think it will take place.

INTERVIEWER: If it did take place, what would you think?

AMY: Oh, God. Well, I'd feel that my father was copping out on us. Since he's an alcoholic, my mother represents guilt to him and what he's done to us in the past. I feel that if he divorces her, he'll be running away from that guilt, and this is what I've told him. It's hard to talk to him now that he's living in the A.A. program. He realizes a lot, but he still has a long way to go.

INTERVIEWER: How do you think your sisters would react if your father were gone, as compared with your brothers?

AMY: My brothers would take the attitude that they didn't care —I think to cover up their feelings—and my sisters would be very, very hurt, and probably be crushed by the fact. My father has said, "If I do go, I'll take the younger kids with me"—that includes my two sisters, one eight and one thirteen. I know my thirteen-year-old sister would just crumble, because she would be taken away from her brothers and sisters, and her mother.

INTERVIEWER: Geri, do you think there would be a difference between the reactions of brothers and sisters to a father's leaving the house?

GERI: Well, I'm the only girl in my family. I have two brothers, one older and one younger. When my parents were divorced, my little brother was around five, and my older brother was around fourteen or fifteen. I don't really think it affects my older brother, Jeff, because he's older. My father was there to support him during the years you need a father. It's hard for my little brother to grow up without his father, but he leans on my older brother a lot. My mother doesn't like it at all, because my older brother isn't a good example for him, or that's what she says anyway. He follows everything my older brother does. I think that he imitates him like Jeff was his father, even though we do see our father.

INTERVIEWER: How does the absence of a father strike one when it happens?

GERI: It affects everyone in the beginning. I remember when it first happened—it affected me a lot. I understood what was happening, but I guess I just couldn't accept it. After a while, however, I just get used to it. I used to see my father once a week, and I'd speak to him every night, but it's hard at the beginning. When you grow up with it, you get used to it.

INTERVIEWER: What do you do in the house to cooperate?

SUE: I do very little around the house. All I do is make my bed on weekends and keep my room straightened up, and that's it. My mother has people come in once a week. They do the house and then —we're trying to sell it—she does the straightening up. The only real housework she does is right before people come to see the house— she gets busy, and all I do is make my bed and clean up my room for them.

DON: Men don't do those things. I try to keep it that way. But when my sisters are at school, I'm the only one who lives upstairs. My mother lives downstairs, so the house gets messy as hell upstairs, and the maid comes every other week and cleans up.

GERI: We have a maid that comes three times a week, every week, and the only kind of housework I ever do is not very much.

INTERVIEWER: Do you cook?

GERI: Oh, I can cook and stuff like that. I don't really do anything in the house. When the maid comes, my room gets cleaned. When she doesn't come, well, unless I'm in one of those really good moods where I want to clean my room. . . . However, that's not very often. If my mother has to go someplace, I'll do the dishes for her—stick 'em in the dishwasher.

SUE: In my family we discipline ourselves. The older kids push the younger kids around a little bit, but as for self-control, we all had to grow up real quick.

INTERVIEWER: Tell me, what do you think of this problem of broken families? Has it affected you in any way?

SUE: Well, every kid from a broken family that I know is messed up in some way, and in some way they all have a handicap. You need your two parents; even if they're lousy people, they're human beings.

INTERVIEWER: What sort of handicap do you mean?

SUE: Well, the fact that your parents have left each other. They couldn't live together, that's all. They just couldn't live together. They couldn't, they just couldn't, try to understand each other. Maybe there're some relationships that are just impossible. But still I think that two people who want to stay together for the kids can try. They can try to get along, because I feel otherwise that the kids are handicapped.

INTERVIEWER: In what way?

SUE: Maturity-wise. Growing up, they need their parents. It's tough to be your own parent.

CHRIS: At the time of the divorce, I didn't really know what was going on, but in fact I did know. One morning I woke up and my father was gone. Then I found out he was living at my grandfather's. I asked my mother what was happening. She wouldn't tell me. I asked my father—he told me.

INTERVIEWER: How might it have been different for you if your parents had stayed together?

CHRIS: I don't know. I don't think I could stand living with my father, having him in the same house for years at a time. I can visit him and I can stay down there for a few weeks, but that's it.

INTERVIEWER: If he had remained with your mother, how might it have been better for you?

CHRIS: I don't know. When I was feeling bad, it would have been nice to have someone to talk to maybe, for companionship.

INTERVIEWER: Might it have changed your drinking and smoking?

CHRIS: Yeah. The smoking maybe not, but the drinking definitely. I could not walk into the house smashed if he was there.

SUE: For me, it would have been a lot different, I think, if they had stayed together happily, not fighting. I would have had someone to lean on with my father there. Most important of all, my father always put me on a pedestal. When someone sets high standards for you, you try a lot harder to live up to them. My mother's more apt to accept me as I am, so I'm more apt to be just as I am, instead of just trying to be a little bit better. I guess that's the only way it would have changed, because actually my father was kind of a silent discipliner. He never played a great dramatic role in my life—he was always there though. He was away a lot, so I had learned to live without him for long periods of time anyway, but then again he'd always come back. In a way, I'm glad they separated, because they were hell to live with. Then again, I think it's very stupid for people to go and get married when they don't even know what living with someone is going to be like.

INTERVIEWER: Would this possibly give you the incentive to live with somebody before you married them, to sort of find out if you could get along with them?

SUE: Definitely. If you're going to obligate yourself to marry someone and have children, I think you owe it to those children to stay there. If it's your decision to have them, you ought to stick by them. I think that before you even get married, and especially before you have children, you ought to learn whether or not you can live together, whether or not it's going to work.

DON: Yeah, I think it would be better, because I don't think my folks would have got married if they had lived together before. My mother didn't know what to look for. If someone's great in bed, they might turn out to be a rotten housekeeper. I think that people should live together, a year or two before, even six months, just to get some idea.

AMY: I think it's a good idea to live together, to get to know the person you're going to spend the rest of your life with, to know them through and through, not to mention that making sure you love each other very much and respect each other. Just to see if you're compatible in every way, that you enjoy the same things, that you're willing to do the same things together. It's good to find out. That's why long engagements before marriage are a good idea. My parents knew each other just four months, and to this day they say they didn't love each other.

GERI: I guess I would think the same way—that you should live with a person before marriage—but I'm sure my parents wouldn't like that idea, because it's the generation thing. I still don't think that would work, because my parents were married fourteen years before they realized that they couldn't get along. Even if they had lived with each other before they got married, it still would have come to that point. So, I don't think even living together before would work.

DON: I think knowing someone—other than just what they look like and their personality—is very important to marriage. I don't really think it would have that much effect on divorces in long-term marriages, but it would cut out a lot of divorces that happen, say, after a year or so. I definitely would want to live with someone before I married her, but I don't know what effect that would have on divorces at all.

INTERVIEWER: What does a good father mean to you?

SUE: A reliable man, one you could count on pretty much through thick and thin, someone with good judgment, someone who was understanding and who I felt had a good set of morals.

INTERVIEWER: Which are?

SUE: Oh, I don't know. I'd want the father to pretty much give my child a set of examples—what happened to people who did what —and then give him the basics and let him go his way with just consultation from the father, knowing he could count on the father when he needed help. A lot of the child's growing up depends on his environment and his friends. I think the parents are only 50 percent of it, and that's only in the very young stages.

INTERVIEWER: How about you, Amy? What would you like your husband to be as a father to your children?

AMY: First of all, I would like him to be a mature adult so that he could understand his children and his wife, and make them know that they could go to him for understanding. He should be a secure person so that he could hold the family together, be the man in the house.

INTERVIEWER: How about you, Geri? What characteristics would you like in your husband as a father of your children?

GERI: A man with responsibility. Someone that you could depend upon, have a good job, could finance a family and me. Someone that leaves in the morning and comes home at night and is responsible. Someone who when he gets married—the day that he's married —that he will spend his whole life with the other person.

INTERVIEWER: How about you, Don? What sort of characteristics do you think you would prefer to have as a father?

DON: I don't know that I'd want to be a father, because I don't think that a father can really comprehend the ideas that are growing in his kid's mind. The gap is widening so fast that I just don't think that a father and son relationship is possible any more. If I were a father, I'd just try to develop the kid's ideas instead of putting them down and trying to insert my own ideas, because my ideas would be obsolete very soon.

Religious Conceptions of Marital Responsibilities

Part Three

In virtually every disolution of a marriage there are religious, moral, and ethical considerations to which individuals have to be sensitive. Part III is designed to provide the reader with current models of the three major religious approaches to separation, divorce, and concern for the welfare of the child.

In presenting the Protestant model, Dr. James G. Emerson, Jr., from his background of long years as a Presbyterian minister, offers a broad panorama of the clergy's role and its current philosophy of coping with broken marriages against a background of changing cultural conceptions, standards, and practices.

Msgr. James P. Cassidy, who is also a practicing clinical psychologist, places strong emphasis on the responsibility of the Catholic parent in a dissolved marriage for maintaining the religious feelings and ideals of his children.

Rabbi Earl B. Grollman, offering a Jewish point of view strongly oriented along traditional lines, bolsters his discussion of the role of the Jewish parent in separation and divorce with excerpts from the prophets and the Torah.

What emerges from the three discussions is a deepened awareness of the concern of modern-day religions with the development and maintenance of an atmosphere conducive to the fullest advancement of the child as a religious, moral, and ethical person, in spite of the vicissitudes of his family situation.

In reviewing the chapters on Catholic and Jewish conceptions of marital responsibilities, the reader will become aware that within these two religious groups are many different viewpoints that diverge from the positions put forward here. The Roman Catholic and Jewish viewpoints presented here are perhaps representative of what has come to be known as "orthodox." Other views may be closer in spirit and practice to the Protestant viewpoint. Certainly the views included below are not the only contemporary conceptions in Jewish and Catholic circles.

JAMES G. EMERSON, JR., Ph.D.

A Protestant View of
Marital Responsibilities

*Dr. James G. Emerson, Jr., for a number of years the minister
of the Larchmont, N. Y., Avenue Church and now director of
the Community Service Society of New York City, provides us
with an informative and thorough Protestant view of marital
responsibilites. A well-known writer in this area, Dr. Emerson
makes clear the whole range of problems for children from
disrupted homes, and is deeply concerned about matters of
their religious and moral education.*

*This chapter affords a deepened understanding not only of
the religious but also of many of the practical problems which
the author has had to handle in the course of his Protestant
ministry.*

The Protestant concern for children of divorce is not so much a matter of doctrine as of process. One can search the doctrinal statements and the formal documents of the various denominations, and little will be found. In magazine articles, church school materials, and guidance literature some material will be found that pertains to children of divorce. Yet even these sources relate much more to the process of living than to the content of belief. In the processes of the parish level and through conversations with individual pastors, we find practices in dealing with children of divorce. That is where the pain is felt, and the church either does or does not become relevant. Unfortunately, there seems little evidence that even these local processes have been developed on the basis of a carefully constructed approach.

In the Roman Catholic tradition, by contrast, activity in the parish is marked by considerable activity at higher ecclesiastical levels. Whether in Rome or the local diocese, there is evidence that the center of responsibility alters the role of the local parish. To a degree, the parish priest is a channel for carrying out the pastoral concern of a bishop who may never know the child involved. In some instances, this type of relationship may be a resource that strengthens what a given pastor brings to a child. In other instances, the relation may mean that the local priest sees himself as little more than a communicator between the person with a problem and the diocese.

For better or worse, the Protestant parish, and its clergy, are almost entirely on their own. They not only must do whatever is done; they also must be creative about what ought to be done. In some instances, this situation means the approach to a child is consistent with a Christian concern for the child of a divorced parent. In other instances, any integrity that binds what happens to a child and what is Christian is purely by accident—if it exists at all.

Until recent years, there has been little in Protestant thinking that does for Protestants what moral theology does for the Roman Catholic. In part, this lack grew from reaction to the excesses of moral theology that developed in the Middle Ages. Even more, this failure grew from inability in the nineteenth and early twentieth century to see that the Reformation dealt as much with the operational side of theology as it did with the doctrinal side.

Since the early thirties, however, the field of pastoral theology, as a theology, has developed and come to take a strong place in most

Protestant seminaries. The field of pastoral theology seeks to look at the operational side of theology from various perspectives—especially the perspectives of nurture, health, communication, and organization. Primarily, pastoral theology seeks to look at the dynamics of personal and interpersonal relationships and discover that which will allow for creative dealing with whatever problem is at hand. In so doing, pastoral theology brings the whole experience of the church back into conversation with all of the helping sciences—medicine, psychology, social work, teaching, psychiatry, and sociology.

What follows, then, stands in the tradition of the current operational approach to understanding faith and nurture in relation to the youngster of divorced parents. In the course of the article, I hope to describe the present situation of the divorced family, point out where the Protestant church has been with regard to this youngster—theologically speaking—and state a constructive basis for approaching the children of broken families from the perspective of Protestantism.

PORTRAITS OF CHILDREN

Who are the children of divorced parents?

The New York subways recently carried an advertisement—a black-and-white picture showing ghetto youngsters sitting before a storefront church. The legend beneath the scene of a child in tattered clothes announced that "Every child is all children."

Despite the emotional impact of the poster, it is inaccurate. For every child is different. Children cannot be helped by an oversimplistic description of their situation. Although no article can do justice to each child, at least certain distinctions have to be made. Children can be described in relation to regions where they live. Their cultural background is a differentiating factor. Economic conditions certainly set off some children from others. Even trends in various parts of a country will leave differing marks on a child.

One way to understand the situation of the child is divorce is to see him or her at one of three economic levels. Trends, regions, and cultures may be blended into that differential. Further, my own sociological expertise is not such that I can properly try to describe children in terms of these other dimensions. Although I have lived in the Far West, the Midwest, and the Mideast, even these areas have changed so rapidly in the last twenty years that mere residency hardly makes one an expert. Yet it is important to recognize that the culture of rural Texas as opposed to vactionland Florida, for example, does have its effect on the child in question. The financial and cultural mood of the Southern church is different from that of the North. Church attendance, large church school classes, and a somewhat literalistic mood about scripture are far more typical of the South than the Northeast.

Another significant difference lies between urban and rural areas. In a rural area, the church may be small, but it is identifiable and clear. In a small town, one person's problem is everybody's problem. The child of divorce, therefore, is not anonymous as in the dense urban area. Such a child may have the problem that "everybody knows"; or he may have the benefit of a church community that surrounds the divorced child with the love and support needed to cope with the experience. The urban child may be free from being labeled in school, but similarly may have to look harder to find love and understanding needed to deal with the family break.

Yet, across every section of the land—North, South, urban, or rural—there may be found economic and cultural differences. Whether or not one can speak of a culture of poverty or a culture of affluence is still debatable. Whether cultural factors cause or result from poverty, there are cultural accounterments that go with each economic level. Because of their accessibility, I pick these as an entry to understand the nature of the problem that is faced.

The first level might be called the level of wealth. Not far from the "Heidi country" of Switzerland, there is a school that has students from all over the world. In New England, New Jersey, California, and Virginia, to mention a few obvious states, there are expensive high prestige schools—all private. The fact that some of these now make an effort to provide scholarships for ghetto children does not alter the picture. Such children are moving into a particular world when they enter these schools; the disadvantaged children do not change that world.

At any one of these schools can be found a certain number of boys and girls whose parents are divorced. One particular boy is suggestive of the situation. He is fourteen. He lives at the school during the academic year. On holidays he may be with one or the other of his parents. More than likely, however, he will be on a tour or at an exclusive camp. Sometimes he is with an uncle.

To many individuals, this boy's situation seems tragic. For some boys it is. In this instance, however, the school is the boy's salvation. He has a good peer relationship. He has developed a friendship with a young teacher and his wife that fills many personal needs. He has found both roots and identity in the school. He is not a star either academically or athletically, yet he belongs. His parents visit him; but they come at separate times. Because of the acceptance he finds in the school setting, this boy finds he can relate to each parent, one at a time, when visits come.

To say that the boy does not have feelings about the divorce would be a falsehood. He is aware of very strong feelings at times, tremendous bitterness. What is important is that the school setting gives him a base in which he is able to deal with his feelings. The fact that this school is Episcopalian-oriented suggests something of one way in which a Protestant church deals with the problem of the divorced child. The church accepts the child as a person and meets his need through a resident school—*if* the child can pay for it.

Whether or not this wealthy youngster is in a private or public school—or in no school at all—there are apt to be certain characteristics. Initially, the family mobility may be quite high. The father may well be established in his work, but his personal travel schedule is likely to be exhausting. The mother may have remarried, and her base for rootage shifts with the experiences of the new husband.

In the area of religion, church for the wealthy may be largely a matter of ceremony. The clergyman is often asked to bless many events. Baptism, usually called "christening," will be private. The minister is expected to be involved in the marriage service and to "read" the funeral service. If the minister speaks out on adultery, that will be accepted as part of his image—not seen as something necessarily to be taken seriously. If he raises questions about remarriage after divorce, he may be tolerated with annoyance, because after all, "it's in the canon." If, however, the clergyman moves into the arena of race relations or integration of private schools and clubs, that clergyman is asking for considerable hostility. Faith is, at this economic level, most generally to be seen as private, individualistic, and not involved in the matter of what a person decides to do about the schooling of his children or the providing for their recreation.

The devoted attendance at church of some wealthy, and the commitment of some church laymen to the matters of education and the problems of children serve both to demonstrate the exception and proof of the rule. In very wealthy areas, the size of church attendance in contrast with that of church roles is the evidence. One layman said to a clergyman in his area, "I will give you money, the privileges of the club, and education for your children; but don't expect me in church or at your meetings."

The result of this is that the average parish of wealth sees relatively little of the child of divorce. Either the parish is not involved in the youngster's life, or the child is living away from the parish. The chaplin at the private school may well relate to this person, and the parish minister may do so occasionally. Yet, in the case of the latter, the relationship may grow more from the pastor's initiative and concern than from the fact that he was sought out by the parish member. The somewhat ceremonial view of the clergyman reduces the degree to which he is sought in the matter of children of divorce. The mood was expressed by one member of a high income area who said, "What would Reverend X know about it?"

The opposite extreme from wealth is that of the low-income youngster. This category includes those who are in poverty pockets, on welfare, and just above the welfare level. In many instances, the Protestant clergyman is the person most likely to be sought because he has contacts, prestige, and some training. The type of church involved is possibly one of the main denominations, but it is more likely to be a Pentecostal, Adventist, or holiness type of group.

The Community Service Society covers a sufficient spread of New York City to give some indication of the portrait of the children seen by Protestant churches. In the year 1969, 17 percent of the Protestant children of divorced parents seen by the Community Service Society were under five years of age; 65 percent were in the school years between the ages of six and fifteen; 18 percent were in the working years to voting age of sixteen to twenty. It is to be kept in mind that these statistics refer to the children of divorced parents only. One-parent families where there had been no marriage are not included. In almost every instance, the children were living with the mother.

At this economic level, the child is likely to be aware of the father, but unaware of where he lives. Whereas the child of the wealthy may see the father on regular bases, the youngster of the very poor may wonder in vain when he will ever see the father. The child of the wealthy may find his identity in a school and be somewhat separated from both parents; the child of all other economic groups must find identity within the context of the mother's grouping.

The size of divorced families, as seen by the Community Service Society in the year 1969, is smaller than it is in the popular image of disadvantaged people. The average white divorced family had 2.2 children. This compares with the 2.85 children of the average white family in New York City, and the 3.3 national average. The average for black divorced families was 2.6 children. The average size for Puerto Rican families was 2.8 children. In New York City, the average size of nonwhite families is 3.19 children, and nationally that average is 3.85.

The *average* size of family, plus the small number of families with children under five, indicates something about divorced groups. A small number of children may result from the built-in birth control of divorce. Equally important, however, may be a concern about having children when the parental relationship is not good. Experience with unwed mothers, and a study of interview material, leads me to believe that there is a higher degree of moral concern for children of divorce in the ghetto than many suspect. For many, having children seems to mean an effort to remain married. As the statistics indicate, for most, the break does not come until the children are in school.

The case of a young teen age girl, whom we will call Linda, explores some of the dynamics involved for a divorced child who lives at this economic level. Linda is one of two children who lives with her maternal grandmother. Her natural mother is often in the home, but at the beginning of the interview relationship was often away and involved in prostitution. The diagnostic evaluation of the mother was that of an "immature dependent." Linda was observed as having a low level of frustration tolerance. She cried easily, but handled routine matters rather well. At summer camp, she was happy, but showed great difficulty in dealing with physical contact. She would pull away from a counselor who put an arm around her. If Linda initiated the action, however, she could accept the appropriate response.

Linda's family was on welfare. She saw adults primarily as

sources for satisfying her needs. Although she could express feelings, she often did so manipulatively. In fact, she did not trust adults. Interviews with her showed a marked interest in her parents—whether the information was good or bad.

In studying Linda's case history, one gets a sense of admiration and pathos. Here is a youngster, black, trying both to gain a sense of identity and afraid of being further hurt by the adults from which she seeks that identity. Her somewhat—but not excessive—lack of interest in peers shows both a dependency need on adult figures and a desire to find identity from her family roots. At the age of fourteen, she was attracted to a thirty-three-year-old man. She also became fond of a woman case aide. Both interests reflected her search for security, but the report also indicates a struggle for an answer to the question, "Who am I?" This identity search, not unnatural at this age for anyone, was magnified by the ghetto problem and the hiddenness of her mother and father.

For Linda, one high point in the year's experience was a bus trip to a resort. This trip was arranged by her church (Pentecostal) and allowed both her mother and her to go. The interviews in the few weeks after this trip indicated of what value the occasion had been. It was not so much the vacation as the obvious chance for Linda to know her mother. The positive result was reflected in several interviews.

Between the extremes of wealth and poverty, there is the large middle-income group. For the purposes of this article, this group encompasses those people from the upper levels of low income and the lower levels of upper income. This is the group most often seen by the traditional Protestant churches, but it is not where most of the divorced children are to be found. The pastor of the low-income church may see the highest percentage of the children of divorced parents. How much a pastor of a middle-income group will see children of broken homes depends on the attitude of the community to the pastor. In a Bible Belt community, or a community with a clear historical identity—such as a town where "Washington slept"—the minister is still seen as *the* person to whom to turn. People in Levittown communities, by contrast, may turn to the minister, but are as likely to go directly to a marriage counselor, lawyer, or school official.

At this economic level, the last ten years indicate a shift in the age of children a minister sees. This statement is based on a sampling of ministerial experience in the New York area. At the beginning of the sixties, high-school groups were strong, and many of the children of divorced were in the upper grade-school levels. Today, there is a perceivable shift downward. The children ministers see are now likely to be in the lower grades and junior high school.

The child of divorce in the middle-income areas may be in private school but probably is in public school. He usually lives with the mother, and the mother probably works locally. There is the problem of financial stability, and especially in a suburb, there is the problem of no father figure. The minister, school teacher, or local doctor may become very important as a father substitute

One case in point is a seventh-grade boy whose father left home and married another woman in a nearby town. The father's work often kept him from home. In the local church, a member of the staff became a father substitute. The boy was in the man's home as often as his own. The boy was at church not just for activities but also to help with preparations for programs. This instance is by no means isolated. When the mother subsequently remarried, the pastor played an important role in helping the boy adjust to the new family environment. Thus, the church played a role in the progress of the boy from identification with an absentee father to that of a father substitute to a "new" father in the home.

What do these three portraits suggest about the needs of children seen in Protestant churches?

Although it is perhaps dangerous to suggest that one need is greater than another, one is outstanding: the need for an environment in which the child of divorced parents can deal creatively with *his* experience of the divorce. I call this the need for a context.

Dr. Seward Hiltner and Lowell Colston have written of the context of pastoral counseling.[1] In exploring the subject of the relative merits of counseling in the context of a parish and of a secular clinic, one piece of evidence was clear: viz, that there are styles of context in which counseling takes place. Whether one speaks of the Rogerian sense of caring or the Freudian sense of the mirror image, therapeutic growth takes place in an identifiable context.

The same truth holds for general interpersonal relationships.

[1]Hiltner, Seard, and Colston, Lowell. *The Context of Pastoral Counseling*, New York: Abington, 1961.

Educational theory, management development, and recreational experience all give attention to the matter of the context in which the education, management, or recreation occur. In all religions, the same concern is gaining more and more attention. Whether it is dealing with church architecture or the openness of a given congregation, the context provided by a church does make a difference in what happens to the church member.

In the instance of Linda, the church—not inadvertantly—played a major role. The church purposely used field trips to provide a context in which people could relate to each other. It certainly provided the context for Linda and her mother. In so doing, the church provided a context in which Linda could begin dealing with her problems and feelings about her divorced parents. There can be no guarantee that such a context will be used creatively. Without the opportunity, however, Linda would have had little change to deal with her feelings in anything but a destructive manner.

A second need is for awareness that the problem of children of divorce is *their* problem. It is true that the youngster did not ask for the problem. It is true that public sympathy is aroused for the innocent victim of adult failures. Yet, the degree to which helping the child grows out of that sympathy and adult guilt, to that degree the real help will be missed. The context a child of divorce needs is one that recognizes that the problem of his or her feelings about the divorce are *his* or *her* feelings. Whether we are dealing with the poverty-stricken Linda, or with the other more affluent children, the real issue is to deal with their feelings about what has happened to them. Ability to help cope would strengthen. Protecting the children against their feelings would only lead to weakness in dealing with future problems.

The reality of a context and the need to deal with one's own feelings mean that the young person also needs certain guiding images that do two things. First, they must help mediate the context that will allow for something to happen. Second, they must be images that recognize the focus of a youngster's problems within his own feelings. What guiding image conveys the sense that "somebody up there likes you"? What conveys the sense that there is something about the young person that is of worth? What communicates the concern that allows one to "own his feelings" and deal with them?

Whatever this context is, and whatever communicates or mediates it, must be at the local and not just the institutional level. Some fifteen years ago, a slogan in the Presbyterian literature said, "If it doesn't happen in the local church, it doesn't happen." Denominational awareness is a factor in making sure that something happens in the local church. Yet, from the perspective of the feelings of the youngster, what is significant is what happens where he is. What happens in the street? What happens in the school or with the people he actually sees?

To enable the young person to deal with his feelings about the divorced family, there is need for some continuity and order. In the instance of Linda, counseling took place over a one-year period. During that time, she had three social agency caseworkers. In the midst of a group therapy session, the second in succession, Linda suddenly got up, walked to the door, and left the room. Was this a sign of hostility? Was it fear? Basically, it was neither. Instead, she went to the office and found a casework aide whom she had come to know from her prior visits to the group. She needed that assurance of continuity which indicated that the context was still there.

This need for continuity provides a problem when a family moves even a few blocks. It provides a problem when a church group moves. The similarity of church groups in different neighborhoods may help with this problem. Similarity in styles of worship, dress of clergy, and procedures of the people all help. However, the cultural differences of even nearby communities break into the continuity of the context. This particular need, in an increasingly mobile society, is a special concern of the urban as opposed to the strictly rural type of community. The need becomes an added dimension in the dynamic feelings of the children that has to be met.

Finally, the child of divorce is in the need of an identity. The search for identity is not unique to children of divorce. The uniqueness lies in the timing. Erikson and others have spoken of the identity tasks in adolescence and early adulthood. For the child of divorce, the identity comes at least then, but perhaps earlier. For most children, the early growing years do not require a clear, firm identity, *apart* from one's family. In the stages of childhood development, there is identity with the mother or identity with the father. The need for self-identity comes at a later stage as one is establishing himself apart from the parental figures. The same is not true for the child of divorce.

Marshall McLuhan suggests that most children of today are losing their childhood years. The implosion of mass media results in the child having to absorb the adult world the moment he can see televison. Dr. McLuhan feels that ours, like other periods in world history, may be marked by the loss of childhood years.[2] Be that as it may on a global scale, it is surely part of the experience of the young person who becomes aware of parental friction. Something is happening in the adult world that affects him. From unclear but real clues in the home to the confrontation in court and determination of custody rights, the child of divorce experiences the implosion of the adult world.

This implosion means not only coming to terms with the adult world but also coming to terms with the loss of the adult constellation as he knew it. As in the case of adolescence and beginning adulthood, this loss requires a new basis for personal identity, but it is required at an early age. Much of the identity problem is usually solved in relation to the mother and the maternalistic experience. The child may be living with the mother. Counselors and caseworkers are often women. The church is referred to as "our mother" by some of the churchmen, and with good reason. Like the school that is called "alma mater," the church carries a nurturing, maternal image. The robes of the clergymen look like skirts. The need for a father is a different matter. The problem of finding a male image is real as the young person—boy or girl—seeks a sense of identity.

These needs are not solely those of children in churches. More than that, these needs can be seen as but further evidence that the problem for the child of the divorced, as for anybody, is part of the problem of humanness. These observations of church children, however, are lifted up to focus on the factors the Protestant parish is facing. Much of divorce in the secular world is dealt with in terms of contracts or of therapy. The marriage license is itself a contract, and many of the laws are basically related to economics. Other laws speak of counseling and therapy programs for the parents or the family. The task, however, is to develop a rationale for approaching the child of divorce that is based on the need to be human. Property, jurisdictional, and therapeutic procedures make sense only within

[2]McLuhan, Marshall. *The Medium is the Massage.* New York: Bantam Books, Inc., 1967, p. 18.

the larger framework of what it is to be human. The church needs to be aware that that is the real focus out of which its relation to the children of divorce proceeds.

PORTRAIT OF THE CHURCH

From a look at experiences of children, we turn to a look at the church. What is the church? Is it the image of love or the image of judgment? This is a historic question. From its very inception, the church debated the issue. There are those who would emphasize Paul's hymn of love when he said, "Now abide faith, hope, love, these three; and the greatest of these is love." (I Corinthians 13). There are others who spoke of firmness in the church with regard to its discipline. In the same letter to the Corinthians, Paul spoke of people who "ate and drank damnation to themselves." (I Corinthians 11) What is the real nature of the church?

As an institution, many today see the Protestant church as austere and judging. The image of a minister who can be a real human being, with fun in his eye, is considered a wonderful exception to the rule. Intellectually, people do not hold to that image, but most jokes and unguarded comments indicate that image which reflects a portrait of the church. The hippie development, with its emphasis on love, and the growth of sensitivity groups are both indications that many did not feel that they found love or sensitvity in the church fellowship. The Middle Age's view of the church with devils and judgment carried the same mood.

Unfortunately, both those who regard the church in terms of love and those who see it in terms of judgment have often missed the point. They have spoken of love or judgment intellectually and doctrinally rather than in dynamic relationships. The Biblical concept of judgment had to do with "right relatedness." The presence or lack of right relations between individuals or God—however one thought of God—might indeed lead to certain consequences. The key, however, was to think of judgment not in terms of a final punishment but of relationships.

By the same token, love in the Christian faith had little to do with passion. Love, in the passionate sense, meant attraction because someone was attractive and lovable. As Paul Tillich so clearly put it, love in the Christian sense meant "love in spite of one being unlovable." As some have gone on to describe this Christian view of love, however, it has become austere and unfeeling in its description. Dynamically, Christian love is best described by the word "concern" or "care." There is great feeling in the Christian view of love just as there is feeling in passion. The difference is that passion develops because of some objective beauty. Concern develops because of regard for a personality even though there may be no beauty.

The concepts of right relatedness and of concern—of judgment and love—must be kept as two poles in tension. Love without right relatedness becomes selfish and narrow. Judgment without concern becomes autocratic and destructive. It is the combination of these two that stands behind the development of Protestant activity. It is this combination that is the basis for a Protestant approach to the question of the child in divorce.

At the time of the Reformation, this balanced view of judgment and love led to rejection of the church structure as then experienced. Luther's approach shattered the structure of the Church. Calvin's approach led to building schools and emphasizing education for children. The result was a move away from emphasis on salvation of souls after death to the nurture of souls—especially of the child—in this life.

In this regard, both Luther and Calvin emphasized the responsibility for the child not of the priest or the pastor, but of the church community. Wrote Luther to people in government, "It is a serious and important matter that we help and assist our youth, and one in which Christ and all the world are mightily concerned."[3] And Calvin emphasized his view of children when he wrote, ". . . let us offer our infants to Him [God], for He gives them a place among those of His family and household, that is, the members of the church."[4] For both Calvin and Luther, the children were to be seen as full persons; and the church and community had a responsibility to deal with them as such.

In Luther's writing, there is a style which even today is becoming part of the approach of many agencies that deal with the problems of the disadvantaged. Luther felt it was not for the church to

[3]Kerr, H. T. *A Compendium of Luther's Theology.* Philadelphia: Westminster, 1943, p. 188.
[4]Calvin, John. *Institutes of Christian Religion.* John T. McNeill, editor. Philadelphia: Westminster, 1960, p. 1359.

do everything for the child, but for the church to push the government to do those things that would help the child. Therefore, with
regard to national priorities, and in a letter to government officials
that might be written today, Luther said: "If it is necessary, dear sirs,
to expend annually such great sums for firearms, roads, bridges, dams
and countless similar items in order that a city may enjoy temporal
peace and prosperity, why could not at least as much be devoted to
the poor and needy youth . . ."[5]

In those days, divorce was not so prevalent that one can find
writings which bear directly on the children of divorce. Yet the
principle is clearly established. The church had a concern and responsibility for the nurture of all children. It sought to push the
public school and public sector to provide for that child. The church
had the responsibility to "open to them the door," as Calvin put it,[6]
that they could be part of the nurture and fellowship of the church
community.

Although today it is almost impossible to find church writings
that deal with the problems of divorced children as such, those principles still hold. In the 1930's, the Presbyterian Church placed a
phrase in its constitution that indicated a child had a right to be "well
born."[7] The phrase meant not that he should be born wealthy but
born with a genuine chance for growth and for life as a person. This
phrase enunciated a principle on the basis of which all children were
to be approached; but significantly, it was written specifically with
regard to the sections of the denominational standards that dealt
with marriage, divorce, and remarriage.

From the Reformation until the present, the average Protestant
church has placed great, perhaps the greatest emphasis on education. The centrality of preaching would lead some to believe otherwise. However, most twentieth century Protestant churches, when
built, began not with the sanctuary but with the educational plant.
The first priority was training the children—and providing a place
where a child could be trained whether or not his family situation
was secure.

In terms of its philosophy, then, the Protestant church to this day

[5]Kerr. *Op. cit.*
[6]Calvin. *Op. cit.*, p. 1329.
[7]*The Constitution of the Presbyterian Church in the U.S.A.* "Director of Worship,"
paragraph 6. Philadelphia: The Presbyterian Church in the U.S.A., p. 349.

expresses high regard for the welfare of the child—and especially for the child in any disadvantaged or broken situation. In the last twenty years, this concern has been expressed not so much by what happens in national or constitutional pronouncements as in church school materials. Before 1950, most materials assumed that the child was white and in a "typical" middle-class family. Before then, most church school materials were primarily doctrinal. Today the mood has changed radically. Church school materials reflect the differences in race. These materials reflect the reality that many of the readers are of broken homes. The Presbyterian church in the U.S. (the "Southern" church) developed its present curriculum around the experience of the family. The problem of brokenness was considered. Materials for junior and senior high discussion groups include background on not only sex, marriage, and dating, but also the problem of brokenness.

The process of today's Protestant church, then, relates to the child of divorce with concern. This concern, however, is usually expressed through the traditional structures of school—church or private—and pressure on the structure of society. Generally, the problem of the divorced child is recognized but not particularly lifted up.

WHAT IS NEEDED

The increasing number of children from divorced homes requires a constructive statement that integrates Protestant thinking on the concern for those children. It is not that such thinking would be very different from Catholic or Jewish conceptions. It is that effectiveness in meeting an issue usually necessitates an institution developing, for itself, a clear, constructive position. Simply because the issue is now of large proportions, and getting larger, the church must become self-conscious about it.

The church needs to see itself not as the institutional therapist for the child of divorce but as the place where that child can grow. It is consistent with Protestantism to say that the church must push for public and private clinics, schools, and agencies to deal with the special needs of the children from broken homes. Whether the needs be for therapy, education, guidance, or recreational opportunity, the Protestant church is not in itself the source of all these. Where the community lacks in providing such a service, a given church may seek to provide it. A position consistent with Protestantism, however, will seek to see that the opportunities are available in the community; and then seek to facilitate the young person in relating to those opportunities.

The place of the church is to be that community where the young person can be free to become truly human. Here there should be the opportunity to come to terms with experiences of clinic, school, and agency. Here there should be the opportunity to relate those experiences to one's values, hopes, and fears. The church, as an institution, must do this in the local parish—for that is where the young person is.

How is this accomplished?

Consistent with the key style of Protestantism, and in line with the experiences discussed in the first part of this chapter, the parish itself must develop its operational approach in four directions:

1. Initially, it must provide a context in which a child can be helped. It must help provide the context of a father identification. This is done not just through the presence of a pastor but also by placing the child in church school classes with male teachers, by training, and by experiences that allow for relating to men in the church. The general concern of the church for the context it provides must now be expressed in response to the question: "How does a parish express the father context as strongly as it has expressed the mother context?" The local parish, in seeking to provide experiences that give guiding images to the growing child, will have to examine the meaning of its structural organizations for their impact on the youngster of divorce.

2. The parish must also provide support for the young person in his struggle. It is a common experience that as a child becomes an adolescent, the feeling of being without two parents is harder to accept, not easier. As there are changes in environment, the parish must be conscious of those who can help in dealing with environmental change and allow the young person a chance to develop a relation to the community that is clear. Whether it is in ushering, some form of service, or some program activity, the parish must be aware of those symbols of "belonging" that give support to a person's life. If I am correct in my view of the adult implosion into a young life that shortens childhood, then this concern is manifestly important. The

bar mitzvah of the synagogue symbolizes manhood. What are the symbols in a Protestant church that symbolize the reality of an early push into adult life? Committee assignments, positions on decision-making groups, and other opportunities become very important.

3. The need for some degree of continuity was expressed in the case studies. Whether it be in liturgical form or Christian studies, or just the existence of a worshipping fellowship, there is a continuity that a church can express. One adolescent of divorced parents found himself in Chicago, alone. On Sunday he wandered into the strangeness of a large church. He listened to the prelude and wondered what he was doing there. When the service of worship began, the congregation stood and sang the doxology. The young man stood; and tears flowed down his cheeks as he sang, "Praise God from whom all blessings flow." In that one moment, he found a continuity with the past. He felt he was in a context that would accept him.

4. The church must also be aware of its healing task. The problem of a child in divorce is not met until that young person can come to terms with the estrangements in his life, the closeness that he does have with one or both parents despite their separateness, and his own feelings. Here, the church may have to have a trained worker to help; but this healing is part of the church's responsibility—whether the healing takes place through a referral or by someone related to the specific congregation.

CONCLUSION

From a theological standpoint, the church must now develop a holistic approach to the problem of the child of divorce. When the local congregation finds a rationale that sees the universe as one, with a life force—God—that works through the secular as well as the religious, it has a basis for ministering to such children. This rationale must then be expressed in the life of the community known as the parish; for when such a community fails to express itself in that way, it will not only fail to help the child, it will fail its mission as a church.

REV. MSGR. JAMES P. CASSIDY, Ph. D.

A Catholic View of
Marital Responsibilities

*Dr. James P. Cassidy, Executive Director of the Family Consul-
tation Service of the Archdiocese of New York, offers a Roman
Catholic point of view not only as a leader of the church but
also from the vantage point of his training as a clinical psychologist. Msgr. Cassidy informs us of prevailing traditional
Catholic views on the nature of marriage, the conditions that
may render a marriage invalid, and the effect of such a marriage upon the children of that union.*

*It is interesting to note that whenever the church permits
a separation or divorce, religious teaching specifies that the
rupture should not affect the child of such a relationship, the
real religious problem, from the Catholic view point, is involved in the parents' remarriage.*

In dealing with the Catholic child of separation or divorce, there are many factors to be considered beyond the usual difficulties. The Catholic church lays great emphasis on the dignity, sacredness, and particularly the indissolubility of marriage. Therefore, every marriage that ends in separation or divorce is in a sense regarded as a "failure." Moreover, if a parent remarries, he or she is regarded as being in serious sin, cut off from the church. If he continues this way of life, he is "doomed to eternal damnation." These considerations, besides the usual ones involved in separation and divorce, have a definite effect upon the children. It is very difficult for the Catholic child to accept the separation or divorce of his parents, and particularly difficult may be his acceptance of the fact that one or both of his parents are cut off from the church, in serious sin, and spiritually lost forever.

In order to better understand the rather unique situation of the Catholic child of separation or divorce, it is necessary to review the teachings of the Catholic church on marriage. The church regards marriage not only as an indissoluble, sacred contract entered into by a man and woman, but has raised it up to the dignity of a sacrament so that it is a means of grace. In the words of Christ Himself, "What God has joined together, let no man put asunder."

The Catholic church is against all separation and divorce. However, in certain circumstances the law may not apply. As regards separations, the canon law of the church permits separation on the basis of adultery or danger of physical harm; separation for some other cause may be permitted by the local bishop.

In most dioceses throughout the United States, the bishops delegate their power of permitting separations to one of their representatives, usually some priest with special training in this area. Originally, this was delegated to the Marriage Tribunal, a church marriage court with lawyers and judges. Most recently, however, as in the archdioceses of New York and Chicago, this power has been removed from the marriage court and given to a counseling service which advises the Catholic couple in their difficulty and helps them to work out some solution.

Technically there is no such thing as divorce in the Catholic church, but a marriage can be annulled or declared invalid. All Catholic marriages are presumed good or valid until proven otherwise. If the validity of a marriage is in doubt, it must be presented to the local church Marriage Tribunal which exists in each diocese under a bishop. The evidence is presented to the Tribunal judges and they make a decision or pass the case on to a higher court, acting according to regular courtroom procedures.

A marriage may be annulled or declared null and void for many different reasons, which must be proven and accepted by the marriage court. If either of the two parties were incapable of entering into the contract because of some defect of age or mental competency, the marriage could be declared invalid. If it can be proven that at the time they entered the marriage contract one of the parties was psychotic, the marriage could be annulled. If at the time of the marriage either of the parties did not intend to enter a permanent marriage or remain faithful, or if he deliberately excluded all possibility of children, the marriage could be declared invalid. The difficulty with many of these questions is that they must have been present at the time of the marriage.

There are other conditions in the Catholic church for declaring a marriage invalid. A marriage is invalid, and is not even regarded as a marriage, if not performed according to church law in the presence of a priest. If a Catholic marries outside the church, this marriage is not regarded as a marriage. Although performed in the Catholic church, a marriage can be dissolved if it can be proven that the marriage was never consummated. If one of the parties is not baptized, the marriage is not regarded as a sacramental marriage and therefore could possibly be dissolved. However, a marriage in the Catholic church between two baptized persons that has been consummated seems indissoluble. Misunderstandings about the teachings of the church have left many people confused.

Whenever the church permits a separation or divorce, the religious teachings on the sinfulness of terminating a marriage really should not affect the child. He may very well have problems about the physical separation of his parents, but the religious factors will not necessarily enter into his difficulties. The real religious problem is involved in the parents' remarriage. Although it is possible for a couple to separate and even get a legal divorce, remarriage for a Catholic means that he cuts himself off from the church and is considered to be in serious sin. If he remains in this situation, he is unable to participate in the life of the church; he may no longer receive the sacraments. If he should die in this state without repentance, he would go to hell and suffer eternal damnation.

The teachings of the Catholic church on marriage, separation, and divorce have been given in brief outline. How this applies to the Catholic child depends to a great extent on how this teaching has been made known to him and how old he is when his parents separate or divorce.

The teachings of the church are conveyed to the child by his parents, by his church, and possibly through attendance at a Catholic school. The concepts of the sacredness of marriage and its indissolubility are taught to him at a very eary age. If the child does not attend a Catholic school, he probably does not have a very good grasp of the teachings on marriage and does not therefore grasp the full religious significance of remarriage. The child in the Catholic school, however, is very much aware of the teachings of the church on marriage. Because Catholic school parents are usually very much involved in the education of the child, the absence, divorce, or separation of parents is quickly known.

For example, if either or both of the parents are remarried, it is impossible for them to receive with the child when he makes his first communion. In front of his whole class and the congregation, a young child of seven or eight may have to go to communion by himself while all his classmates go with their parents. Because of the great emphasis on the importance of the family taught in the Catholic school, the Catholic child of divorced or separated parents can suffer greatly.

The suffering of the Catholic child in a separation or divorce is very often more intense than that of a child of little or no religious background. Beyond the usual psychological difficulties and insecurities that develop, he finds at least one beloved parent acting contrary to his whole sense of values. This can lead the child to reject completely this parent. On the other hand, children of separation and divorce often have a tendency to reject all moral and ethical standards. Because of their attachment to a loved parent, they want to identify with him and therefore they, too, reject religious and moral values. The Catholic child that is caught in this bind has to compromise in some way. He either has to reject the parent or his religious standards and values. Unlike the child from a religious faith that accepts divorce, the Catholic child has not only the usual tremendous problems involved in the separation or divorce but also its very serious religious implications.

For the parent of the child caught in this dilemma, we can only counsel patience. It would be most helpful if emphasis were rightly placed on the particular teachings of the church that would help all concerned to accept the situation. The Catholic church as Christ Himself teaches that the sin is to be condemned and not the sinner. We can think of Christ and Mary Magdalene, He loved her the sinner but hated her sins. The child should be helped to grasp this distinction. The child may hate his father for deserting him and still feel he should love his father; he often feels guilty about his mixed feelings. He must be made to understand that he can still love his father, or mother, yet hate what he does. He must also be made to understand that only God can judge because no one else can know all the factors involved.

The first and primary rule of the church is that God loves us: "I have first loved you." If the child really knows and feels the love of God, then he can be secure in that love that will never desert him. He will be able to accept a situation such as the separation or divorce of his parents knowing that God in His good time will work it all out. The child of a separation or divorce needs a firm knowledge and understanding of moral and religious values; otherwise he may reject these standards and find only confusion in his life.

For the Catholic child, there must be a deep understanding and awareness of all his problems, particularly of his religious problems and their implication. Only with an awareness of these problems and a fuller understanding of his faith—especially of those teachings that affect his conflict—can he overcome his difficulties and grow into a normal, healthy Catholic child.

RABBI EARL A. GROLLMAN, D.D.

A Jewish View of
Marital Responsibilities

Rabbi Earl A. Grollman, of Belmont, Massachusetts, provides us with a traditional Jewish view of children of separation and divorce in which he indicates that the family has historically been central to the Jewish way of life. However, if a Jewish marriage is regarded as invalid, it may be dissolved.

Rabbi Grollman also points out the role of children, the importance of an intact family, and the consequences for children upon its disruption.

His discussion illustrates the manner in which the traditional Jewish religious leader develops a frame of reference for ordering his perceptions of interpersonal relationships, and how this frame work is based on age-old religious teachings and doctrines.

Marriage has been described as the one enterprise in which we expect 93 per cent of our people to enter and 100 per cent to be successful.

When a marriage begins to founder, couples with children face three difficult choices. They may decide to stick it out for the sake of the children; they may try the long and painful process of repairing the marriage; or one or both parents may decide to obtain a divorce.

Divorce may solve many problems. But, inevitably, it creates a new set of dilemmas, particularly when children are involved. There are the practical questions of custody, support, and remarriage. There are the emotional problems of guilt, bitterness, and hostility. The world of the single parent is society's never-never land. It is fraught with social isolation, frustration, and loneliness.

The strongest formative Jewish influence, continuous and permeating, has been that of the home. Through family life, one serves God. "Man cannot exist without woman, nor woman without man, and both of them without the Lord." Ideally, every human being should live as a unit within a family, for the family is the ideal human group.

The reciprocal relationship between marriage and religion is clearly seen in Judaism. The important religious rituals are mostly home-centered. Jewish family ceremonials are marked not only by extended family visiting but also by the use of distinctly Jewish foods associated with that particular holy day. Religious observance requires the recitation of blessings at mealtime and at frequent intervals throughout the day. Festivals such as Passover involve extensive participation by family groups in their homes. Some psychiatrists have noted that Jews, more than members of any other group, have reported experiencing their highest religious feelings in a family setting. Yet, the regular celebration of these holidays does not mean that Jewish ritual practices have remained unchanged. On the contrary, since the first three decades of this century, there has been a marked alteration or abbreviation of home ritual ceremonies on the part of most American Jewish families. However, it is not the extent of these ceremonies which is of concern but their *function* as a binding influence on the family.

Within the Jewish family setting, customs, associations, and values have helped the family withstand many of the disruptive influences of modern life. By preserving these practices, the Jewish family has, in effect, preserved itself against some of the disorganization that is currently widespread in American family life.

Yet, despite the importance of family life, divorce is acceptable in Judaism. In Judaism, people are more important than institutions. The stability of marriage must, if necessary, be sacrificed to the right of the individual to attain personal fulfillment. Marriage was made for man, and not man for marriage. Rashi, the popular expounder of the Bible and the Talmud, wrote: "If thou hatest her, then put her away; but act not cruelly by retaining her in the home if thou art estranged from her." The futile act of preserving the union at all costs is neither desirable for the couple nor the general welfare of their progeny.

Judaism believe in the holiness of marriage but does not preserve the legal family at *all* costs. Mosaic law does not subscribe to the view that "what therefore God hath joined together, let no man put asunder" and that "the wife departeth not from her husband." Divorce may be a tragedy; but if the marriage was ill-advised in the first place, it may be an inevitable one.

As a Jewish institution, divorce had its origin in pre-Israelitic times. The Torah states: "When a man taketh a wife and marrieth her, then it cometh to pass if she finds no favor in his eyes, because he hath found some unseemly thing in her, that he writeth her a bill of divorce and giveth it in her hand, and sendeth her out of his house" (Deuteronomy 24:1).

The Jewish sages realized that divorce was a difficult and shaking experience, especially for the children of divorce. Separation means the end of family life as the child has known it, the end of feeling that his parents are there whenever he wants or needs them. Judaism thus offers religious and moral teachings as a guidepost in the ensuing encounter with helplessness, guilt, loneliness, and fear.

The Jewish faith is concerned with the youngster and how he is first told about the impending divorce. Judaism speaks to the divorcing parents and says that nothing is more disturbing to their child than a change he does not understand. Parents must help their offspring to face reality, just as they, too, must face it. Be honest with the youngsters about the divorce. It may be painful, but so is an unexplained separation. If there is no possibility of reconciliation, do not mislead the child with distorted hopes.

The former husband and wife should not deprecate each other, for they still remain father and mother. Personal grievances must be pushed into the background for the sake of the offspring. "Be not like a fly, seeking sore spots. Cover up your mate's flaws and reveal them not to the children" (Eliezar ben Isaac, *Ornot Hayyim*). Do not malign or disparage the other partner: "Cruel talk kills three: the speaker, the spoken of, and the listener" (*Numbers Rabbah* 19:2).

Children should never have the guilty feeling that they are to blame for their parents' tensions. Parents often say to their youngsters: "If it weren't for you, I wouldn't have to worry about so many things." The children, therefore, feel they are responsible for the unrest and unhappiness. A Judaic dictum admonishes adults to be very cautious in what they say to the young: "The talk of the child in the streets is that of his father and mother" (*Sukkah*, 56b).

Parents should not take out their aggressions on the offspring. When one is vexed with their ways, one should remember the days of his own youth. On the other hand, the children should not be overindulged in order to compensate for one's own failures. The Talmudists blame the corrupt character of Absalom, who led a revolt against his father, King David, upon his pampered youth. The proper course is balance: "To push away with the left hand and draw them near with the right hand" (*Semochoth*, 2:6).

One should not try to impose impossible standards on children. No matter how the subject of divorce is presented, the youngsters' lives are changed. Even if the family were to remain together in peace and harmony, *all* children have difficulties in growing up. If their goals are set too high, both parents and children are hurt. Nor should parents bring unhappiness by insisting that the children make up for their own failures. Some parents deny it, but they are frequently looking for victories and satisfactions for themselves rather than for their offspring.

Parents should listen to what their children are saying. Many parents are so intent on explaining their "side" of the divorce that they do not take time to hear and heed what their offspring have to say. Children should be able to express their feelings, even those of fear, anguish, and hostility.

To empathize is to reverse roles and to imagine how the children might feel during this time of crisis. The former husband and wife must be patient. Do not expect miracles overnight. The children are probably doing their best to make painful adjustments. But it takes time and forbearance. The ability to wait and not overwhelm requires courage and strength; patience is the preserver of peace and the teacher of perspective and time is sometimes the wisest counselor.

The young need praise as well as older people. At a time of crisis, children need to know that they are wanted and needed. When they are deserving of commendation, on-the-spot recognition does much to demonstrate that they are appreciated. Yet there is something sweeter than receiving praise—the feeling of having merited it. From truly earned praise, the children experience justifiable self-worth and esteem. Approval may be one of the most important ingredients in affording the children encouragement and reassurance at this difficult time.

Each child's response to divorce is different. A Chassidic rabbi said it this way: "Each person experiences distress in accordance with the stature of his soul and the tolerance of his body." Just as no two blades of grass are exactly alike, so no children are precisely the same, even identical twins. The sages drove home this point in a vivid parable. "A mortal king," they said, "when he wishes to make many coins, creates one mold. With that form, he stamps out all the coins he needs. Each coin is exactly like every other coin. God, however, created all men from one. Yet no two individuals are exactly alike." Each youngster is unique in himself and his own life situation. No one in the world duplicates him. That which is relevant is only that which is meaningful to a particular child at a given moment. Help him to discover and develop his own uniqueness.

Of course children are pained by the separation. But life itself cannot be described without the element of hurt. What gives light must endure burning. Children might be bitter at first, but they must learn to face adversity. Pangs belong to life and cannot be eliminated either through flight or fancy. Sweetness alone is impossible for a complete existence. Darkness and light, joy and sorrow, success and suffering—all of these are indispensable strands. Neither parents nor children seek a crisis, but when it comes, they must make the best of it, not in surrender but in constructive action. There is no predicament that we and our offspring cannot ennoble either by doing or enduring. Divorce can be transmuted into an instrument to enhance a child's spiritual nature by enlarged sympathy, courageous acceptance, and active determination; that is, to reshape hardship into hardihood, misery into mercy, and to strive for that keener insight that finally allowed Job to cry out even in travail: "I know that my Redeemer liveth. . . . In mine own time will I see God" (19:25).

The most important help to children's suffering is love. The power to love is a privilege which God has given us, and not a pistol with which to hold up and control others' destinies. In the story of the Akedah (Genesis 22), Abraham was in danger of loving God so much that he would have destroyed his own son, Isaac. The ancient patriarch finally understood that Isaac needed his love more than God wanted it. There is no more critical moment when one's off-spring require parental affection than during the crisis of divorce. They have every right to fear the future. Their home is split and they feel abandoned. Let them know that they are wanted and needed even though husband and wife no longer live together. For there is one facet of a marriage neither parent need ever relinquish—he or she can always be the children's loving parent. Banish fear and anxiety from their gates by inviting love and security within their portals.

The goal now is to return to the task, renew one's efforts, and restore one's strength. There is the story of a student who sat before the *Zaddik*, "the righteous," Rabbi Mordecai of Nadvorna. Shortly before the Jewish New Year, the young man asked for permission to be dismissed. The rabbi asked: "Why are you hurrying?" The student answered: "I am a reader in the synagogue, and I must look into the prayer book and put my prayers in order." The *Zaddik* replied: "The prayer book is the same as it was last year. It would be better for you to look into your own deeds and put yourself in order."

How to help one's children during the crisis of divorce? A great deal depends on how the parents first put themselves in order. May they use their lips for truth, their voices for prayer, their eyes for pity, their hands for charity, their hearts for abiding love.

Children from Economically and Socially Deprived Environments

INTRODUCTION

Part IV deals with two of the many economically deprived groups in American society—the Spanish-American and the Puerto Rican.

Dr. Leonard P. Campos, a clinical psychologist of Stockton, California with much experience with Spanish-American groups largely of Mexican origin, offers the reader a highly informative picture of a whole culture in a state of transition, moving from traditionally defined social and family roles to those increasingly similar to the roles of the community that is assimilating them.

Writing of another segment of the Spanish community, Dr. Jose Nieto concentrates on Puerto Rican familes. He stresses the background of Puerto Rican folkways, formed on the Island and removed by emigration to the mainland New York City area.

Drs. Campos and Nieto offer a better balanced understanding of two economically disadvantaged sectors of our society and their special problems with their children of separation and divorce.

There is no separate chapter on the blacks, born and brought up in the larger American culture. In general, their problems are similar to those of the larger community and do not appear to be unique to their race.

LEONARD P. CAMPOS, Ph. D.

The Spanish-American Child

In this chapter, Dr. Leonard Campos indicates why it is neces-
sary to make a distinction among those members of American
society of Spanish descent. There are about six million Mexican-
Americans, concentrated in the Southwest; one million Puerto
Ricans, chiefly in the New York City area; and close to a million
others, such as Cubans, largely in Florida. In many ways, there
are as many differences among these group members as there
are similarities.

Dr. Campos concentrates his attention on three types of
Spanish-American family styles: first-generation families, who
are minimally assimilated into the American culture, whom he
calls "traditional"; second-generation families that are "transi-
tional"; and the more or less "assimilated" group. It is interest-
ing to note how well ideal family roles are defined in the
Spanish-American subculture.

The result of the author's efforts is an up-to-date, informa-
tive, and highly understanding view of the customs of a signifi-
cant minority group.

The existing state of knowledge about separation and divorce in Spanish-American(SA) families provides very little to those who wish to understand its effects on parents and their children.[1] Back in 1948, Jones described the lack of scientific studies about the Mexican-American (MA) family; over two decades later, the MA still remains the "forgotten American" (62). Heller (24) states that very little factual knowledge exists about the MA. Yet more studies exist about the MA than about the Puerto Rican(PR), and hardly any at all on the Cuban-American (74).

As a minority ethnic group in America, the SA child must adapt to the effects of minority group status: attitudes of discrimination and prejudice, unequal opportunity for education and employment, stereotypes (often carried by the mass media), a language barrier, a host of social class and economic factors ("culture of poverty"), and varying degrees of assimilation into the Anglo-American culture.[2] Whatever we say about the SA family must consider the vast difference between the broken family of the lower-class migrant farm worker of California and the educated upper-class affluent businessman of New Mexico.

At the present time, with about six million Mexican-Americans (concentrated in the Southwest), one million Puerto Ricans (concentrated in New York), and close to one million other SAs (such as the Cubans who are mostly concentrated in Florida), it would be untenable to overlook the vast heterogeneity of this population. Significant differences are found in families of persons who are first generation or foreign born (in Mexico, PR, or Cuba); native born (in U.S.) of foreign-born parents (second generation); and native born of native-born parents (third generation and later).

[1] Similarities in the description of Mexican-American(MA) and Puerto Rican(PR) families in three decades of studies justifies the general use of the term "Spanish-American"(SA). We recognize that differences do exist. Lewis(35) has pointed out that the MA has a stronger identification with his past heritage than the PR. PR women have less of a martyr complex than MA women. PR men are less concerned with proving their *machismo* than MA men. Responses to family separation may also differ; there is less asthma in the PR than the MA child (35). Nor do all persons of SA heritage identify themselves as similar. Clark(5) has pointed out how the PR in California holds himself aloof from the MA.

[2] Authors show conflicting points of view about how rapidly such assimilation is occurring; some feel the SA is assimilating rapidly (14 and 16); others feel it is slow and difficult (21 and 35). Indeed Gordon states that the PR is "substantially unassimilated culturally." Lewis feels nevertheless that the PR family has assimilated more rapidly than the MA family.

In fact, three distinct SA family patterns can be identified corresponding to these differences in generation which are related to differences in education, social class, urbanization, and assimilation. An early or first-generation rural family of low educational and social class status, minimally assimilated into the Anglo culture, best fits what we shall describe as the "traditional" SA family. The later third-generation urban family of high educational and social class status, maximally assimilated, corresponds to the "modern" Anglo family. The second-generation family in the process of transition between the traditional and the modern SA family will be called the "transitional" family.

This is a broadly characterized continuum of SA family life which does not overlook the wide variation across different families throughout the U.S. Authors who have drawn generalities about the SA from studies of the traditional family are often out of touch with significant changes that have occurred in SA family life. At the outset we can dispose of any myth that perpetuates illusions of a homogeneous SA group in America. Penalosa (53) has emphasized how many textbook descriptions are anachronistic. He points out that, contrary to popular stereotypes, for the most part the MA subculture is actually a variant of the American working lower-class culture; that it is more correct to talk about the "Mexicanized American" rather than the "Americanized Mexican." a large number of data exists to show that differences between ethnic groups in America may be more a function of social class status rather than "ethnic" status (67, 17, and 73). Any inference that there exists "the MA family" or "the PR family" without correction for differences in social and economic status seriously detracts from our understanding of how children and parents adapt to the broken SA family. To cite one example, unassimilated Spanish speaking wives hold on to traditional family values, whereas the English-speaking MA wife shows an Anglo-type marriage contract which is more companionate, egalitarian, and sexually gratifying (64 and 71).

The social distance between the SA and Anglo diminishes with increasing intermarriage or marriage outside of one's ethnic group.[3]

[3]Mittelbach, Moore, and McDaniel (46) have found that, overall, 75 percent of the MA in Los Angeles(LA) county married other MAs. With each advancing generation, MA brides tend a little bit more to marry out of their community. In the traditional (first-generation) family, 87 percent of grooms and 80 percent of brides stay within their ethnic group; in the second-generation transitional family, it is 77 percent and

In the traditional lower-class culture ethnic identity in marriage is maintained. As the SA moves away from immigrant status, solid kinship and family ties increasingly weaken and divorce rates increase. As Mittelbach, Moore, and McDaniel (46) point out, a third-generation MA is more likely to marry an Anglo than either a first- or second-generation MA. Many authors point out that in spite of the transitional status of the SA family, *the family* is still the "bulwark of tradition" (63). Although Penalosa (53) criticizes current textbook descriptions of the MA as anachronistic, he (54) confirms the existence of traditional Mexican family roles in the contemporary MA family.

A COMPOSITE PORTRAIT OF THE TRADITIONAL SA FAMILY

Madsen (38, p. 17) has stated: "The most important role of the individual is his familial role, and the family is the most valued institution in Mexican-American society." Rogler and Hollingshead (58) and others find this to be also true in the PR family culture. The SA mother and father raise a family within a network of kin and with a strong sense of kinship. Parents and offspring may form the nucleus of the family, but the bond between parents and child extends over three generations, and familial obligations of respect and obedience extend to grandparents, uncles and aunts, and cousins. First cousins can be as close as a brother and sister. Two entire families behind the marriage bond create relationships that are difficult to break, and make for enduring marriages. Regardless of the difference in class status and degree of Anglo assimilation, family bonds are stronger than those of the Anglo family. *Compadres* or coparents are established as additional ritual kin in ceremonies during baptism, confirmation, and marriage, although several authors have minimized the importance of compadres in childbearing (35, 53, 58, and 61). In the traditional family, the Catholic church's influence makes marriage vows sacred and the idea of divorce sinful.

74 percent respectively; in the more advanced transitional or modern third-generation family it is 70 percent and 68 percent respectively. Women outmarry more than men. The highest rate of ethnic inmarriage is in the lowest occupational levels. Nearly 87 percent of MAs had no previous marriage. Divorce reduces MA ties to the ethnic group. Marriage outside the MA community is more likely when either spouse had a previous marriage dissolved by divorce.

The ideal roles of mothers, fathers, and children are precisely defined. A mother who separates herself from a child whether in thought, emotion, or action, to the extent that a father can, deviates from the mores of good motherhood and is labeled *mala madre*. To be described as a "bad parent" or "bad son" is the most disparaging and insulting label to put on a family member (58).

Minuchin, Montsalvo, Rosman, and Schumer (44) have given an excellent description of how, because of prior child-rearing, husband and wife roles are submerged or absorbed by parent roles. Mothers validate themselves through the mothering role and even in their relationship with men see themselves mostly as mother. The mothering role provides a sense of self-fulfillment (especially the role of nurturant parent). Mother as daughter, in relation to grandmother, often does not grow up to become a mature daughter capable of mothering as an autonomous adult because the transition from child-daughter to adult-daughter is not clearly established. Rainwater's (56) study of marital sexuality points out how the Puerto Rican husband identifies the wife as a "second mother" and hence has potent reasons for not regarding her as a gratifying sexual object. Several authors (7, 8, 9, 39, and 40) have described a "family neurosis" created in men by the traditional first-generation family expectations: a tendency for child-rearing influences to interfere with the marital relationship (love for mother versus love for wife), tensions associated with overcoming strong maternal influences, anxiety about sexual potency, conflict over asserting virility versus loving tenderness, and rebelliousness toward authorities.

We have adopted the view in this chapter that understanding the transactions (transactional analysis) during and after marriage in family encounters prior to separation and divorce adds immeasurably to our understanding of what separation and divorce do to children in the SA family. Simply put, transactional analysis is the analysis of the kinds of overt and covert messages that are communicated among family members (43). Below adult awareness, SA men and women begin marriage and the family guided by unspoken messages communicated to them by prior child-rearing. What a SA man and woman does or expects of marriage and the family depends on the structure of his or her personality, transactions within the family and across extended kin lines, transactional "games" played (transactions in which advantages are derived from satisfying ulterior motives), and important nonverbal messages sent by parents to children during the first few years of child-rearing.

Men and women show distinctly differentiated sex roles. The woman is expected to be submissive; the man dominant. She is expected to be virginal; he, *muy macho* (manly). The message to boys is "Be virile (but don't grow up)." A strong parental message conveyed even before birth is "It ought to be a boy" (7), so that at birth greater status is accorded the male child. The son is prepared for manliness; the daughter for modesty and seclusion before marriage. The message to girls is "Be a woman but don't be sexy (be virginal)." Infant boys can exhibit their genitals; girls are not allowed to touch their genital area. The girls are prepared for maternity, so that a girl's self-concept of femininity is strongly associated with the message "A woman's place is in the home." Both boys and girls are taught to accord high esteem to motherhood.

In order to defend himself from parental accusations of being a *pendejo* (literally, pubic hair), an *añoñao* (dependent, incompetent), or, worst of all, a *maricón* (vulgar term), the boy goes to great lengths to prove he is a man. Sex role differences obviously affect premarital behavior and the beginning of marriage. In marriage the male often continues to prove his *machismo* by feeling free to engage in extramarital affairs.[4] Remaining submissive to her husband, the wife's personal needs as a woman are disregarded as she plays out a *Virgen de Guadalupe* complex in marriage (38). As *ama de la casa* (the "soul" of the household), she develops a martyr complex while she plays out her mothering role with self-sacrifice. While father maintains his unquestioned supremacy, she is expected to bear and rear the children.[5]

After having been cloistered with fear that they will not get

[4]In the Rogler and Hollingshead (58) study of PR marriages, to the question of what a spouse should do about infidelity, approximately 90 percent of the spouses thought the husband should divorce or separate from an unfaithful wife; only approximately 27 percent thought the wife should divorce or separate from an unfaithful husband; 68 percent of the husbands and 65 percent of the wives claimed their father had been unfaithful to their mother.

[5]The proportion of large MA families (six or more persons) is three times that of Anglos; one and a half times that of the nonwhites in the Southwest (47). A California State report shows that 25 percent of SA families in California have six or more persons in the family (68). In San Jose, California, Clark (5) reports that the proportion of MAs with four or more children is twice as high as that of the Anglos. Sexton (66) reported that in New York City's Spanish Harlem, the birthrate of PR girls under twenty years is five times greater than among non-PR whites.

parental approval to marry the man of their choice, some women turn to eloping and establishing free or consensul unions (marriage without a civil or legal ceremony).[6] Many women enter marriage already estranged in their attitude toward men. "My mother told me that men are not to be trusted; they are bad. They try to feel you up and talk you into doing bad things" (p. 58, 133). When they marry they often view the sex experience with great aversion.[7] The message is "Marry but don't trust men (men are bad)." When the babies come, child-rearing messages received by the parents when they were young influence the messages they send to their own children. In relation to their sons, mothers are indulgent and overprotective in their discipline; mothers program their sons for loyalty and dependency on them. Individuality is discouraged and replaced by family loyalty. The child is trained to be a "good child" who must never discredit the family. The message is "Don't be yourself" and "Don't grow up." Mom's relationship with daughter is also close, especially when they ally themselves in handling a male-dominant home.

The expectations for fatherhood are different. The relationship of father to son is often distant, severe, and demanding of respect and obedience. Daughters are expected to be obedient to Dad, too, but there is less open conflict between them. Father's position in the home is well reflected in the quote of a sixty-year-old father. "In my home, I am judge, jury, and policeman" (61). To defy that kind of authority brings on the *castigo de Diós*. In the father-absent home, the oldest male wage earner plays out the father role. The younger sibs respect the older ones; girls respect the boys, while the sister-sister relationship remains close. There is a lot of sibling rivalry as they compete for maternal affection.

[6]Consensual unions are often formed because of a "cloister rebellion" among girls against parental authority. According to Dohen (10), 25 percent of the marriages in PR were of this kind. In another area, Lewis (34) found that 50 percent of the marriages were of this type. In the U.S., the consensual marriage of the parents must leave the SA child confused (18). In the U.S., the children of the consensual union are identified as "out of wedlock" or illegitimate by community agencies. They probably have special problems when the family breaks up.

[7]Rogler and Hollingshead (58) found that 85 percent of the PR men and 7 percent of the PR women had sexual intercourse prior to marriage. The men view their first sex experience in favorable terms; women, in unfavorable terms; 83 percent of the women associated sex with terms such as painful, frightened, nervous; only 18 percent of the men responded this way. Because she has been programmed to be "virginal," she responds with terror and shame at the violation of sacred norms.

Children are constantly confronted with parental advice. Parenting comes with a lot of "don't" messages which relate to the power of the parental figure. "Don't do that because you make me nervous" or "Don't do that because I say so," etc. The children learn to define the limits of permissible behavior by respecting parental mood responses. The effect of parental self-identity is to absorb parents in issues of interpersonal regulation rather than intimacy. The message is "Don't be close (intimate)." Even among siblings, transactions are governed by power operation ("I will not give you the ball until you pay me back for my glasses," etc.).

Physical punishment and use of fear are the two very common methods of discipline. The mother invokes the threat of paternal authority to control the child's behavior. This style of discipline is common to the family of lower economic status. Mothers do not foster development of internal controls in the preschool child; they set down strict roles for inhibiting unwanted behavior but do not explain reasons for the rules (44). Hence a strong message to the child is "Don't think for yourself."

Minuchin *et al.*(44) state that *respeto* (respect) is "the cornerstone of Puerto Rican child-rearing." Rubel (61) states, "Respect for one's elders is a major organizing principle of the Mexican-American family." Parents accompany their discipline with the familiar *para que cojas respeto* (so that you learn respect). According to Stycos (70), "love" between parent and child is not as important as respect and obedience to the parents and the parents' provision for the physical needs of the child. Peck (51) and Peck and Diaz-Guerrero (52) show that U.S. samples of students show higher and more positive valuation of the concept "love" than Mexican-American students. One-third of almost three hundred Mexican-American students associated love with blindness, deceit, and disillusionment. In another study, Diaz-Guerrero (9) showed how MA youth respond to the concept of respect with fear and awe.

In the Minuchin *et al.*(44) study of PR and black families that have produced delinquent children who end up in the Wiltwyck School for Boys in New York, an in-depth study of a PR family reveals significant family characteristics that seem to lead to the inevitable separation of father from mother and children. In most of the families producing at least one delinquent son, more than three-fourths of the children had no father or stable father figure.

At the very beginning, the marriage is affected by ostensible anxiety on the part of the woman to assert her rights for fear of aggressive responses from the husband. Because of his own child-rearing, he wants to be dominant, but he also exhibits boyish dependency. An almost furtive alliance develops between mother and son against dad. Father feels displaced by the children and has difficulty feeling integrated into the family. The father accepts his feelings of isolation due to the absence of intimacy in his earlier child-rearing. Since he has no right to expect tenderness (that would be contrary to *machismo*), he finds it difficult to express his positive feelings. Transactions between father and son are often antagonistic because of programmed "Don't be close" messages. While the PR male feels isolated and defeated by the alliance of mother and child, the woman feels enslaved, exploited, and deserted by her husband. With these feelings, transactions are set up between husband and wife which leads to separation.

When the father leaves home and the son gets into trouble, mother the martyr believes herself to be blameless. While she has ostensibly sacrificed herself for the child, she is angry with him and does not accept responsibility for the outcome. "What can a (good) mother do?" In homes with unstable father figures, the child-rearing responsibility delegated to mother from father is met with anxiety, and this is communicated to the children. Mother relinquishes her authority to the older sibling or "parental child." If she does not do this, the family authority may be relinquished completely and the family abandoned altogether. When the sibling system is used to maintain authority in the family, if the older sibling is delinquently oriented, the delinquent values will be assimilated by the younger children.

THE SA FAMILY IN TRANSITION

In transitional families, much of the above composite portrait of the SA family before breakdown does not apply. Sex roles are changing definition with increasing assimilation of men and women into the Anglo culture. Trent (72) points out that in transitional PR families undergoing change, women show increasing self-dissatisfaction (increased discrepancy between descriptions of real and ideal self). As women leave home to work, they feel freer to challenge old role definitions (50). And just as the role of the woman is in transition, the men show increasing ambivalence about their sex role and increasing anxiety about the adequacy of their supposed masculinity (35).

In the family undergoing transition, marital conflict increases as wives become less accepting of husbands' extramarital affairs. Sex becomes one of the most frequent causes of quarrels. The working wife begins to threaten the male *machismo* which the man depends on for self-esteem. As social class rises, men do not feel so secure with the "dominant" role; nor are they so inclined to run father-dominated households. Parental discipline becomes less authoritarian (73). The disapproval of divorce is still higher than in the modern SA family, but it becomes increasingly attractive as a solution to marital unhappiness. Satterfield (64), and Tharp, Meadow, Lennhoff, and Satterfield (71) have shown that, whereas the unassimilated Spanish-speaking wife defines herself by home and family values and associates sex with physical pleasure, the assimilating English-speaking MA wife depends less on "familial" values and more on a companionate intimacy for self-esteem.

In the transitional family, tensions begin to develop between father and son over arbitrary use of authority. The underlying resentment built up in the child of the traditional family becomes expressed in more open rebellion and direct challenge to arbitrary parental authority.

PRELUDE TO FAMILY BREAKDOWN

To understand the effects of separation or divorce of parents on the child many confounding factors have to be unscrambled. Because of the nature of existing studies, it is difficult to discern the effects of breakup from the effects of factors like economic status. Aside from the many comparisons of "disadvantaged" (which includes many SA children) and nondisadvantaged populations, there does not appear to be any existing research comparing the difference in adaptation to separation or divorce between the SA and the Anglo or black child. Since the SA mother will rarely desert her child at the time of the breakup except when she is mentally ill or alcoholic, the voluminous literature on "maternal deprivation" obviously has limited relevance to our study of effects of family breakup in the SA family. Investigators have found that there are more adverse effects on children of separation and divorce in the Catholic than in the Protestant family (60) or in the middle-income white family than in the low-income black family (23). Whatever psychiatric disturbance occurs with divorce, social and economic factors will be found to co-vary with it (33 and 67). Hospital admissions for foreign-born PRs of recent migrant status are greater than that of the rest of the New York PR population (67 and 41).

As mentioned earlier, much of SA family functioning is studied within the context of the "culture of poverty" (75). Usually more divorce is found in families of lower socioeconomic status (19). Yet when we look at divorce statistics, we find that there is less divorce but *more separation* in the SA family than in the Anglo family (5, 24, 45, 46, and 47). A frequently cited reason for desertion of men from their wives and children, aside from the costs of divorce, is the infidelity of husbands. In the Los Angeles area, MA men separate from their families more often than black males separate from their families. In the "modern" or later generation MA of native parentage, the rate of divorce is approximately that of the Anglo's. In the SA family that is transitional between the traditional and modern, the increasing urbanization and trend toward the nuclear family household brings an increased divorce rate (20 and 65). In the traditional family, widows and widowers are expected to remarry, but remarriage among divorcees is met with social disapproval and is not condoned.

Separation and divorce should also be looked at in the light of the extended kinship system (15, 25, 58, and 61). In the traditional family, even unions of the consensual type can be enduring because of the family support accorded them (34 and 57). In the nuclear Anglo family, breakup often signifies an interruption of a "loving" bond between parent and child. How the child handles family breakup may be quite different in the extended kinship system where his relationship to family members extends to many kin. Hence the concept of family "disorganization" may not be tenable when applied to the traditional SA family. Rogler and Hollingshead(58) found that in fifteen out of forty ruptured families, the orphaned child is reared by grandparents or aunts and uncles. The PR parental family serves as a source of support when the family breaks up. The picture is further complicated when we note that migration among PRs between New York and Puerto Rico may leave family members separated for years.

AFTERMATH OF SA FAMILY BREAKDOWN

Very little has been said about the effects of divorce on the SA child, though much of what has been said about the Anglo child no doubt applies in varying degrees to the SA child. Whatever the ethnic identity of the child might be, the effects of the breakup depend on parent characteristics, child characteristics, and the nature of the parent-child transactions. Generally speaking, probably the happier the home has been to the child, the more adverse will be the effect of the breakup (31); or the younger the child, the greater the effect of the loss of the parent. The assumption that the effect of divorce on the child *has to* be adverse has been seriously questioned by several investigators. Landis (32) mentions studies showing that few differences emerge between children of unhappy nondivorced parents and children from divorced parents.[8]

Reviewing the outcomes of breakup in the SA family is severely limited by the paucity of existing scientific research. Perhaps the SAs have not been as accessible to study because of their avoidance of public agencies where research is carried out. Moustafa and Weiss (48) have confirmed this author's experiences in the difficulty of getting the MA into Anglo mental health facilities in California. Studies show that the MA is underrepresented at psychiatric facilities. Some reasons cited are that the MA can return to Mexico if he becomes seriously ill; the language barrier "masks" symptoms; and he can depend on the extended family for support. Families in transition toward the Anglo nuclear family become increasingly accepting of the Anglo psychiatric facility.

One significant outcome of separation and divorce in the SA family is the high incidence of father-absent homes and, consequently, mother-centered households. As Herzog (25) concluded after an extensive review of the existing data on fatherless homes, the often found relationship between father absence and confusion

---

[8]Studies on the personality characteristics of divorced or separated parents are few. Loeb and Price (36) compared the personality of separated or divorced mothers with that of continuously married women on a personality inventory and found them to show higher disturbance. The children of such mothers were more often rated "aggressive." Dunteman and Wolking's (11) replication of the study found only one significant difference in their samples: separated or divorced mothers were higher on sociopathy. One trend found was that children diagnosed as "behaviorally disturbed" came from the disrupted homes.

about sex identity, delinquency, peer dependency, and other out-comes is confounded by a host of many uncontrolled factors.[9] Her conclusion that a sense of "familiness" may not necessarily be a function of presence or absence of divorce is certainly applicable to the extended SA family. Thus, in reviewing the problem of sex iden-tity found as one effect of fatherless homes, the point that male models may come from outside the home is especially applicable to the SA child, because of the extended bonds of familiness beyond the immediate nuclear family.

A particularly strong problem for the SA boy or girl in the father-less home broken by separation or divorce is related to the strong training by the mother for dependency on her. Field, Maldonado-Sierra, Wallace, Bodarsky, and Coelho (13) reviewed several studies supporting findings of a high-need dependency in PR boys and ex-treme responses to separation from the mother. This has been re-peatedly related to passivity in the SA personality (1, 5, 28, and 38). In comparing the manifest needs of SA and Anglo male college stu-dents, Campos (4) found that next to need for dominance, need for nurturance was significantly higher among the SA population. The fatalistic *qué será, será* philosophy often mentioned in literature is strongest in the traditional SA but becomes mythical when applied to the advanced transitional or modern SA family. "Passivity" or dependency on others or outside events for self-direction and control may be related to the way the young child subordinates his individu-ality to family kinship expectations. In the power-oriented traditional family, responsibility for mental or physical illness is often attributed to some powerful outside agency such as God's will or witchcraft (61). Madsen (38) quotes a Mexican Texan as saying, "The Latin doesn't think he missed the bus because he arrived too late. He blames the bus for leaving before he arrived."

This passive-dependency may also be a function of a family sys-tem in which responsibility for one's actions becomes the responsibil-

[9]Herzog and Sudia's (25) critique of studies of the effects of fatherless homes shows that of a core group of fifty-nine studies, twenty-nine or about 50 percent supported the classic view of adverse effects of separation and divorce. However, only seven of these studies were judged to be reasonably sound in method; seventeen studies challenged the classic view with again only 7 rated as sound in method. Thirteen studies had mixed conclusions. Besides finding varying definitions of the "broken home," few studies compared the conflictful intact home with the conflictfree one-parent home or related father absence to availability of other relatives.

ity of the other members of the family system—thus limiting the development of individual autonomy (44).

If separation from the father and closeness to the mother leads to extreme separation anxiety, the child may be expected to have difficulty adapting to school away from home. Many authors (29) have concluded that divorce adversely affects school performance.[10] Even aside from the effects of family breakup, the SA child has been reported to show problems of adapting to the Anglo middle-class school (55). Manuel (42) found that high school students related most of their problems in school to an inadequate command of English in the first grade. Glazer and Moynihan (18) have pointed out how the SA child with his Spanish accent finds it difficult to maintain his self-dignity. Home, then, becomes the child's sanctuary where he can retain his self-respect and receive maternal comfort. Supporting the negative response to school are parental attitudes often found in the traditional family that "downgrade" the American school as an alien Anglo institution (35 and 49). Lewis (35, p. 212) quotes a PR mother in New York as saying,

> ... And let me tell you, if a Puerto Rican child learns only English it's because his mother wants to show off. But all she does is create problems for her children because people say, "Look at that kid. He's Puerto Rican and he thinks he is an American." I wouldn't want my children to forget their Spanish. If they came home from school saying, "Mami, whatchmaycallit," in English, it would be a problem for me. My children learned Spanish from me and speak Spanish, and they'd better not start speaking English to me because I'd kill them.

Extreme dependency on peers is another characteristic found among SA children from broken homes, particularly among the boys. Training for dependency in the traditional or early transitional family may account for some of this, but it may also arise out of the influence of the more "individualized" Anglo culture on teen-agers in these families. A distinction is drawn between the nondelinquent associations of young male chicanos called *palomillas* and the delinquent associations such as the *pachuco* gangs (61). Heller (24) reviews

---

[10] The highest school dropout rate in the nation is among the MAs (24); 31 percent drop out before high school graduation as compared to an average of 19 percent for other groups. Some studies show that the poorest school achievers come from father-absent homes (27).

studies which show that MAs exceed Anglos in the proportion of offenders whose parents have been separated or never married (when divorce is included in the statistics, there is no difference between MAs and Anglos). Many authors have suggested that delinquency is high because of the need to rebel against strict parenting in authoritarian families. Then again, the MA boys may feel rejected by the Anglo culture or in turn reject the Anglo culture by grouping together for self-defense and offense. In January, 1970, this author examined the histories of the MA population of delinquent boys in a California Youth Authority institution. Of sixty-seven boys located, twenty-three or 34 percent came from intact homes; thirty or 45 percent came from homes where parents were separated or divorced (including desertions); five or 6 percent were totally abandoned by both parents; nine or 15 percent came from homes broken by the death of one or both parents. Even in the intact homes, there were a great number of "multiproblem" families (arrest history, unemployment, drunkenness, etc.). A study of the "personality type" of these MA boys indicated that they make up the large proportion of boys classified as "cultural conformist" (3). Their delinquency is an outcome of handling conflicts with adult authority against whom they are alienated and distrustful; they reject expressions of emotion (except anger), and they tend to gravitate toward delinquently oriented peers. It will be recalled that in the Minuchin *et al.*(44) study of the PR family in the New York slums with at least one acting-out boy, the older delinquent sibling can serve as a model for the younger brothers, especially if he has to serve as the parental child of the family. Incidentally, the passivity mentioned earlier found in SA children was also found in the California Youth Authority sample. When confronted with why they get into trouble, they are often heard to say, "You never know what's going to happen to you."

A great deal has been written about the self-image of the disadvantaged SA child in the U.S., with most authors agreeing that it is low or negative (6, 35, 42, 49, and 75). Minority group status brings with it a lowered positive self-image. The self-esteem of the advanced transitional family or modern chicano family is probably higher. In interviewing boys about their reactions to the separation of their parents, they report a loss of pride or self-respect. It becomes a *punto de honor* (point of honor) to maintain peer solidarity from which they derive more self-acceptance. This same pride in *la raza* (the race) is found in the traditional family and explains the finding by Dworkin (12) that Mexican-born MAs recently coming into the U.S. show a more positive self-image than native-born MAs.

Another frequently cited way the SA youth of broken families adjust to their home situation is in the high incidence of alcoholism and narcotics use (2, 22, 24, and 48). Moustafa and Weiss (48, p. 33) state that the selection of narcotics and alcoholism is "the culturally preferred means of dealing with psychiatric stress" among MAs. Green (22) asserts that drunkenness in the PR male is an expression of aggression against the heavy family demands of *respeto*. From a transactional point of view, alcohol "turns off" the stern parental state of mind or self-image and allows the individual to have child fun. Rosenberg (59) found that young alcoholics, under thirty, when compared to older alcoholics, show a history of significantly more father-absent homes in which the relationship with the mother was an overdependent one. This will have to be validated on a SA sample. Consistent with our point of view, Steiner (69, p. 105) describes the young alcoholic's transactions with his mother:

> The young alcoholic is usually rebelling against his mother's overprotective attitude, which means, in essence, "I'm O.K.(good), and you my son (because you are a man or because you're like your father), are not O.K. (bad)." Offspring in this situation can safely rebel by saying, "I agree, I'm bad, since I'm a drunk, and you are good (ha ha)." Every time he gets drunk he provokes his mother into presenting him with ample evidence for the validity of the "ha ha" since she will, typically, lose control and show her angry, persecuting child which is definitely not O.K. . . . This game can be considered a son's rebellion against a mother who insists on appearing blameless when, in fact, she is quite angry at her husband and son.

AN OVERVIEW FOR THE NEW SA GENERATION

We have stated that the existing state of knowledge about separation and divorce in the SA family is inadequate to help us understand how parents and children adapt to such a situation. So much has been written about the "disadvantaged" SA family that little distinction can be made between the effects of family breakup peculiar to the ethnic identity of being "Spanish American," and the effects of social and economic factors. We have to agree with authors such as Herzog

and Sudia (25) and Schwartz (65) who call for a radical improvement
of methods of study and critical reexamination of the current assumptions about divorce—particularly in any attempt to understand
its effects on the SA family.

By recognizing that SA families in America vary on a continuum
from the relatively fixed "traditional" family, through varying degrees of transition (the "transitional" family), to the "modern" Anglo
family, we have attempted to discard any assumption about
homogeneity of "the Spanish-American family."

When we look at the high rate of separation of fathers from
wives and children, or the high rate of delinquency in sons, the
contradiction between these facts and the ostensible commitment to
"family solidarity" is striking. We have seen how the marriage of the
MA or PR couple can start off with covert estrangement between the
sexes that surfaces to consciousness when family members begin to
assert their rights of individuality or autonomy. The lenient, overprotective mothering or strict fathering of children during child-rearing
serves to perpetuate a pattern of transactions with the expectation
that children acquiesce their individuality to the needs of "the
family"; while women are supposed to prepare for marriage by sacrificing their personal needs for motherhood and the man's needs.
The rupture of surface solidarity occurs when underlying resentments and drives toward adult autonomy lead to rebelliousness
among the children and conflicts among the parents.

We have adopted the view that analyzing transactions or the
overt and covert messages communicated among family members
before, during, and after marriage and divorce will aid immeasurably
to understanding why families break up. When Lewis (35) refers to
the slum PR family living between New York City and San Juan as
showing an "inexorable repetitiveness and iron entrenchment of
their behavior patterns," he underscores the degree to which the
autonomy of many SA parents and children is restricted by the fixed
way in which the transactions of the SA family culture are communicated from generation to generation.

The young chicano's current resurgence of pride in *la raza* (37)
is related to an attempt to overcome feelings of passivity and powerlessness and move from dependency to dignity and self-respect
through greater adult autonomy. As the generations change, the MA
and PR young are freeing themselves from the fixed expectations of

earlier generations that have predetermined family transactions as though they were outside the control of individual members.

Intensive treatment work with the unstable SA family such as that demonstrated by Lance (30) offers clues to helping SA families confronted with potential breakup. Lance describes a father with a strong need for mothering and a mother who feels she has no control over her own life; they are faced with a retreating, depressed eldest daughter. The treatment plan consists of teaching the parents *adult responsibility* and helping the mother not to expect so much "parental responsibility" from her disturbed daughter.

SA children's greater capacity for spontaneity and intimacy will depend on their parents being willing to encourage adult autonomy that allows for enjoyment through rational parental authority. This may go counter to strong unconscious covert messages communicated within the family that inevitably lead to family breakdown.

In fact, the new SA generation may recognize that much of their status of being "traditional" or "modern" can be a matter of *individual choice.* In the same way, the decision to assimilate or not to assimilate into Anglo culture, to speak English or Spanish, to separate or not to separate (or divorce), can be a free and conscious decision in the service of greater self-esteem and adult autonomy.

JOSE NIETO, Ph. D.

The Puerto Rican Child

Dr. Jose Nieto contrasts the social and cultural standards of Puerto Rico with those common to mainland United States. He presents examples of approved and desirable relationships on the Island which clash decisively with those expected of continental fathers and mothers.

Puerto Rican families who emigrate to large cities in the U.S. are often bewildered by the strange standards used by their neighbors to judge their family relationships and responsibilities. The Puerto Rican child, however, does not necessarily suffer the same emotional difficulties commonly encountered by Anglo children from disrupted families. The conception of the Puerto Rican family as a "clan" cushions the shock for the children, who often find their peers in the same situation, with substitute fathers readily accessible for advice and support.

The relevance of the concept of "frame of reference" is accepted today almost unanimously in sociology,[1] psychology,[2] and psychiatry.[3] It would be impossible without the frame of reference or cultural context to distinguish between the symptoms of a real mental illness and several cultural conventional forms of behavior, such as seeing spirits, hearing heavenly voices, and believing in the power of killing by magical rites. Even in the so-called "developed countries," it is hard to distinguish between psychopathology and certain types of bizarre behaviors if the cultural context is not fully explored. Thus, the frame of reference should be the starting point for selecting the facts and defining categories; in short, it should be the means for studying each step involved in the scientific method. On the other hand, it is practically impossible to find a country with an exclusive and monolithic frame of reference in today's world; however, in every nation with a few centuries of history since its political birth, only one frame of reference is generally outstanding. This main frame of reference gives emotional charge and moral meaning to the language used and the specific words chosen to represent the idea which this paper is presenting.

To begin, changing the frame of reference means that the connotation of the terms "separation" and "divorce" also changes, besides carrying its impact over the behavior of human beings. "Separation" and "divorce" are two juridical labels whose power depends on the complete sociocultural system; and their dramatic appeal relates inversely to a concrete kind of family and parental union considered as the only one that is legal, moral, and admissible within the frame of reference concerned. Notwithstanding, one can always find several types of frames of references, some of which are in conflict, in a fight to prevail or to survive in the urban and industrial societies of the present world, and more specifically in those societies undergoing rapid change. In culturally pluralistic societies, it is the people or the observer who selects one set of values in order to describe and to qualify the facts and the happenings. This election

[1]Bloch, Herbert A. *Disorganization: personal and social.* New York: Alfred Knopf, 1953, p. 11.
[2]Horney, Karen. *La personalidad neurotica de nuestro tiempo* (Cultura y Neurosis). New York: W. W. Norton and Company, 1937.
[3]Mead, Margaret (Ed.). *Cultural Patterns and Technical Change.* New York and Toronto: Mentor Book, The New American Library, 1955, pp. 263–65.

of a frame of reference is related, of course, to the particular reference frame of the individual or collective observer. What the scientific method tries to diminish is precisely the prejudice contained in the so-called point of view which every researcher has in mind and which is often reflected in the hypothesis which he proposes to test.

In the case of Puerto Rico, we can see that some scientists trained in psychology in the United States, with the principles which apply to certain classes of the American population, expected to find in the Island a very similar situation to that accepted almost unanimously for the children of separation and divorce in the United States. Some researchers have expressed their surprise when the weight of proof did not speak in favor of their assumption, but against it, although others have maintained their *a priori* beliefs. This is, in fact, the general impression gathered from the readings of the existing bibliography on this theme—a very rich bibliography, indeed, since "the geography, the cultural history and the rapid social-economic revolution in which Puerto Rico has been caught up for more than two decades has made . . . of this island . . . a magnificent laboratory" for behavioral scientific field work. An academic joke describes the typical present-day Puerto Rican family as consisting of "fathers, mothers, children, grandparents, and the resident social scientist".[4]

In 1945, a thesis was presented for a Certificate in Social Work[5] on the problems of conduct affecting children of school age from homes where the parents are not living with their children. The author says that the assumption was that there would be more problems of behavior among children from homes where both parents were absent; that there would be fewer problems with children living with both parents. Contrary to the expected results, according to what the researcher believed had happened in the United States, it was found that there were fewer children with problems among those that came from homes where both parents were gone; that the mean was represented by those children who lived with both par-

[4]Fernandez Marina, R.; Von Eckardt, Ursula; and Maldonado Sierra, E. *The Sober Generation* (A Topology of Competent Adolescent Coping in the Modern Puerto Rico). Puerto Rico: University of Puerto Rico Press, 1969, p. XI.
[5]Cruz Apellaniz, Angelina. *Estudio de los problemas de conducta evidenciados en niños escolares de hogares donde faltan los padres.* Trabajo para el Certificado en Trabajo Social, Departamento de Trabajo Social, Universidad de Puerto Rico, 1945. Aceptado para la maestria en 1955.

ents, and that the maximum frequency corresponded to the homes where only one parent was living with the children.

Another thesis for the Master's Degree in Social Science, of which an abstract was published in the Revista de Ciencias Sociales in 1961, expresses a similar conclusion. "There is no relation between the school comportment and the degree of instruction of the parents, nor with the fact of living with the parents, or the type of family relations in the home."[6]

The papers presented at the Congress held in Puerto Rico in 1959 under the auspices of the Commission on the Child were published in November, 1961. In one of them,[7] seven groups of children with behavior problems (but without having any relation with the police) were studied, and it was found that 64 percent of the sample lived with both parents.

On the other hand, the ideas of Benjamin Fine have influenced the psychologists and psychiatrists of Puerto Rico. Professor Ramon Ramirez Lopez has summarized the prevalent opinions in this manner: "The child that is not loved . . . is predisposed to develop a super-demanding and aggressive personality." . . . Here in Puerto Rico the broken home is mentioned repeatedly as a causal factor."[8]

Although there are some works of a psychological nature on the possible relation between broken homes and child psychology, it is obvious statistically that juvenile delinquency claims more attention than other forms of maladjustment. In Puerto Rico between the years 1956–63, the number of interventions by the police due to the behavior of minors rose by 592.9 percent, while the population of less than twelve years of age increased only by 9 percent, and the general population of Puerto Rico by 2.3 percent.

[6]Borges, Carmen L., y Mendez de Alicea, Teresa. *Comportamiento de alumnos de nivel elemental residentes en una urbanización con facilidades minimas en Puerto Rico, y su relación con las estructuras y valores socioculturales de sus hogares.* Tesis para Maestria en Trabajo Social, U.P.R. Publicada en extracto en la Revista de Servicio Social, San Juan, Puerto Rico, Año XXII, 1961, Numero 3 y 4, julio-octubre, 1961, p. 18–20 y 61–62.

[7]Comisión del Niño, Estado Libre Asociado de Puerto Rico. *Memorias del Tercer Congreso del Niño de Puerto Rico.* Ponencia presentada por Beatriz M. Cruz sobre *"la actividad de siete grupos orientadores en Ponce, con niños que presentaban problemas de conducta."* Departamento de Hacienda, San Juan, Puerto Rico, 1961.

[8]Ramirez Lopez, Ramon. "Entrenamiento psicopedagogico del adulto con relación a la delincuencia juvenil." En la revista *Pedagogia*, Universidad de Puerto Rico, Volumen X, numero 2, 1962, p. 13 (Cita a Fine, Benjamin. *1,000,000 Delinquents.* New York: *World Book Co., 1955*)

If it were true that maladjusted personalities were a link between broken homes and juvenile delinquency—considering the latter as an expression of hostility toward the parents and the society that deprived the child of affection—a positive correlation should exist between children of separation and divorce, and juvenile delinquency. Nevertheless, the specialized studies do not agree with this correlation. It is also true that the opinion of the specialists in the United States is not unanimous either. As Jorge Marrero points out very well, in reference to a study carried out in Michigan on juvenile delinquency in this "Age of Anxiety":

> A high percentage of children referred for delinquency lived with both parents . . . 59 percent of the children have parents who are married and living together. This trend was contrary to what was expected, because, generally, broken homes have been associated in the popular mind with the problems of delinquency. Moreover, 19 percent of all cases come from homes where parents are divorced; in 5.7 percent the parents are separated or deserted, and in 7.9 percent of the cases, the father is dead.[9]

Commenting on an article by Eisenberg on autistic children in relation to the "schizophrenic mother" and the "autistic father," Carmen Rivera de Alvarado[10] calls attention to the fact that of the 131 brothers and sisters of the 110 autistic children studied, only eight presented some kind of emotional disturbance. She indicates, too, her scepticism regarding the existence of a casual link between broken homes and maladjusted juvenile behavior.

Henry Ellis Plyler[11] refers to the most popular explanations of maladjustment in children as myths, and he even says that "Probably the most overworked of these misconceptions are the working mother and the broken home as causes of delinquency."

But, in spite of the contrary opinions, the truth is that the general public in the United States and in Puerto Rico insist on the causal relation between broken homes and the inadequate conduct of minors. But, "It is difficult to determine the number of maladjusted

[9]Marrero, Jorge. "Some Social Aspects of Juvenile Delinquency." En la revista *Pedagogía*, Universidad de Puerto Rico, Volumen X, numero 2, 1962, pp. 103, 104, 111.
[10]Rivera de Alvarado, Carmen. "Las relaciones familiares y la delincuencia juvenil." En la revista *Pedagogía*, Universidad de Puerto Rico, Volumen X, numero 2, 1962, p. 62.
[11]Plyler, Henry Ellis. "A Theory of Social Problems and Juvenile Delinquency." En la revista *Pedagogía*, Universidad de Puerto Rico, Volumen X, numero 2, 1962, p. 77.

young people except as they evidence their emotional difficulties and attract the attention of formalized institutions. One such institution is the police."[12] The statistics of the Puerto Rican police show repeatedly that the large majority of their interventions with minors are caused by children who live with both parents. Of the 2,290 children who were referred to the juvenile court during the year 1960–61, 47 percent were living with both parents, 35 percent were living with one parent, 12 percent with other relatives, 1 percent transient, and 5 percent unaccounted for. Forty-nine percent of the 2,444 minors who were on probation during the same year lived with both parents, 38 percent with one parent, and 12 percent with other relatives.[13]

Despite some possible errors in the police and juvenile court reports, the statistics are impressive enough. Besides, many other studies and research material based on other sources of information and applying other methods confirm the results arrived at by the police and the juvenile courts.[14] It seems, then, that in Puerto Rico the existence of a causal relation between "broken homes" and "maladjusted juvenile personality" (measuring the latter in its most dramatic expression—juvenile delinquency) has not been proven. In the presence of this situation, admitting that such a relation does exist in the United States, we ought to ask ourselves what are the factors existing in Puerto Rico that prevent the appearance of a similar relationship. The explanation resides in the fact that the words "broken home," "divorce," and "separation" do not describe in the United States and Puerto Rico real equivalent situations nor do they

[12]Bodarky, Clifford, J. "Juvenile Delinquency: Some Shibboleths." En la revista *Pedagogía*, Universidad de Puerto Rico, Volumen X, numero 2, 1962, p. 95.
[13]de Judkin, Isabel. "Algunos datos estadisticos sobre la delincuencia juvenil en Puerto Rico." En la revista *Pedagogía*, Universidad de Puerto Rico, Volumen X, numero 2, 1962, pp. 68–70.
[14]Palau de Lopez, Awilda. *Proyectos exploratorios sobre la delincuencia juvenil.* Programa de Investigación en Bienestar Social, serie sobre Delincuencia Juvenil, patrocinado por el Departamento de Salud y la Escuela de Medicina de la U.P.R. (mimeografiado). Departamento de Salud, Oficina de Investigación Científica, febrero, 1963, p. 5.
    Palau de Lopez, Awilda. *Ponencia sobre la delincuencia infantil.* Publicación numero 4 de la serie sobre delincuencia juvenil (mimeografiado). Departamento de Salud, San Juan, Puerto Rico, marzo, 1965. (Contiene el dato de que hay menos delincuencia infantil en los distritos donde las madres trabajan fuera de la casa.)
    Otero de Ramos, Mercedes. *Estudio socio-ecologico de la deserción escolar y la delincuencia juvenil en Puerto Rico.* Centro de Investigaciones Sociales, Programa de Criminología (Mimeografiado). Agosto, 1966, pp. 38, 103.
    Policia de Puerto Rico. *Datos estadisticos.* Delincuencia juvenil. 1959–68.

have the same impact on the modulation of juvenile personality.

It is true that Puerto Rico has changed very fast in many aspects of its vital system. From 1940 to 1968 the individual income rose from $118 a year to $1,000, though in Orocovis it was $194 and in San Juan $1,980. Life expectancy in the same period rose from 46 to 70 years. Illiteracy was reduced from 35 percent to 13 percent. In 1968 there were two hundred thousand telephones, compared with sixteen thousand in 1940. In this same year, 1.3 million of the island's 1.8 million people lived in the countryside, while more than half of today's 2.7 million inhabitants live in the cities, many of them in substandard housing, or in sprawling suburban "bedroom communities." The horizontal and vertical mobility has increased drastically, and, in the new urban and industrial society, a new urbanized middle class has emerged that refuses to accept the old, rural-oriented way of life. This urbanized middle class, with 47 percent of the total voting power, gave the victory to its candidate for governor in the last elections, in November, 1968, in spite of the fact that 53 percent of the electorate were against him but favored other candidates. As anyone can deduce, this new class is not the majority in Puerto Rico, and yet, on the other hand, as a newcomer it keeps many traditional values hidden underneath its commitment to the new goals.

There are no studies of what happens with the children of broken homes in this emergent social class. It seems probably that one could apply to them what has been found applicable to the children of the U.S.A., although attenuated by the residues not yet totally assimilated of the previous culture. In roughly more than half of the population of Puerto Rico represented by 53 percent of the votes cast in the last elections, the traditional frame of reference still dominates, and the situation is different from the one that is supposed to exist in the United States.

In the first place, the law of Puerto Rico had never given juridical status to the ancient classification of children as legitimate, natural, adulterine, spurious, incestuous, *manceres*, or sacrilegious. But the law of Puerto Rico was more progressive, and the law in force at present does not recognize any juridical difference among children due to the marital status of the parents. With rare exceptions, statutes usually follow a real situation, and the law of the land in Puerto Rico does not discriminate between the children of ritual marriage and those of *de facto* unions, revealing that the conscience of the majority of the people does not make a drastic distinction either. The union legally called at present "consensual marriage" has a long historical tradition in Puerto Rico (23.6 percent of the unions in 1950 were consensual marriages), and it continues to have a considerable statistical frequency at present. Historical and teluric circumstances neutralized the efforts of the church and of the successive legal systems that influenced Puerto Rico in such a manner that, in the large majority of the population, the taboo or the guilt complex was not created: usage prevailed against the law. It is easy to understand that not attaching undue value in any dimension to ritual marriage, the dissolution, separation, or divorce in Puerto Rico cannot produce the moral shock that it could cause in other cultures.

On the other hand, the concept of the big clan family still prevails in Puerto Rico. The family as such is not only constituted by parents and children that surround their privacy with a wall. It is rather a complex net of long threads that become thinner until they get lost in the distance, centered around a female figure, generally, and in which are intertwined all the blood relatives, the in-laws, the half brothers and sisters, the adopted children, the relationships of *compadrazgo*—godchildren—and an infinite line of varied shades of family ties. The family has many homes, and the relatives meet and eat in any one of them. Divorce, separation, or a trip to the U.S.A. is something that cannot break the family structure of the clan. The source of the big family coincides with a hill, a valley, or a portion of land, whose population grows to the extent that the family does, without losing the emotional dependence from its center. Children do not live together with their parents alone, or with their brothers and sisters. They go together with their second and third cousins; the brother-in-law of their sister may teach them to work; they obey the elder aunt, and take shelter in the grandmother's home. The phrase "In this *barrio* we are a large family" is not a mere phrase, but rather the expression of a reality that is emotional, social, and economic at the same time. The large family is the subject of important events: "Birth, like the rest of the life cycle, including death, is not an isolated ocurrence. Few experiences in the child's life will be unknown to his family and community. Far from resenting this lack of privacy, he will come to delight in it and to expect likewise to share the experiences of others."[15]

[15]Landy, David. *Tropical Childhood*. New York: Harper & Row, 1965, p. 157.

The children of previous marriages also belong to the large family: children previously begotten by men who marry women of the clan, sometimes are loved by those women more than they love their own children, especially when the father abandons them. The stepmother is a figure of positive polarity in the large family against the negative value that accompanies her in the legal marriages and in other cultures. This reality has been presented in literature in a play by Rene Marques, *The Ox Cart.*[16] Although this observation may be considered out of the strict field of the present study, the sense of belonging to the large family continues to exist for the members of the clan who are far away, and many times they reconstruct in a distant place a sort of subclan family structure, a kind of metastasis.

These circumstances do not create the conditions that would lead the child of a broken home to construct an unfavorable "specular image." And at the same time that his emotional security depends on the large family group rather than on his parents, his economic security is not deeply affected either by divorce, separation, or death of one of the parents. On the other hand, the law of Puerto Rico, although it is liberal in relation to the classification of children, is strict insofar as imposing alimony on the parents. The impact of the mother who works out of the house is not a deep one either, since the child is accustomed from the time of his birth to the fact that the mother may work, habitually or sporadically, outside of her home, although she always returns at night.

Regarding this point, there is a very important study that proves the reality of this fact, even in a class considered to be superior. Research in this field has shown that a comparison of juvenile delinquency in districts where women did not work out of their homes with juvenile delinquency in those districts where they did work out was significantly less in the latter. As a mere hypothesis, the author proposes, as an explanation of what she considers a *surprising phenomenon*, that the absence of mothers has given place to the appearance of other structures that substitute them with advantage.[17] If this is so in a class considered superior, it confirms the important vicarious role of the clan family structure in the class that is not superior. This

[16]Marques, Rene. *La Carreta*. En teatro puertorriqueño, IV Festival, Instituto de Cultura Puertorriqueña, Barcelona, 1963, pp. 317–563.
[17]Palau de Lopez, Awilda. *Ponencia sobre delincuencia infantil, op.cit.*

observation also confirms the minor importance attached to the identification with the father in Puerto Rico.

There is another study about a superior social class, in which we
find this assertion:

> Both girls and boys found such support outside the nuclear family
> and thus the horizontal relationship with the parent of their own
> sex could be coped with. Whenever grandparents, aunts, and un-
> cles were available to the adolescents they found support in coping
> with difficult parental relationships. Many admired their grandpar-
> ents and sought to consciously emulate them in their own attitudes
> and behaviour.[18]

There are many interesting studies carried out through the
method of individual studies, as for example *La Vida* of Oscar Lewis,
about a family in the subculture of poverty. Naturally, his conclusions
would not apply outside of that subculture, which is not by any means
the most representative of Puerto Rico, but could rather be applicable to other expressions of the same subculture in other places of the
world. In the introduction of the above-mentioned study, the author
explains a valuable evaluation of the method of individual cases, and
I am going to summarize here an example of a case study that is to
be published soon.[19]

AXY is a forty-five-year-old woman. She lives in the country, at
a distance of only six kilometers from a city located on the western
coast of Puerto Rico. She owns, by inheritance, a small plot of land
on which she has built her own one-story house. She has two older
sisters who dwell in houses located nearby. The two older sisters are
married to men who work sporadically, and who do not contribute
regularly to the support of their households.

AXY married legally when she was eighteen. She continued
working as a domestic. Of that first marriage she had two sons and
a daughter. In spite of the fact that AXY only went to school for a
couple of years as a child, she is able to write quite correctly, she
reads the newspaper habitually, acts as a primary teacher to her
children, and values education to an extraordinary degree. Her husband left for New York and divorced her when the three children
were still very small. AXY remained in her house, working as a

[18]Fernandez Marina, *et al., op. cit.* p. 794.
[19]Nieto, Jose. *Un clan matriarcal en el Monte.* In press.

domestic for well-to-do families of the neighborhood. The children grew up in the country within the pattern of the clan family.

When AXY was about thirty years old, she lived in a consensual union with a man who was married to another woman and was not divorced. She had three more children: two daughters and a son. The father of these three children also separated from her and went to New York. Although he lives far away with another woman, he has maintained a cordial relation with the children of AXY, writes to them occasionally, and sporadically sends money. AXY has continued working as a domestic. All the children of both fathers live together in great harmony and in absolute equality, although the age of each one establishes a certain hierarchy that imposes at the same time the right of the older ones to be respected by the younger ones and the responsibility of the older ones to protect the young ones. All of them have attended school, although some have profited by it more than others because of individual differences and circumstance.

The elder daughter has married in a consensual union and has remained in the mother's house with her husband. This couple has a baby daughter who is cared for and pampered by all her uncles and aunts, and by her great-aunts and her grandmother, who treats her as her own child.

The second son of AZY is an epileptic. While AXY works outside as a domestic, his older sister and brother take care of him.

The third son is also living in a consensual union with a girl who was already pregnant by another man. This couple also came to live in the house of AXY, who added a little room in the rear of her house to shelter them. The baby was born there, and although the real father remained a stranger to the family, the girl's child was received as if he had always belonged. At present this couple have another child of their own, making a family of four within the larger family. This son works sporadically in the country, but AXY is the one who regularly provides for the needs of this couple and their family.

The first daughter of the second husband of AXY is in high school at present, on a scholarship which she earned with her good grades. The grandmother, the great-aunts, and the sisters and brothers help her in many ways in order to make possible the continuation of her studies. They all consider her academic success as if it were their own.

The youngest children, a girl and boy, are in the rural elementary school, a short distance from their home.

Besides the money that AXY makes and what the father of the second group of children sends once in a while from New York, they receive some help from the Welfare Office of Puerto Rico. Everyone in this family dresses properly and they are well nourished; with the exception of the son suffering from epilepsy, they do not show any physical or mental deficiencies. AXY's sisters repeat in their patterns of life a situation similar to the one described.

None of the younger members of the family present symptoms of wanting to abandon the country or the house on the hill with their mother-grandmother, nor the desire to change their type of life. In successive circles, this clan family extends into other analogous units, in such a manner that the hill is inhabited by relatives in varying degrees, directions, and types of relationship.

In spite of the economic motivations offered by the neighboring industrialized urban setting (the city is six kilometers away), the majority of the members of the large family continue to live as they did many years ago. It is not infrequent to see the few members who do leave return to the primary structure that gave them emotional and economic security, after experiencing the adventure of urban living. The members of the large family go to town in order to buy the food that is not produced in the country. They do not go to the movies, and their only amusements are the festivities and family reunions in which they and their neighbors act as musicians, singers, and dancers. The great events, in which *"la casa se echa por la ventana"* (the house goes out the window), are, outside of Christmas and Epiphany, the wakes, the celebration of a baptism, or the commencement celebration when a student graduates from school.

No member of the family described has shown any sign of anxiety or insecurity. There are no drug addicts among them, although there is an old alcoholic who has remained single, and a gambler who is married to one of AXY's sister. Among the wealthy and upper-class families who live in luxury residences and share with the clan family the hilly countryside, they have a reputation of being honest, faithful, and dignified; they do not feel inferior to anyone for any reason. Limiting ourselves to the children of AXY, we can see that neither separation nor divorce has caused any problems for them, and, what is more significant, AXY herself has taught the children respect and love for their absent fathers, whose image they do not even remember. AXY says: "Those men abandoned me, but they are the fathers of my children."

The case described coincides in general with a typical matrifocal clan family, with a very ancient root among peasants and small landowners. It responds to an anachronical system of values to which these people remain emotionally faithful, and thus it continues to perpetuate its defining power on human life in all its directions, including the material aspect.

Although this kind of rural Puerto Rican family, completely *jíbara* (hick), was common thirty years ago, it was by no means the only existing type of family. There were also families of a higher social class who adhered to many of the values of the middle Spanish colonial class. But, neither in this traditional middle class nor in the new emergent middle class of the present do we fail to find residues of the traditional family which we have described.

Among the cases studied in *The Sober Generation*,[20] all the adolescents belonged to the superior middle class and were excellent students from elementary school to college, where their scholastic work was of the highest caliber. Among them, there are three children of divorced parents who did not show any trace of disruption due to the early separation and divorce of their parents. Even in the social middle class, one can see that the mothers, in spite of having remarried in some cases, have some continuity with their first union. Overcoming their personal feelings of animosity, they express the wish that the children continue loving their fathers.

Accepting the risks that all generalizations imply, and on the basis of my own interpretation of the data, it seems safe to state that the repercussions of divorce and separation on Puerto Rican children are not comparable to the effects that supposedly results from broken homes in the United States.

[20]Fernandez Marina, *et al., op. cit.*

Socializing and
Educating the Child

Part V sets forth the challenges that face separated and divorced parents in meeting the social and emotional needs of their children. The several chapters provide a kind of chart of the essential steps that parents may follow in the long, ongoing process of socialization and education of their children.

Dr. F. H. Klatskin, looking at the child's developmental processes from birth through adolescence, places special emphasis on related emotional and psychological factors. When the family in which a child has developed a feeling of emotional security becomes disrupted, we need to know how the child is likely to react. Dr. Klatskin proves to be a good guide and a sensitive counselor.

Dr. Hanna Kapit, from her long experience in working with the emotional problems of divorced couples, provides a view of what knowledge and understanding may be required to help parents face, appreciate, and ultimately come to terms with their problems. Dr. Kapit offers hope for the effects of psychotherapy upon both the divorced couple and their children.

Mrs. Lois Kriesberg and her husband, Dr. Louis Kriesberg, concentrate on the processes of education of the child that contribute to his state of well-being. They direct their attention to both the formal and the experiential dimensions of education, within and without the broken family unit.

In the final chapter Dr. J. E. Garai presents a useful and stimulating view of the central importance of sex education for children. He offers an informed and sensitive awareness of the crucial significance of parental responsibilities in this area. The reader will gain fresh insights into how to approach an often sensitive area and how best to meet his children's needs.

E. H. KLATSKIN, Ph. D.

Developmental Factors

Dr. E. H. Klatskin of the Department of Pediatrics at the Yale University School of Medicine provides us with an interesting and helpful overview of the developmental factors that may play an important role in problems that children of separation and divorce present. Dr. Klatskin looks at these developmental processes in relation to their emotional and psychological outcomes, particularly as they may have an effect upon the security of a child who becomes threatened by disruption of his family life.

A well-known psychiatrist once remarked, from his point of view as a parent, "If you have children, you have problems!"

Unfortunately, from the child's point of view not only is a parallel rueful comment often true, "If you have parents, you have problems!" but even the process of growing up is itself a succession of problems which have to be solved and tasks which have to be mastered. For every child, each stage in life presents to some degree problem situations which he has to face and work through if he is to grow to be a healthy adult, both physically and emotionally.

Therefore, if parents understand the normal developmental sequence during the period when a child is most dependent on them for physical and emotional support, then they can better be prepared to anticipate and understand the problems which may arise when their child's life is disrupted by their separation or divorce.

It is a truism to say that the time of his life when a child needs his parents most is from birth through early adolescence. Though there may be later periods when he will seek counsel, and even as an adult will want the continuing knowledge that he has his parents' support and understanding, the parent-child relationship is obviously most influential when he is most dependent on them for physical care and emotional gratification.

What, then, are the developmental tasks which a child faces as he moves from infancy into the preschool period, and through the school years into puberty and early adolescence?

As a newborn, the infant has to learn to live outside the protection of his mother's body, and to make multiple physiological adjustments to extrauterine life. The moment he is born, he has to establish such automatic functions as breathing and heart rate, and to adjust to temperature changes. Very shortly thereafter, he has to adapt to "eating" the food provided him, to make muscular adjustments to being handled, and to learn to sleep despite what may be going on around him.

As an older infant, he needs to learn to conform more and more to a daily schedule of eating and sleeping, usually set by his parents rather than by himself. Paradoxically, he has simultaneously to achieve more self-reliance and self-control, particularly in the use of his body. Between birth and eighteen months or two years, he has to attain mastery over his body—first in sitting, then in creeping, in standing, and in walking. By the time he is two, he is expected to have learned to control his bowel function, if not yet his bladder. He is beginning to understand that his needs are met more effectively if he makes them known through words rather than through the howls and frantic thrashing about of his earlier infancy. And, most importantly for his future psychological development, he learns to distinguish between strangers and those people in his small world—most often his mother and father—on whom he can depend for nurturance, comfort, and affection.

In the preschool years, the toddler has to establish increasing control over his body and its physical functions. By the time of entering school, or around the age of five, he is expected to have developed regular patterns of eating, sleeping, and toileting, and to be able to use language easily as a means of communication. Paralleling this increased physiological mastery, he has to adjust to the fact that, if he wants to get along with adults and peers, he has to accept limits imposed on his behavior by society. He has to learn to moderate the self-centered activity of infancy and to curb his impulsive acting out, particularly of his anger. He begins to learn the meaning of "good" and "bad" behavior, and to experience feelings of shame, guilt, love, and a desire to please. It is during this period also that the child becomes very much aware of anatomical differences between the sexes, and begins to be curious about his parents' relationship. In the process, he may act out sexual and aggressive urges toward both parents, and become quite possessive of the parent of the opposite sex.

The "problems" which the school-age child faces are, by and large, more those of mental and emotional than of physical origin. The focus for the child shifts from tasks of body growth and development to those of intellectual and emotional growth and development. He responds to the structured learning situation in school, as well as to the unstructured learning situation of his expanding life experience. During this period, he has to work toward greater independence from his parents, to develop relationships with his peers, and to move toward a sense of his own identity as an individual. And, as he approaches adolescence, he has to clarify and accept his sex role and sexual identity.

As he reaches puberty, the adolescent is faced with the complex task of coping with his sexual development and accompanying rapid body changes. Hs has to consolidate his identity and self-concept not only through increasing independence and emancipation from his family but also through meaningful relationships with his peers. And he has to move toward realization of his intellectual potential, in anticipation of the time when he will be a self-sustaining adult.

To recapitulate, in this time span from birth through early adolescence, the sequence is one of emphasis on body mastery in infancy; physical and emotional mastery in the preschool years; intellectual and emotional mastery in the school years; and intellectual, physical, and emotional mastery in early adolescence.

What, then, are the particular problems which the child of separation and divorce may develop as he moves through this life sequence?

If the parents' separation occurs during the pregnancy or early in the infancy period, the greatest potential hazard for the child is that the person on whom he is most likely to be dependent for his physical and emotional care—namely his mother—may be so overwhelmed by her own depression and grief at the breakup of the marriage that she is unable to offer herself to him in an adequate mothering role. If the quality and quantity of care which the infant experiences from his mother is unsatisfactory, there are likely to be disturbances in his patterns of feeding, sleeping, and elimination. He may become excessively irritable and difficult to comfort, as well as develop dependence on body satisfactions such as rocking and finger sucking, which are irritants to his already depressed and quite possibly guilty mother.

It has been shown that extremes of maternal deprivation may result in such a medical syndrome as "failure to thrive," where the infant shows a delay in physical growth, or in such a psychological syndrome as "infantile autism," where the child becomes unresponsive and withdraws into himself. One certainly does not anticipate that a separation or divorce during this early period will result in emotional deprivation severe enough to cause such profound reactions in the infant. Nevertheless, the mother's depression and apathy about his care may cause the infant to develop mild to moderate symptoms like those which characterize infants with failure to thrive or infantile autism.

Since the important need during this period is for affectionate and consistent nurturing, the most straightforward solution to the infant's developmental problem is to provide a mother substitute until the mother herself is sufficiently recovered from her depression to be able to respond with more emotional give-and-take to her infant. This is particularly indicated if the separation occurs during pregnancy or in the immediate postpartum period, when all women are emotionally and physically vulnerable, and the woman who is separated from her husband does not have the supportive relationship of the child's father.

The infant born into a family with older children is somewhat better off than a first-born infant, as his older siblings will undoubtedly give him some of the care and stimulation he might otherwise lack. However, it seems doubtful if, under these stressful circumstances, they will be capable of the mature handling and emotional reciprocity which can be provided by a more mature adult. It will probably be most advantageous to seek the aid of a grandparent or other mature relative, who herself has an emotional investment in the newborn. Then, as the mother begins to regain her emotional stability, and as the infant begins to establish less demanding patterns of behavior, she will find herself increasingly able to assume her proper role in his care, and to take joy in his development.

If the marriage breaks up during later infancy, the mother, who is the parent most likely to have care of the child, may transfer to him the love which would normally be given to her husband. Because of her own affectional needs, she may become overprotective and set the stage for patterns of child-rearing which will prevent growth toward age-appropriate independence in later years. If her overprotectiveness is too indulgent, the result may be an aggressively undisciplined or "spoiled" child, while if it is of a dominating sort, the result may be a passive and submissive child who is lacking in self-reliance. For her own sake, therefore, as well as for that of the infant now and her child's development in the future, it is desirable for the mother to continue or seek activities outside the home which will provide her with additional sources of pleasure and satisfaction in accomplishment.

Although separation and divorce may be the culmination of chronic emotional upheaval in a family, if it occurs during the preschool period, it presents the young child with an acute crisis situation as well. For, unlike the infant who has never known a home with both parents, he has to cope with the additional problem of the loss of a family figure. Although he may have been aware that there was something "wrong" in his parents' relationship, he is now faced with an abrupt change in his daily life patterns because of the absence of father or mother. Further, he is not yet old enough to comprehend the causes of their separation, and will probably have difficulty understanding even the simplest and most straightforward explanation he may be given.

During the early part of this age period, problems are most likely to manifest themselves in the area where the child is most vulnerable —his recent acquired mastery over his body functions. There may well be a breakdown in the controls he has learned. It is possible that he may begin to soil or wet his pants during the day; become a picky eater; show sleep disturbances such as night terrors; and become subject to temper tantrums. If a parent can understand that such regression is the child's way of expressing the anxiety and grief he feels but is not able to verbalize, it will help him not to compound the problem by punishing the child for his "babyish" behavior and thereby increase his sense of alienation from the parent with whom he is living. Since the child is responding not only to loss but to a break in routine, with the establishment of a new routine, he will usually regain the controls he has temporarily lost.

Later in this preschool period, when the child is having difficulty coping with the anxiety associated with his increasing concerns about birth, death, and sexual differences, the problems are most likely to be one of a psychological nature and more likely to be overlooked because they are not as obvious as are the problems of regression.

If the young child does not see the parent who has left the home, he may conclude that he is dead, or build up elaborate fantasies about the "good" and "bad" parent which he cannot test against reality. Experience indicates that some children see the parent who has left the home and deserted him as the "bad" parent, while others feel it is the "bad" parent who has remained and driven the "good" parent from the home. Such ideas are akin to those of many normal children, who at this age often imagine that they are adopted and that their "real" parents would be better to them than the parents with whom they are living.

A complicating factor at this age is that many, if not all, children begin to develop strong affectional ties to the parent of the opposite sex, and obviously competition between father and son for the favors of the mother, or between mother and daughter for the favors of the father, may occur. It is not unusual to find a child of this age fantasizing or daydreaming about the death or removal of the rival parent. Consequently, when separation or divorce occurs, the child may find himself in the now unenviable position of having his daydreams come true. Under these circumstances, he may develop very irrational but nonetheless very real guilt feelings about having himself been responsible for the breakup of the marriage.

In a stable home, during this period of oedipal fantasies, the child has the presence of both parents as the reality to check his possessive and destructive fantasies. Therefore, in the broken home, the presence of the absent parent, even for brief intervals of visiting, will help to allay the anxiety associated with ideas that this parent is dead or has abandoned him. It will also reassure him that though his parents are no longer living together, they both continue to love him and both are still his parents.

It has been suggested by some marital counselors that periodic visits with the "other" parent are unwise, since they may arouse fantasies in the child that his mother and father will be reunited, and because after each visit he may relive the initial grief reaction which followed their separation. It is recognized that the young child may misinterpret the meaning behind such a contact with the separated parent, and that it may be difficult to cope with his tears and anger after such a visit. However, in the long run, the results obtained from helping him to accept both the reality of the "other" parent's absence from the home, as well as his continuing relationship with this parent, would appear to outweigh the short-term disadvantages of a temporary emotional upset.

The parallel is to be found in the adjustment of young children to hospitalization. Until fairly recently, it was felt unwise to permit parents to visit their hospitalized children, because the children became so upset following their departure. However, it has been shown that upon their return home, children who had contact with their parents during their hospitalization made a much quicker emotional recovery from the experience than did children who did not have contact with their parents. The lessons learned from "humanizing" hospital experience would appear equally applicable to parental separation and divorce.

During the preschool period, the child's home environment has been the primary influence in his life. Now, as he enters school, other influences will progressively assume increasing importance. The most significant of these are the demands made by his teacher on his intellectual ability and the demands made by his peers for conformity to their social norm. Therefore, as the child grows older, he will begin more and more to think for himself and to make comparisons between his own family situation and that of his peers. He will quarrel less with reality but, as he becomes more objective about his life experiences, he will show less acceptance of interpretations and conclusions based on adult authority and will more and more himself engage in critical thinking. Regrettably for his parents' ego, he is moving from the "my mother and father know everything" conviction of his preschool years to the "neither of you know anything" belief of his adolescence.

During this period when all children begin to think about themselves in relation to the world around them, the child from a broken home has an additional circumstance which he will have to integrate in his perception of his environment.

In view of the frequency of separation and divorce in the American culture at the present time, the difficulties which may arise for the child in this school-age period are more likely to be those of disruption in the intellectual function from emotional problems than of stresses within his peer group. As far as his friends are concerned, it is highly likely that there will be several other children whose parents have been divorced and possibly remarried, so that his changed situation will not be a unique one.

The cases of two children brought for evaluation to a clinical psychologist because of their underachievement in school illustrate how learning difficulties may result when children are caught in the stress of the breakup of their parents' marriage.

David was a boy of eight, whose mother and teacher were concerned about the fact that he was not achieving up to his grade level. The mother's interpretation was that he was of superior ability and was bored in a noncompetitive public school placement. The teacher questioned whether he was even of average ability, because of his short attention span and inability to work for any length of time unless closely supervised. Examination of David showed that he was of bright but not superior endowment, and also revealed him to be a very anxious and insecure boy, with a vivid imagination. The content of his fantasy was quite threatening, but was displaced from real-life situations in that it dealt with "ready-made" themes such as fairy stories and television space programs. In the subsequent conference with his mother, the interpretation was made that David's preoccupation with his anxiety-arousing fantasy was responsible for his short attention span in school and inability to work unless closely supervised, but that the basis for his feelings of vulnerability were not clear from the testing. The mother then brought out that she and his father were in the process of divorce, but that she assumed the children knew nothing about this as they had merely been told that their father was working in another city. The boy's improved school performance after his mother and father were able to discuss the situation with him openly made it evident that his disrupted intellectual function resulted from his awareness of the disruption in his home life.

In the case of Matthew, his parents' divorce had occurred when he was three, and both had subsequently remarried and had children by their second marriages. Matthew, now eleven, was also brought by his mother because he was felt to be of superior ability, but was underachieving in a competitive private school. The results of the intelligence tests did indeed show that Matthew was of very superior ability, while the results of the personality tests revealed him to be an extremely introspective boy who apparently ruminated a lot about problem areas and tended to lose himself in fantasy. In his case, his fantasy related quite directly to past and present family events, and showed his confusion about his role in the family constellation, his uncertainty about whether he was to identify with his father or his stepfather, and his perception of himself as pushed around in the situation and not allowed to make decisions for himself. During the interpretation of the test results to his mother, she questioned whether the fact that the two families were on very intimate terms with each other could be contributing to her son's confusion. As an example of the contact which took place between them, she described the marriage of her present husband's daughter by his first marriage, which had been attended by her former husband, his second wife, and their children. In this situation, it did seem probable that the intimacy of the two families was contributing to Matthew's confusion about his identity role, particularly in relation to his two "fathers." However, in this case the boy's identity crisis appeared to be sufficiently serious that psychotherapy was recommended.

While the cases of David and Matthew illustrate the emotional impact which separation and divorce may have on a child's ability to learn, they also illustrate mistakes which well-meaning parents may make in assessing how the child interprets or misinterprets the situation before their divorce and their subsequent relationship to each other after it.

As has been seen in the case of David, it is a mistake to assume that if the child does not ask questions, he is unaware of what is taking place within the family. Rather, if the separation occurs after the child is five or six years old, he will undoubtedly be even more aware of the "emotional divorce" preceding the legal divorce than he was in his preschool years. However, because of his own guilt feelings or desire to avoid confronting a painful life situation, some children like David may show no outward reaction to their parents' dissension and separation. This is a considerably less healthy reaction than if the child is able to express his confusion and need to know what is going on. Under these circumstances, it is best if the parents can find an opportunity to acquaint the child with what is taking place and help him acknowledge his awareness of the impending breakup of the family.

Assuming that the child will ask questions, as most will do, it is to be hoped that the parents can steer a course between extremes which may compound his confusion and emotional turmoil. On the one hand, to refuse to answer questions and brush the child off with such statements as "Don't ask me questions—you're too young to understand" or "I don't want to talk about it" may put a stop to his questions. It will not, however, put a stop to his curiosity, and lack of explanation will very likely lead to even more distorted ideas about what is taking place than is actually the case. On the other hand, it is equally inadvisable to go into detailed explanations of marital incompatibility which imply recriminations against the other partner. Use of this latter type of "explanation" has been likened to the use a drunk makes of a lamppost—not for illumination, but to gain support.

When the parents recognize that their incompatibility is leading to separation, it is best to inform the child in simple terms that they can no longer live together, but that they both will continue to love him and will still be his parents, though they are living apart. Questions about when the divorce will take place and what the subsequent living arrangements will be should be answered honestly, even if the honest answer is that the parents themselves do not yet know about the details of legal proceedings and custody plans.

How the parents continue to relate to each other following their divorce will, of course, be a function of many variables, including the circumstances surrounding the divorce, and the successfulness of the ongoing life each must now make independently. For the child, however, the custody and visiting arrangements and parents' attitude toward the divorced partner may perpetuate his confusion and conflict about their separation. As far as custody and visiting arrangements are concerned, obviously there are many alternate solutions appropriate to the circumstances of the divorce. Of greater importance to the child in maintaining his emotional security and minimizing his ambivalent feelings toward his parents is how they now communicate to him their perception of each other. Here, again, negative and positive extremes of behavior are to be avoided. If one or both parents is constantly trying to discredit the other, their accusations may lead the child to feel that he should ally himself with one against the other. At best, the result will be to set up a conflict of loyalty accompanied by intense guilt feelings, and at worst the possibility that the child's negative perception of the parent of the opposite sex may make it impossible for him to establish harmonious heterosexual relationships later in life.

On the other hand, if the parents continue to maintain an overly intimate relationship with each other in the belief that this is best for the child, their conduct may trigger fantasies both that they will be reunited and also that their separation must somehow be his responsibility. The younger child, prohibited from seeing his parents' divorce as the product of their own incompatibility, in searching for a reason for their separation may not unreasonably conclude that he is in some way at fault.

The older child, in contrast, will sense the hypocrisy behind the compatible behavior of two people who at best can only be ambivalent about each other. As a result, he may begin to question the sincerity of his parents' behavior in other situations.

It is understandable that when divorced parents have contact with each other, both hostile and affectionate feelings may come to the fore, no matter how businesslike their meeting may be. However, there is no need to display either extreme of these emotions before the child, and it will be preferable if they can maintain a civil but formal relationship.

If there is ever a time when most parents feel with certainty that "if you have children you have problems," it is when their children reach adolescence. For, under the stress of adjusting to the internal bodily changes of puberty and to the external changes in the socio-cultural role he is expected to play as he moves toward adulthood, even the most stable and affectionate child is likely to become inconsistent and unpredictable in his behavior, and to show openly high ambivalent attitudes toward his parents.

Therefore, in the one-parent family it is as likely to be the parent who is disadvantaged during this period as it is the child. The parent with whom he is living will very likely receive the brunt of the negative expression of the adolescent's ambivalence. Further, the normal depression felt by parents in anticipation of the time when their children will grow up and leave home cannot be alleviated by a marital life fulfilled apart from the child.

It is to be hoped that a sense of humor plus recall of their own adolescent difficulties can give single parents enough detachment to weather this period in their child's life.

Adolescence has been described as the time in life when the "I's" have it—referring not just to the self-preoccupation of this age, but to the three major tasks which the adolescent faces: *industry* in learning, increasing *independence* from his parents, and establishing *intimacy* with his peers. Further, as the child enters adolescence and faces these tasks, he brings with him a legacy of experience from his past which will in large part determine how he solves the problems of the present. Important aspects of this legacy are whether his home life has been discordant or harmonious, the identification models his parents have provided, and the attitudes each has expressed toward the marital partner, either in the presence or absence of separation and divorce.

As far as industry in learning is concerned, experience suggests that during adolescence it is more likely to be the remarriage of one or both of the divorced parents rather than a divorce itself which may lead to disruption in the learning process. The child whose parents have divorced earlier in his life has by now made his adjustment to this situation, while the child whose parents divorce during his adolescence is old enough to be able to understand some of the complexities of his parents' relationship and to comprehend their verbal explanations. The child at any age may interpret a parent's remarriage as an additional loss, and to feel that his mother or father has abandoned him for another person. However, if the remarriage occurs during adolescence, it confronts him with another rival for a parent's affection at a time when, in the process of struggling for independence and emancipation from his family, he may be reliving old oedipal conflicts.

His efforts to cope with the upsurge of psychosexual drives he is experiencing may not be confined to ambivalent outbursts toward his parents but may for a period make it difficult for him to concentrate on his studies, with resulting erratic school achievement. The situation may be particularly complicated for the boy or girl whose father remarries during their adolescence, since under these circumstances it is more likely that the new stepparent will be closer to them in age than will be the case if their mother remarries. It will be most helpful in resolving the child's conflict if the parents can reassure him of their support and affection, while steering a course between excluding him in their preoccupation with their new life together and heightening his anxiety by relating to him as an age peer.

In his striving toward increased independence and in his efforts to consolidate his role as another adult within the family group, the adolescent's ambivalence toward his parents is often clearly evident. If possible, however, his ambivalence toward his own changing age role is even more apparent. He varies between acting half his age, and thus expressing his wish to remain a protected and nurtured young child, and aping the behavior of adults, reflecting in his pseudomature mannerisms his wish to be accepted by them as a peer.

In any home, the greatest threat to the young adolescent's developing emotional maturity lies in the possibility that his parents may unconsciously abet one or the other extreme of the ambivalent feelings he has about himself. In the single-parent home, this is even more likely to occur because of the divorced parent's fear of impending separation from the child. He may, therefore, discourage attempts at independence in the unconscious wish to perpetuate childhood, so that the son or daughter may become overconforming, find themselves incompatible with peers, and be unable to assume the responsibilities of increasing autonomy. Or because of the fear of alienating a son or daughter and losing a source of emotional gratification, the parent may be unable to set any limits on their behavior, with the result that the child may become defiant, unreliable, and possibly delinquent.

During this period of young adolescence, when a boy or girl is no longer a child but is not yet a man or woman, the mature parent will allow and encourage reasonable independence, while neither setting prohibitive limits on freedom nor allowing complete autonomy when the adolescent is not yet mature enough to assume full responsibility for his behavior.

Paradoxically, during the period when the adolescent is striving to become independent of his parents, he must simultaneously begin to relinquish some of his independence in his relationships with his peers, if he is to establish the kind of intimacy which will eventually lead to a stable heterosexual relationship in his own marriage.

In this process, his developing heterosexual attitudes will depend greatly on the identification models his parents have provided and on the attitudes each has expressed toward his former marital partner. The adolescent's own self-esteem will not only reflect the self-image of the parent of the same sex but also will be influenced by the qualities attributed to that parent by the opposite partner. The child who has been exposed to repeated recriminations between his divorced parents, which have been phrased not just in terms of their specific faults as perceived but toward them as a man or woman in general, may well think not only of himself but of members of the opposite sex in negative terms. As a result, he may unconsciously try to establish distance rather than intimacy in his peer relationships, in an effort to protect himself against a potentially painful involvement.

The above is not to imply that the parents should deliberately distort a negative perception of their divorced partner, as again the child will be aware of their hypocrisy. Rather, it is to suggest that they should not use their emotions destructively for the child's future heterosexual development, by implying that the negative aspects of the divorced partner are characteristic of all individuals of the same sex.

The foregoing discussion has been focused on problems which may arise in the behavioral development of the child of separation and divorce. However, divorce is not the unique situation in which a child may live with and be raised by only one parent. The death or incapacitating illness of a parent or separation of parents because of military service will all have the same result. Further, developmental problems are not necessarily the sequel to the breakup of a marriage. Since the child's emotional development is more likely to be related to the conditions which are present in his home than to those which are absent, his experiences in a cohesive one-parent home may well be more constructive than those in a chaotic two-parent home. Divorced parents can reassure themselves that a one-parent family is still a family, and a one-parent home is still a home.[1]

[1]In organizing the ideas contained in this chapter, the author has depended heavily on the excellent Developmental Schema Charts contained in *Problems in Child Behavior and Development,* by Milton J. E. Senn, M.D., and Albert J. Solnit, M.D. (Philadelphia: Lea & Febiger, 1968). Their section on the special problem of divorce (pp. 239–43) was particularly helpful.

She also wishes to acknowledge the use of the section of "Growth and Development" by James J. Gallagher, and Allen D. Calvin, Editor, *Psychology* (Boston: Allyn and Bacon, 1961, pp. 45–183), as well as two papers by Melvin Lewis, M.B.,B.S., "Child Development in the Problem Family" (*Journal of American Medical Women's Association*, 1968, 23:44–53) and "Psycho-sexual Development and Sexual Behavior in Children" (*Connecticut Medical*, 1968, 32:437–44), and a paper by Martha F. Leonard, M.D., "The Impact of Maternal Deprivation on Infant Development" (*Connecticut Medical*, 1968, 32:466–573).

Discussion with the following colleagues was also fruitful: Richard H. Granger, M.D., Associate Professor of Clinical Pediatrics; Herbert S. Sacks, M.D., Associate Clinical Professor of Psychiatry; and Ruth L. Silverberg, M.S.W., Instructor in Pediatrics (Social Work).

HANNA E. KAPIT, Ph. D.

Help for Children of
Separation and Divorce

What are the possibilities for success in a second marriage for parents whose children are having difficulty in making a healthy adjustment to the new family situation? Dr. Kapit provides information and advice from her numerous contacts with just such problems. This chapter is not restricted to how to cope with common situations after the family disruption but also discusses how most productively to inform a child of the impending event, how to deal with problems of placement and custody, and how to anticipate personal and emotional reactions to being a single parent. Dr. Kapit has found that new relationships, new values, and a new atmosphere of security and stability often accompany the new marriage relationship, encouraging the emotional growth of the children.

Rose, eight years old, sat on the edge of the chair in the therapist's office, her face intensely serious, her hands folded in her lap, her voice urgent.

"I can't understand why people get divorced. Why did my mother and father stop loving each other? She told me they just stopped. They couldn't even talk to each other anymore. My father wanted to get a divorce for a long time, but my mother didn't. Finally she had to agree. Now she is remarried and so is he. He went to South America to work for a while and found a new wife.

"It's so confusing. Weekends I have to go to my father's house and I hate to go there. I hate his place. He has moved four times in the last three years.

"Another thing I don't understand is why a person who knows nothing about another one says bad things about him. My father always tells me that my mother and Fred—that's my stepfather—don't want to work. My father doesn't know and he isn't right. Fred works—he just has the kind of job where he has to think a lot. My father always tells me he doesn't want to pay the four hundred dollars for me and my brother Ronny. But Fred pays four hundred dollars for his *one* son who lives in Cleveland.

"I like Fred. He's fun. He teases me.

"My father is an optometrist and many times I have to sit in his store for hours with nothing to do. It's so boring and he yells so, I can't stand it. I'm afraid of him so I don't say anything to him. If I have the choice between going to the movies with him and staying home with my stepmother, I stay with her. She is nice and peaceful. When I stay with her, Ronny goes with my father.

"When I grow up, I want to get married only once. It's all wrong what they say at the ceremony: for better or worse, through sickness and health. My mother shouldn't have said those words. Then she wouldn't have had to be so unhappy.

"I was only two and a half when they got divorced. I wish I had been born nine years earlier. Then it would not have been so hard on me; I would have taken it better if I had been older. I would like to be fifteen or sixteen now. Then I'd be independent.

"Do I have to go to my father's house? I don't want to. Last summer I ran away the day I was supposed to go. Ronny ran after me and pulled me into the bus. He said he was going to hit me. But I don't want to go. Why does the law do this to kids?

"I never know what to do. At my mother's house I never make my bed. At my father's house I have to make it. And everything is different. I never know what to do where. All that moving back and forth . . . it's bad for a kid. A few days here, a few days there. I just don't understand it, I feel torn apart.

"I don't understand why people get divorced in the first place. I wish my parents would still be together. Or that I would be grown up. But, no, I don't want to grow up either. And I never want to marry. I don't know what I want.

"But I know I don't want to go to my father's. Do I have to go?"

The therapist had been asked to see this little girl by her mother, "Not because she has any problems, she is very well adjusted. The divorce didn't affect her at all, but because all the others in the family are in some form of treatment and she feels left out, she wants to have somebody to talk to also." Suspecting that the child was not so untroubled as the mother wanted to believe, the therapist agreed to see Rose and was not surprised to hear her pour out her confusion, misery, and conflict.

CHILDREN OF CONFLICT

"Happy families are all alike; every unhappy family is unhappy in its own way." (Anna Karenina)

Every child is different, and every child's position in the family as well as his experiences prior, during, and after separation and divorce are different; so each child's needs will vary. Approaches toward helping these children weather the storm with a minimum of scars or shipwrecks will also vary and will depend on the severity of the individual situation. Helping methods might include one or more of the following: education of parents concerning their child's problems; counseling with the child alone; counseling with parent (parents) and child. Help may range from slight short-range intervention to intensive, long-range therapy.

Some parents may want to hold onto the belief that children are not affected by their parents' conflicts. The contrary is true: every child experiencing a separation and/or divorce suffers. Serious long-lasting conflict between parents threatens the security of a youngster, causes anxiety and worries, and poses questions that are impossible for a child to answer. Adults often get embroiled in these common controversies—"Is a divorce better for the child or is it better if the parents remain together in a tense situation?" "Does the child or the parent suffer more?" "Do neurosis, delinquency, homosexuality, etc., stem from broken homes?" In any case, such questions can only be answered for the individual situation and concerning individual families. But they are completely irrelevant as far as the individual child is concerned. Any child of an unhappy, unloving marriage and any child of a breaking or broken marriage feels insecure and most probably will need help. The parent knows his child, the counselor or therapist his patient.

In fact, the child's anxieties and conflicts are aroused as soon as the parents' problems begin, as the marriage starts disintegrating, and it is as early as that that the child needs to be considered and protected.

Though the child's experiences are difficult to measure and though no exact studies exist, it is today commonly agreed upon by behavioral scientists that the separation and divorce experience is damaging to the child. The wounds and scars depend on the child's constitutional makeup, his childhood experiences up to and the actual circumstances of the conflict situation. The damage is not caused by the separation and divorce itself, but by the divided house, the tensions leading to the separation, and the events thereafter. The emotionally healthier child—one in a less bitter overall situation—if caught in a violent and resentful battle will suffer less and resolve his conflicts more easily than the already weakened child. All these children, however, will need the sensitive and understanding help of their parents (or at least *one* parent) or of some professional outsider —and some will need it desperately.

THE FORTUNATE CHILD

The child will be able to deal with his feelings when his mother or father—or both—are concerned with his emotions and reactions and are sensitively aware of his needs in a time of crisis. The parent or parents will encourage the child to understand and express his normal and natural feelings and fears, put them in perspective, and resolve them. They will be able to assure the child of their love, his worth and blamelessness and his place in both their lives.

In addition, a child who is only minimally embroiled in hostility and guilt will believe more in his parents' love for him and can preserve his own love for them without too much damage. If he can remain emotionally receptive, he will be able to use his parents' guidance to develop an ability to relate, to love, and to find happiness in personal relationships. If he has been helped by his parents, he may never come to the attention of a counselor or therapist.

THE TEMPORARILY NEGLECTED CHILD

In the case of parents who are either not very sensitive to start with, or who temporarily forget the child's needs because of their own unhappiness and bitterness—a separated or divorced woman is often a selfish woman, a separated or divorced man is often a selfish man —the child is forgotten or, worse, used as a pawn between the parents. This child is often neglected by the parents at a time when he needs special protection.

Parents ought to be reminded of their children's needs, and many sources of help are available. This book and others like it attempt to educate and help parents. Lectures and discussion groups by psychologists, marriage counselors, and psychotherapists—sometimes under the aegis of such organizations as "Parents Without Partners" or "Single Parents"—are available to many parents, as are professionals dealing with children in conflict. Often clergymen and usually lawyers, present in situations of separation and divorce, are in a good position to draw attention to the children's needs and problems at this time.

Professionals working with parents in a therapeutic relationship are often justified in directing parents' attention to the child's anxieties and problems. Though at the time this may distract from the adults' needs, for many parents it is helpful to be reminded, to become concerned, and to avoid later occasion for guilt and regret. To save the child problems and misery will save parents problems and misery, too.

With such slight intervention, many parents are able to calm themselves enough to listen to their child, to become aware of the child's needs, and to fulfill them. If, because of their own disturbed state of mind, parents find themselves incapable of dealing with their child's anxieties, they may want to see and discuss the problem with a counselor.

In this still rather benign situation, the counselor will attempt to help the parents understand how their own problems may interfere with their being open with the child. Such parents, motivated and-flexible, can become aware of their own attitudes and how they may interfere with both their own recovery process and their relationship with their child.

Being familiar with their own conscious as well as unconscious feelings about this phase of their life will help parents be more understanding and accepting of their child's feelings, and helping the child will in turn bring greater awareness and resolution to the parents.

Most often *one* parent (usually the mother, who has custody of the child), will be the one who comes for help with a desire to "do right by" her boy or girl. But there have been instances in which both father and mother together have come for assistance with their child. Such interest on the part of the parents, the fact that they can cooperate, their willingness to understand, help, and do the best, most often assures sensitive and accepting handling of the child, frequently with only minimal help from a professional.

THE CHILD GETTING HELP FROM NEITHER PARENT

The parent who has left (usually the father is the absent parent) may assure and convince the child of his concern and love, but his very absence will cause pain. Even if very troubled and destructive to the child, this absent father rarely involves himself with the child's therapy. He often refuses treatment when recommended, or may go for help individually that has no connection with the professional care of child.

The mother who has custody of the child may also be very disturbed and incapable of helping her child. She may have been poorly adjusted before the marriage break or may be reacting to an intensely upsetting separation and divorce with a great emotional handicap. She may come for help on her own accord or be sent by school, church, or place of employment.

If the therapist sees that a mother is not likely to recover reasonably quickly and will not be able to take proper care of herself and her child, he will suggest professional help: counseling or therapy, depending on the situation.

Whether the recommendation for treatment—for child or either parent—is accepted often depends on the parents' sophistication and psychological, intellectual, and emotional state. If a parent refuses counseling or therapy, nothing will be accomplished; if a parent is not motivated to receive help, therapy becomes difficult or impossible. In some instances, when the mother is recalcitrant, the pressure of school or some other agency may persuade her to agree to treatment at least for the child alone. Though far from ideal—especially when the mother with whom the child has to spend day and night is difficult, hostile, detached, or depressed—treatment for the child alone is better than if neither mother nor child can be reached.

If the parent, however, can be convinced of the need and efficacy of treatment for both, the first battle is won, and the situation becomes more optimistic. In some agencies, convinced that a child can only be helped in conjunction with treatment for *one* parent, at least, the organization will not accept the child alone.

Treatment for mother and father may range from counseling to psychotherapy to psychoanalysis, one to five times a week. Different treatment methods depend on such circumstances as the kind and severity of disturbance, availability of time and finances, as well as the professional's expertise.

Though some professionals prefer to keep treatment of different individuals separate in parent and child situations, team therapy is often the preferred approach. To therapists or counselors working closely together and concerned with the effects of one patient's treatment on the other, may well work toward a common goal.

For the small child not yet able to verbalize his feelings, play therapy is the medium through which he can express his conflicts, fears, and anxieties. With the help of dolls, toys, water, clay, crayons, etc., the child communicates his feelings to the therapist, whose interventions and interpretations may be made verbally—if the child understands—or via play. It is sometimes possible to see the child's anxiety and agitation abate in successive sessions, as he feels understood and accepted and can work through the confusions and conflicts he could not untangle by himself.

The older child, emotionally and intellectually able to express himself through words, symbols, and ideas—remember Rose, who gave us a most vivid description of her feelings in the introduction to this chapter—can be helped to clarify his confusions, find answers to his questions and doubts, and learn to understand and deal with both the external and internal conflicts which beset him.

CUSTODY OF THE CHILD

In approximately 95 percent of custody decisions, the mother is awarded the care of the child. Most often the father agrees to such an arrangement, which fits in best with his cultural and social position. The role of breadwinner has taken the father out of the house, child care skills have been deprecated, and the child has been left in the mother's hands to a large extent before the separation and divorce and, fortified by our legal and judicial system, to an even greater extent afterwards.

The mother, though most often wanting the child's custody and fighting for that right, may also resent being saddled with the child. Unrelieved responsibility for the care of the child will restrict her freedom, and a degree of resentment is natural. Jealousy over her husband's freedom of action may be added to her frustration and bitterness. If understood, accepted, and put in its place, such feelings can be handled.

There are times, however, with a very difficult, hostile, detached, or depressed mother in which her relationship with the child becomes so explosive that custody arrangements may have to be questioned by the counselor. His concern for the child's welfare may dictate the child's separation from the mother. Some mothers can be helped to see this to be in the best interest of the child, but with others the suggestion may cause great opposition and may have to be referred for legal action.

At times a boarding school placement may be an interim solution. Other times, the question of optimal placement, temporary or permanent, with father, relative, or foster parent has to be decided on the basis of merits for the individual case. At such a time the counselor's interest and concern for mother and child may be a big help.

The mother's resistance, resentment, hostility, and guilt—and the child's perception of desertion and abandonment with its consequent resistance, resentment, hostility, and guilt—have to be dealt with and understood with respect to the maximum benefit for the child.

A SEPARATION OR DIVORCE IS NOT A DISASTER

A separation or divorce is not a disaster. It can be a correction of an unhappy, disturbed marriage and is often a relief that may bring a happier and healthier adjustment for all.[1] At the time, however, it is a disruption of life and the focus for realistic as well as unrealistic feelings, fears, fantasies, and projections in adult and child. For the child, confusions and misunderstandings are often added. Clarifying, understanding, and accepting those reactions, and putting them in proper perspective, help the child and allow him to adjust to the situation and make the best of it.

Louise Despert, in her helpful book, *Children of Divorce*, says, "A child who has been able, with his parents' or outside help, to weather a divorce has a better chance for healthy maturity than a child of unhappy marriage who has not come through his stormy experience."

The understanding of a child's conflicts, responses, and concerns resulting from the rupture in the parental relationship is a prerequisite for helping a child handle this unfortunate experience.

PROBLEMS OF THE CHILD OF SEPARATION AND DIVORCE

Unfortunately, as we have mentioned before, the first problem of the child is that he rarely is being helped—by parent or professional—when his anxieties first start, when he first begins to sense conflicts around him. This may be *before* the parents are aware, or have admitted to themselves, that their relationship is in difficulty

Depending on the age of the child, he will sense and react differently. Even the youngest child, though not understanding what goes on, and therefore more threatened and afraid, will sense his mother's anxiety by the way he is held, will react to angry or cool

[1]Morton M. Hunt, in his interesting book, *The World of the Formerly Married*, says, "Divorce clearly appears to be a highly moral act, not only in many specific situations but in a broader sense. It is the necessary corollary of our elevated ideal of marriage, our valuation of emotional health, and our respect for the individual's right to seek happiness."

voices, and be aware of the tensions between the parents, in the house and all around him—and will be frightened by this atmosphere of an unseen, not-understood disturbance.

The child's security, his very life, depends on the parents' love and nurturance. Feeling the love withdrawn, the child is afraid that he will not be taken care of, not be fed, or protected. Not being told, and not understanding, are more threatening to the child because he cannot know what he has to deal with. Not being told deprives him of tools to handle the imagined danger, leaves him completely in the dark, and makes him feel inadequate.

Tension and hostilities between the parents will be interpreted by the child not only as a lack of concern for him—"Mother is involved with other issues than me!"—but it will also stir up his own aggressions. The dangers that the child will see in the parents' conflicts may make him afraid that one or the other, or both, will leave, that they may hurt or even kill each other—and that then they may possibly even turn their wrath toward him, the helpless child.

These frightening thoughts will naturally be resented by the child—"Why are they doing this to me? They are nasty and mean!"-Hand will lead via another road to intense anger and resentment. Such hateful emotions are difficult for children to bear, especially when directed against parents whom they need and love, and will therefore be accompanied by excessive guilt. Such feelings, if borne by the child in silence and alone, are overwhelming and destructive. If, on the other hand, a sensitive parent or a trained professional, in an atmosphere of acceptance, helps the child express his feelings, they can be exposed to the light and understood. Once understood, they can be accepted by the child as a natural response to the situation and do not have to undermine the child's belief in himself as a worthwhile person.

WHO SHOULD TELL THE CHILD

The parents worried about "telling the child" often need help also. Their anxiety and guilt about hurting the child, and their worry about how to deal with the child's reactions, make this confrontation an intensely emotional situation for them, which they often delay and evade. When parents delay, the mystery and unknown horror of the conflict continue, seem more frightening and dangerous, and encourage more misinterpretations on the part of the child. The little boy or girl, or even older children, must conclude "If my parents, big people, are afraid and cannot face this problem, it must really be horrible. And if the big people can't deal with this, how can I do it, being so small?" Bringing the problem out into the open takes away the dark horror.

Wherever possible, it is best if both mother and father can sit down with the child and explain the facts of their disagreements and their plans for the future. Experiencing father and mother together, even though in some conflict, gives the child the assurance that both care and are willing to work together for his good. Some parents, feeling that they wanted to cooperate for the sake of the child's security but might not be able to succeed have gone for professional assistance. Through counseling, they have received confidence which they can hand on to their child.

If parents, however, have reached a state in which they cannot be together without fighting, it is better not to impose this on the child. In that case, when one parent tells the child, that parent should be reasonable, calm, and controlled, should understand that the child *will* be hurt, but also that there is love and hope for the future. If the parent is very upset, depressed, and resigned, having given up hope for his own life, this pessimism will be handed on to the child. The more acceptance and confidence the child can hear in a parent's voice and see in his eyes, the more confidence and trust will he have in being taken care of toward a brighter future.

A child should not be told more than a parent is sure of. When problems start, the child may need to know that his parents have conflicts but are trying to straighten them out. Not until parents are sure that a separation and/or divorce is in the offing does the child need to be told that fact.

A father and mother who are vacillating, separating and coming together again repeatedly, not able to decide, make it difficult for their child to accept, adjust to, and come to peace with an always changing, always disturbing situation.

The child need not be told intimate details of his parents' troubles. He is burdened enough by the conflicts around him and need not be pulled in to the personal problems of his parents.

Above all, tell the truth! Children are sensitive and know when they are deceived. Dishonesties only worry and anger children more

—"Why don't they tell me the truth? Am I too weak to hear what is really going on, or do they think I am stupid?" Most often, the child has heard and seen and sensed correctly, and he wants and deserves to have his impressions confirmed and clarified.

A child has to be told that there is something wrong or unhappy between his parents, that adults sometimes make mistakes, that their marriage has been a mistake which they are trying to correct for their sake and for his sake, also. Admitting that the troubles between them have made them angry and nasty—not only with each other but also sometimes with the child—will appease the child's doubts and fears that he has been the cause of the conflicts, a battle which is already raging in him.

How much a parent tells a child depends on the child's age, his personality, and on the parent-child relationship. It is important to explain as much as the child can understand, to reassure his child that the situation is sad but not tragic, and, most importantly, that *both* parents love him and will see to it that he will be well taken care of and protected. The child has to know that he is safe, loved, and appreciated.

It is important to gauge the child's feelings and reactions after the parents' explanations to make sure that the child's responses and reactions are included in the total communication between the child and his parent. This prototype of the parent-child relationship can contribute much to convincing the child of his importance to both parents. It is good for him to express his emotions, even if they are bitter and resentful, to know that he has a right to them, and that his parents accept and understand them. It is also essential for the parent or counselor to hear the child's responses, fears, and interpretations—so they can be further explored and corrected. The idea is to get the child to understand his internal and external reality, not to spin frightening fantasies and remain a worried youngster.

A PARENT LEAVES

At the time when one parent—usually the father—leaves, the conflicts in the child are accentuated and aggravated. Every new step and development in separation will stimulate fears and anxieties anew, even in a prepared child who, hopefully, understands the reasons and issues of the separation or divorce. An unprepared child will be that much more anxious and fearful.

Any child will feel rejected and abandoned when somebody as important as a father or mother leaves him. Being left by a parent gives rise to feelings of rejection and abandonment. The child asks himself: "Doesn't he love me? If he loved me, he wouldn't leave me; his deserting me is proof that he doesn't love me . . . he is my security, my protection . . . I need him . . . I am afraid what will happen to me—and Mother—Mother is not strong like Father . . . we are both in danger . . . and why is he doing this to me . . . us . . . me?"

Since a young child sees everything in relation to himself, and older children also relate their parents' actions to themselves, the child will ask himself: "Did Father leave because I was bad and is he therefore angry at me?" and will remember some angry act or thought in the past for which he believes his father is punishing him by leaving. The fact that the child may have overheard his parents quarrel about him makes it even more likely that he will fear that he drove the parents apart and the father away, and this will make even more understandable his feelings of guilt. Again he asks himself: "Why is this happening to me? Why are they doing this to me?" Resentment leads to guilt, and guilt to more resentment in a full vicious cycle.

The child not helped by parent or counselor to understand and resolve his feelings, and stop the resentment-guilt cycle, may well be left with psychological scars that hamper his optimal development.

In his later development, the child may establish a love-hate tie with the absent visiting parent, wanting him and pushing him away at the same time, or denying any feeling altogether. Excessive demands by the child, fulfilled or not by the father, may be a constant part of the conflict, and the perception, "I never get enough, I want more," a trait of the child. The demand to be given, especially material things, manifests a need for a constant proof of love, proof that the child is worthwhile and also that the father is good and loves him. If he does not fulfill the demand, the father is bad and can therefore be hated or ignored. But since the demand is insatiable, infantile, and removed from reality, it can never be really gratified, and the relationship can only be unsatisfying for both sides.

The father's own attitude may contribute to that of the child. Some fathers feel deprived by not having closer contact with their children; others feel guilty about their "desertion." Gifts, money, things, may be substituted for affection and closeness or may be used to buy the child's love.

One father visited his son in Queens twice weekly, took him for expensive dinners, gave him a color TV set, and planned to send him to an expensive camp. Questioned why he was wearing an old shabby overcoat and had not had a vacation in years, he was shocked. It was difficult for him to understand that his overgiving was unrealistic, not good for himself, and, even worse, an encouragement for his boy to become a revengeful, demanding, selfish youngster.

A child must learn to understand how his pain at the father's absence has made his distrust his father's love. Otherwise he will always demand constant proof, take constant revenge, and be unable to sustain an affectionate give-and-take relationship with his father.

This troubled relationship may become the example for all later emotional contacts. The young adult, growing up without an ability for warmth and love, will alienate others and remain an isolated, lonely individual. To reverse this trend, and help such a young person get satisfaction in mutually giving and loving relationships, therapy may be needed. In the therapeutic relationship, he can explore and learn to understand his basic mistrust and the roots thereof, and can turn his desires and abilities away from self-destructive attitudes. He may learn to utilize his feelings for loving and being loved.

THE CHILD'S REACTIONS TO THE REMAINING PARENT

Finally finding himself really alone with *one* parent, usually the mother, the child may find his adjustment to his new situation made more difficult by exaggerated fears and worries.

The immediate doubts may have to do with the question: "Can Mother alone take care of me?" The mother's own anxiety and misery may be transmitted to the youngster and, depending on his age, be felt in different ways. But even with a relatively secure and adjusted mother, the child, knowing that he used to have *two* parents and that most children are protected by two parents, may feel insecure with only one parent.

Since, for the child, parents are supposed to be all-powerful and all-nurturing, the child will add to his doubts about his mother's ability to take care of him the question, "Why did she allow this to happen? Maybe she is responsible for Father's departure; she may have driven him away. Maybe she is bad." And since the absent parent may be idealized and the yearning for his return be constant, he may be exculpated; the remaining parent may become the target for all resentment and hate and may be blamed for all unhappiness. This may work in the opposite direction also: the child may hate the departed father and idolize the mother, as discussed earlier.

In fear, also possibly via projection of his own hostility and wishes, the small child may worry: "Father left already, maybe Mother will leave also." A week after her father had left, little Mary was left with neighbors. When her mother returned half an hour late from the lawyer's office where she had gone to discuss custody procedure, she found Mary in tears, sure that "now Mother left also and I'll be all alone. Who is going to take care of me?" No assurance from the neighbors had helped her. At the sight of her mother, she first threw herself into her arms, then started biting and kicking her for what she felt had been a hostile act of her mother's.

These fears and resentments, natural childhood responses to a traumatic situation, have to be accepted, understood, and resolved. Otherwise they may shift from a temporary place in the child's personality, understandable under the circumstances, into part of the child's permanent character makeup that may harm him for life. The earlier he can be helped to understand and not blame himself, the better will he be served.

The parent or a professional will have to help the child with another problem. The youngster, growing up in a home where love and closeness reign, will be able to develop in his relationship to both parents, love them both, resolve his dependency, and approach later relationships with maturity. Of course, this does not proceed without hurdles and loyalty conflicts under the best of circumstances. If parents, however, live apart and also resent each other, the child's difficulties will be more pronounced and the solution of the loyalty conflict more troublesome. The child may feel that loving and identifying with one parent and doing what this parent expects of him means hating the other. Taking the side of one parent feels like disloyalty to the other. In addition, hostile parents often set up enemy camps and attempt to alienate their child from the other parent. They compete for the affection of the child on the principle of "divide and conquer."

One of the most tragic situations—and there are no more vicious legal procedures than divorces—are those in which a parent uses his children as weapons in the fight against a hated spouse. In his revenge, each parent blackens the other with malice, using the children to carry the messages, abusing them with his hate, rather than protecting them. Such children, not able to defend themselves and feeling deserted by both sides, do not know which way to turn and need help desperately.

Unfortunately, since they are needed for the neurotic revenge motives by both parents, these children rarely receive help until some serious symptoms appear that can no longer be ignored, or until an outsider—lawyer, friend, teacher—forces one or the other parent to stop, look, and listen, and admit his difficulties and destructive behavior. If neither parent is willing or able to fight for such a child, the child is in dire straits, because therapy will not be offered him either.

However, the parent who has custody can sometimes be convinced of the child's needs. The child must be encouraged and reassured that loyalty to one parent does *not* mean disloyalty to the other, that in spite of the parents' conflicts he has the right to love *both or one,* to be loyal to *both or one,* and even to be angry at the situation in which they have placed him. He has not only the right; it is essential that he learn to defend himself against being used. The counselor or therapist must help the child disentangle and clarify his feelings, and help him develop the strength and the ability to handle tools for self-defense. Later, if therapy is successful, the child will be able to see his parents as individuals with their strengths and weaknesses and have affection for one or both.

Some mothers who have custody of the child legally or illegally discourage or prohibit the child's contact with the father. Though in very rare situations this may be realistic and justified (if, for example, the father is destructive), most often it is damaging to the child, who needs to know his father. To the child, the unknown father is an abstract concept that cannot be made concrete and may therefore be made into a hero or a monster, both unrealistic images. The mother, often with a counselor's help, might need to understand the damage done to the child by banning the father, and might therefore want to consider reversing the ban. If not possible because of the mother's resistance, a counselor can gradually give the child perspective than enables him to retain an open view. He may first be asked why he thought his mother was abusive about his father, why she prohibited contact with him; understanding his own reactions, the child can gradually learn to accept his mother's and father's short-comings. He may want to draw his own conclusions when he is older and more independent and can hopefully reestablish contact with the father on a mature level.

Mothers are sometimes able to understand that every child needs to relate to a man in addition to the relationship he has with the mother, a woman. To provide the child with a male figure—a Boy Scout leader, guitar teacher, choir director, counselor, etc.—not only gives the child the opportunity to relate to a man but may also indirectly assure him that his mother approves of, and is not hostile to men. A woman who may be seen by the child as "having sent Father away," who discourages contact with him, may well give the child the impression that she dislikes men in general. It is hoped that the mother will be able eventually to give the child evidence of her wish and ability to sustain a *close* relationship to a man.

One more very important situation needs to be discussed because it occurs so frequently. Every child has to be helped by his parents to develop from childhood to maturity, from dependence to independence. A child feeling abandoned by one parent may need —at least temporarily—the other parent more and may lean on him or her more. A mother, in turn, feeling deserted and lonely, may well enjoy and encourage this increase in the child's dependency, which provides her with love and company. This may prevent the mother and the child from moving out into the world and finding friends appropriate to their level. Such mutual dependence also contains domination and underlying resentment. A woman separated from her husband for five years, ever since her little boy was born, had never left the child for one minute. When her son went into a raging panic at entering kindergarten and refused to let her leave the class-room, she was first surprised, then horrified, but finally agreed to treatment for both. In therapy the mother's and child's pathological interdependence was slowly dissolved, and they were helped to establish independent lives and independent goals. Today the mother has remarried and the boy is on good terms with his father and stepfather. He is a teen-ager who enjoys school and sports and who wants to become a veterinarian.

THE SOCIAL STIGMA

Many children feel a sense of shame about living "only with a mother" or "having an absentee father," which may stem from several roots: feeling "different" from or "worse" than others; believing that a parent's absence is evidence of "something wrong" with the child. Or it may stem from their guilt about fantasies that they have come between their parents, are responsible for separation and divorce, and are therefore unlovable and bad. The social stigma prevalent against divorce—although in large urban areas less than in much of the small-town America—reinforces the feelings the child is already burdened with. A little boy, whose mother had hung a framed photo of his father in the boy's room, believing that it would please the child and strengthen the loose tie that existed between father and son, surprised her by hiding the picture. He explained: "I don't want my friends to ask me where Father is, why I live with you alone. It is embarrassing: I don't know what to say, and I don't want to be reminded all the time."

Anything that reminds the child of the altered circumstances or that brings to the attention of his friends the fact that his parents are separated is painful and needs to be avoided. Those are topics that the child needs help with, not with physical reminders but with emotional support.

Other issues that are continuous reminders of separation and divorce and are continuous irritants to parent and child are the mother's return to work (which increases their income but deprives the child of care and time) and visits with the separated parent.

Under the best of circumstances, the father's visits lack the natural flavor of a father's and child's natural togetherness. Whether the mother is present or not, whether the get-together takes place in or outside the house, both father and child have to make special efforts, set up extraordinary plans and entertainments, and go through unnatural activities that are unnecessary in an intact family. The enforced times, sometimes inconvenient for all, possibly taking everyone away from other more desirable activities, and the frequent interference of the other parent, make visitation often a painful rather than enjoyable undertaking. And worse, the visits have to be explained to the child's friends.

Gail, a fourteen year old, met her father every Sunday with demands for money from her mother. Her father was furious with the girl and attacked her verbally but gave the money to her. The parents were vengeful and resentful; the girl needed to act out her guilt and shame. As it turned out in treatment, Gail gave part of the money to her mother. Gail wanted to satisfy her mother and also atone for the sense of guilt she felt about fantasies—possibly based on wishes—in which she had caused the divorce and was responsible for her mother's unhappiness. Especially important were the clothes she bought with part of the money she kept. She paraded the clothes before her friends to prove that she had a loving father, that there was nothing to be ashamed of, and that she was loved and good.

In therapy Gail learned to understand her feelings of guilt, her doubts in herself as a worthwhile human being, and her consequent inability to defend herself against the unfair exploitation by her parents. She learned to trust her judgments and her rights. Gail was encouraged to see her own needs and her parents' selfishness, which allowed her to be angry without feeling too guilty. She could accept her parents' love for her when they were *not* intent on punishing each other, which allowed her to trust the possibility of having a relationship with them and work toward it.

Though the father refused therapy and is today a lonely man, the mother seems to have solved some problems and calmed herself. Her understanding and relative openness have helped her remarry, and Gail, entering college this fall, seems to look forward, believing in herself and in relationships of closeness, and in the future.

In similar instances, especially when the child is younger, a counselor may also want to explore alternate ways of dealing with visitation, money, etc., and mediate between parents for the good of the child.

AN UNFIT PARENT

Until now we have discussed children whose parents, though separated or divorced, were more or less responsible, more or less upset, and more or less loving. Such children could be told truthfully that they were loved by both parents. Though the child might have questioned and doubted the existence of this love initially, finally accepting and understanding that it existed helped him accept the fact of separation or divorce. He could also accept the people involved— both his parents and, most importantly, himself—in a positive and constructive way.

What about the child loved by only *one* parent and not loved by the other? Not every adult is capable of love, and some parents' difficulties manifest themselves in an inability to have or show affectionate feelings. A serious alcoholic, a psychotic, hospitalized or ambulatory, an infantile individual—such parents will somehow have to be explained to the child. This is the most difficult situation—most difficult to tell the child, and most difficult to help him understand and accept. Whether this person be the father or mother, the child's basic trust will be shattered, his faith temporarily broken, and his view of life upset.

A parent taking care of his child, possibly with the assistance of a counselor or therapist, can heal the wound and help the child recover his faith in one parent and therefore also in the other parent and in himself. It is likely that the child, with a child's sensitivity, has already noticed, worried, questioned within himself "What is wrong?" Bringing the problem into the open, clarifying and making it less mysterious and dangerous, will take away the edge of fear.

The child has to be told, on the level of his age and understanding, that the absent parent has a problem and that his unloving behavior is his way of expressing this problem. The child, wondering why the remaining parent had ever chosen one with problems, asks: "Why did you marry a person like that?" and should be answered honestly: The marriage had been gone into with hope and with a wish that it would work; it has been a mistake and unfortunately even adults are fallible and make such sad mistakes. It is important to emphasize that the unfit parent's problem had existed a long time ago, long before the child was even born, and was in no way his fault or doing.

The child should also know that though he is the product of both parents and has traits of both, he can experience and learn warmth, closeness, and love from one parent in the relationship with that parent, and possibly through his treatment with therapist or counselor. "Love is enough," according to Louise Despert, even if experienced in a relationship with only one parent.

ABANDONMENT

The problem of a parent's abandoning a child is psychologically the most difficult situation to handle. Though the child's life may seem to be simplified by the fact that the conflicts between two ex-mates are eliminated when only one is left, not even this is sure. The other parent may some day show up, and he has to be reckoned with.

Fortunately, in the middle and upper classes, this is a rare occurrence. It is more often the father that leaves; though if a mother leaves, for biological and psychological reasons she has been earlier and longer so much closer to the child that she will be more needed and more missed.

The child of separation and divorce feels rejected, hurt, angry, unloved, and guilty, but he can also see the other side of the coin. The abandoned child is completely rejected, and for him there is no other side of the coin. Although for the separated and divorced parents there are mutual agreements and rules, for the abandoned mother and child there are none, and no hope, or anything to look forward to. For the mother there is not even the hope of another marriage; she is bound to disappointment, frustration, and loneliness, serious emotional and most likely serious financial deprivation.

The child's reactions, of course depending on age, will be serious. A mother's abandonment, especially of the smallest child, will give rise to intense depression even if an immediate and effective substitute is provided. The very young child, not yet having had a close relationship to the father, not aware of and not needing him, may not react seriously to the father's abandonment unless the mother's reaction and depression transmit themselves to him. In any case, not very much later, when the child understands that other children have mothers and fathers, he will start wondering, worrying, and asking questions. If he can ask the remaining parent, he is fortunate. If he feels, however, that such questions will hurt or anger his parent, he will have to keep his worries in and thus feel more alienated and isolated, and find it harder to sort out his feelings.

Having been abandoned, the child will at first have intense feelings of loss and depression, soon to be followed by resentment: "Why are they doing this to me?" Since a child has difficulties experiencing or expressing anger at a parent, the next question may be: "He, Father, can't be bad; it must be me. I must have done something to make him angry [and a child can always think of a nasty thought or act in the past which he has committed] and make him leave. I am really the bad one." This depression, the inability to handle aggression, and the accompanying guilt are all often found in children of separation and divorce, and found even more abandoned children.

Additional fantasies, varied and intense, may focus on illegitimacy and "immaculate conceptions." An attractive, intelligent twenty-nine year old, whose father had left shortly after her mother had given birth, entered treatment as an adult. (It was sad that her mother could not deal with the child's fantasies or provide treatment for her when she was young.) In therapy she remembered her childhood fantasies of having been conceived out of wedlock and the shame that went with this. This meant to her that she was conceived without love, without either her father or mother really wanting her. Other fantasies revolved around the possibility that "there never was a father," that she had been conceived immaculately without sex, and that a father, a man, was "not necessary for anything." This, of course, gave her comfort, but also made it impossible for her to solve problems in an important area of her life. On the basis of what she felt her father had done to her *and* her mother, her refrain in treatment was "What do I need a man for?" and "Men are cruel. Look at what they do! I don't want a man!" On the other side, she looked for, and hoped to find, a father in every man; and then, equally afraid, pushed him away, revealing her ambivalence.

She had never had a close or sexual relationship with a man and was deadly frightened of marriage. What to have said to that woman when she was a child—what to explain to a child whose parent has deserted? This is the most perplexing of questions for parent and therapist. Though several approaches are possible, none entirely answers the problems or is able to ease the pain for the child. Being abandoned causes wounds and leaves scars.

Telling the child that his father did not love him and that therefore he was a bad person will make the child feel utterly unlovable, directly via reaction to the desertion, and indirectly via identification with the father. The psychological elements of the situation will point in that direction, and even language contributes. The mother who talks about *your* father, even if not expressing hostility about her husband, unknowingly is saying, "Your father left. He left you and me and hurt us. He is *your* father, you are *his* child. You are like him and therefore you are bad also." Of course the end result in the child's mind will be: Father's leaving proves that he did not love me and that I am no good. If I were good, he would not have left!"

Telling the child that the father has deserted him because he "is sick" or because he "has problems" makes it harder for the child to recognize and allow his very justified resentment and anger to surface; he will then have to turn these feelings against himself, feeling bad and guilty, and possibly he will punish himself in varied ways.

The imperfect but optimal picture a parent can give a child embroiled in such sad and confusing problems is: "None of this problem was caused by you. Your father left because he had a bad problem and cannot be a father to anyone. What he did was very bad!" and "I love you. Together we will do everything to help you grow up into a happy, healthy, and adjusted youngster and adult." The aim is to make the child feel lovable and worthy, and not guilty; the explanation tries to distinguish between the parent as a person and the parent's deed: the parent is not bad but the action is bad. Though this explanation may be meaningless to a small child and even not quite understandable to an older one, it leaves the road open. The child, maturing and finding more answers, can gradually sort out his feelings and understand his father, even if he may not be able to forgive him. The older child must understand his own actions and emotions and forgive himself—and find that since they were understandable feelings, there was really nothing to forgive himself for.

This attitude may be transmitted to the young child via doll play: "This doll leaves his children. The grown-up doll has problems, but leaving a child is nevertheless a very bad thing to do; it must make the child unhappy and angry . . ." With the older child the mother or therapist can talk (not nag) repeatedly about the wound inflicted on the child. This repetition is necessary because an injury so severe will affect the child for years to come and needs airing and resolution many times. For the mother it is most important not to blame the child and to keep the anger at the father away from the child as much as possible. The fact that most children have a drive toward normality gives hope that even this, the most serious of all wounds for a child, will leave not too serious a scar.

THE CHILD'S REACTION TO DATING AND MATING

After the child has had to react to the parents' conflicts and separation, he may soon face a completely new set of circumstances, confusing, upsetting, and threatening.

For the parent there is first an initial period of loneliness and adjustment, for it is the rare divorced parent who jumps into new relationships immediately. Also it is better for the child if he does not have to face this jump too early, while his wounds are still open and painful. Eventually a need for companionship, love, and sex will stir in the new single parent. This may well be a period when the mother and father will think carefully, and possibly discuss with a counselor, about what effect their actions will have on the child, how to proceed in the child's best interest, and how to protect him from major confusion, conflict, or injury. It is also the time for aiding the child in an acceptance of further new adjustment—the adjustment to the possibility of a new stepparent in the future and, most likely , a new way of life.

At a moment when the child's shock is still strong and missing his father is still an acutely painful feeling, he may need his mother's presence and consolation more than normally. His mother's hours out, her time spent with others, and the fun she shares with men may increase the child's sense of rejection and abandonment.

Later on, when the child is more secure and can understand that the mother has her own life to lead, the mother can begin to introduce her own social life into the family. At this time a counselor has a twofold function. First, he has to help the mother accept her needs and recognize that her own fulfillment may be the best present she can give her child. Second, he has to help the child accept and deal with a new relationship and come to terms with a stepparent.

At this juncture, mothers and fathers often have to be guided to be cautious and discreet in how much they allow their youngster to see. In the initial stages of dating, it may be wiser not to involve the child in new and short-lived relationship and not to expose him to too much emotional experience prematurely. Becoming attached to somebody and having to give him up can occur over and over and may tax the child's trust too much. When, however, a relationship becomes more serious, the child will have to be included gradually and carefully, and prepared for what is to come.

It is possible that initially the child may accept the mother's new friends because "They are *my* friends, they bring me presents," especially whey they attempt to make contact with the child in order to facilitate the relationship with the mother. This acceptance will change to jealousy, resistance, and resentment when the child senses his mother's more serious intentions. The man will then be seen as an intruder and a threat, and he will be hated.

No child wants to share love. Having lost one important love object recently, he finds the threat of losing the other unbearable and infuriating. If a little boy sees that his mother is looking forward to seeing the man who is picking her up for an evening out, and sees that she is in a good mood a minute after she has scolded him for not wanting to go to bed, he will feel that she is being unjust to him. The experience may be a blueprint for further suffering. The boy wants to be the best loved, the one his mother smiles at and pays attention to. At all times, but especially soon after a separation or divorce, or after a prolonged period of too close and exclusive a relationship with his mother, the child will suffer from jealousy, anger, and doubts as to his mother's love for him.

When the absent parent, (usually the father) dates, the situation is not so serious or intense in its effect on the child. The privacy this man has permits dating to proceed more unencumbered. The distance and periodicity of visitation contacts decreases the importance to the child of the father's new relationship. But even this relationship has to be handled carefully and sensitively, and the child must be introduced to a potential stepmother gradually and with affection.

A loyalty question also enters the picture. Through accepting a stepparent with affection, a child who is still very attached to the absent parent and who still hopes and wishes for his return, may consider the stepparent an intruder. The child may feel that his affection for the stepparent means giving up his love for the original parent.

Liking the potential stepparent may also cause conflict and guilt. If the absent parent disapproves of the stepparent, the situation holds even more conflicts for the child and needs more sensitive handling of the child by parent and stepparent, or additional counseling. Only the understanding and working through of the idea that loving one is no disloyalty to the other, that it is O.K. to love parent *and* stepparent, can help this child.

Often a child attempts, and unfortunately sometimes succeeds, in destroying every attempt a mother (or father) makes at forming new close relationships. The threat of being displaced, the loyalty conflict, the hope that the parents may still get together again, and even the fear of more children being born from the new union (meaning more sharing) are painful and unacceptable possibilities to the already insecure child. The little girl who told her mother that she would "elope" if her mother let another man sit in her "old daddy's chair" expresses a very natural feeling and wish.

The complementary emotions in the mother (or father) may include doubt about the parent's own rights versus the need of the child. The mother may feel that she has to listen and give in to her child; she may give up any thought of remarriage if she believes it would be bad for the youngster.

Such feelings, parents' as well as child's, are understandable and met with frequently. But they are not realistic and are therefore harmful and destructive to everyone. A happy and fulfilled mother and a good marriage—after some adjustment—will enhance the child's life, lighten the emotional load on mother and child that the incomplete family imposed, and give pleasure, warmth, and joy to the members of the new family. To see love between mother and stepfather and to live in a peaceful atmosphere will show the child that closeness and intimacy can exist, that life and marriage can be good, and that the child can look forward to a similarly satisfying adult life.

It is not practical for the incoming parent, who is most often seen as a trespasser, to take over too quickly. The youngster can accept restriction and punishment only when an accepting and friendly relationship has been established. The wise newcomer will not expect love immediately, will be patient and understanding of the child's difficulties and resentments, accepting of his jealousies, and of the child's perceptions that "He is taking Mother away from me!" He will try to prove that he is genuinely interested in the child's welfare and wants to add to his good feelings rather than take love away. He will show the child that the new arrangement will make life for him and his mother fuller, more relaxed, and happier.

Overt expressions of love or of sexual feelings between parent and new parties are better avoided. They remind the child painfully of his sense of rejection and make him feel left out and more jealous. The child may also be stimulated sexually by such behavior on the part of the two adults. Overt sex may tax his excitability and, because of his age and vulnerability, may lead to greater frustration, resentment, and guilt.

Some men and women planning remarriage wish to consult professionals on how to handle the situation with their children, sometimes even two sets of children, which makes it more complex and difficult. When parents understand the needs and feelings of everyone concerned, they will find the best way to proceed.

No two situations are the same and no two children will react alike, but they will all need some help and understanding of the issues involved, and some assurance that they will be well taken care of. At this stage, a counselor or therapist can be of incalculable value to parents in their efforts to prevent preferential treatment, to avoid setting "my children" against "your children," and to minimize jealousies. He can help the child in learning to accept and not destroy the new relationship and can help to reduce the frictions that any new adjustment like a remarriage unavoidably brings with it.

Situations where the father or mother, or both, enter into one marriage after another, not capable of good lasting relationships, demand more adjustments of the child than he may be able to make without help. "I have three daddies and two mommies" is confusing and disturbing to any child. Providing this child with the one steady, secure relationship to a therapist may give him strength, help him be only minimally drawn into the emotional turmoil of his many "parents," help him not identify with their instability, and guide his life in a more rational, constructive direction.

CONCLUSION

The child's first world, that of his family, is usually the sample he carries along into adulthood and uses to judge the whole world. Although he has experienced a disturbed family relationship, the child can be shown in treatment that later relationships do not have to be replicas of the important earlier one. He can learn to see how childhood events have influenced his feelings, thinking, and behavior and how as a result he often contributes to his own self-destructive behavior. Accepting and understanding neurotic behavior—*i.e.*, alienating others, hating every man because "Father left me," or clinging to women because such behavior was encouraged by the mother —will be a step toward a more realistic and healthy approach to relationships. The child can learn that he is not merely a passive pawn sucked into unhappy relations, but that he can be an active participant, capable of responding and behaving constructively and lovingly, and of being loved in return. Developing constructive behavior problems rather than destructive or alienating ones is the job of therapy or counseling.

Helping the child—either by himself or with the assistance of treatment—not only gives the parent the satisfaction of having done the best for his child but also clarifies emotional issues for the parent. In understanding the child, the parent has the opportunity of understanding himself; in helping him, the parent helps himself. The parent's own childhood disappointments and pains, probably aggravating the emotional upset of separation, may be illuminated through insight into the child. Healing the child's wounds may well start the parent on the road toward healing his own.

An unhappy, disturbed parent will most likely have an unhappy, guilty, and anxious child. The child of parents who have resolved their conflicts and have established affectionate and satisfying relationships learns trust and is free to find gratification in his own life.

Many a child of separation and divorce has been helped through a labyrinth of confused and hurt feelings, coming through well adjusted, happy in his relationships to parents and stepparents, and strengthened in his belief in a satisfying future and the possibility of a happy and loving marriage for himself.

LOIS ABLIN KRIESBERG, M. A.,
and LOUIS KRIESBERG, Ph. D.

On Educating Children

As an educational institution, the school is no longer considered to be restricted to simply the imparting of techniques for reading, writing, and mathematics. Contemporary society now demands that the school accept responsibilities ranging far beyond its traditional scope, many of them overlapping territories once exclusively the prerogative of the home.

Combining their experiences with the results of social change on the institution of the school in American life, Dr. and Mrs. Kriesberg apply their knowledge to the problems of the single parent concerned with the emotional and scholastic well-being of their children. In the process of discussing the school as an aid to single parents, they emphasize that raising and educating a child in a one-parent home is not necessarily doomed to failure. Their discussion is supplemented with practical advice concerning relevant educational techniques as well as goals to consider during their children's developing years.

There is much evidence that seems to indicate that children from intact families do better educationally than children from broken families. Before blaming the single parent or offering him or her advice, we need to look at the evidence. We need to know to what extent coming from a single-parent family actually handicaps educational achievement, and what it is about growing up in such a family that is handicapping. We will then have a firmer basis for determining what action would reduce whatever handicaps there may be.

One issue must be confronted before we can go any further. Terms such as "intact" and "broken" families usually imply that families with a married couple raising the children is correct and normal, while a family with a man or woman alone responsible for the children is abnormal. Our use of the terms is not intended to have such implications. To draw such implications betrays a class, race, and usually a sex bias. This should be clear if we consider the variety of ways in which children are actually raised. Probably about one-fifth of American adults have spent most of the time until they were sixteen in "broken families."[1] Even more persons must have experienced a broken family for at least a short time while growing up. Moreover, the proportions are greater among nonwhites and the poor. Thus, in the year 1966, 10 percent of all children were in female-headed families; 27 percent of all nonwhite children were in such families; 30 percent of poor, white children lived in female-headed families; and of poor, nonwhite children, 44 percent lived in female-headed families.[2] Finally, since most single-parent families have females as heads, the assumption that a single-parent family is incomplete and abnormal implies that the mother is inadequate. We reject these implications and assumptions. Their general acceptance, however, constitutes a problem for single parents and their children.

Interpreting the findings regarding the educational achievements of children from single-parent families is not a simple matter. A consideration of the difficulties will help illuminate the meaning of growing up in a single-parent family. The basic way of assessing the consequences of this experience is to compare children from one-parent families with those from two-parent families. But what group

[1]Calculated from Beverly Duncan and Otis Dudley Duncan. "Family Stability and Occupational Success," *Social Problems*, 16 (Winter, 1969), Table 1, p. 275.
[2]Orshansky, Mollie. "The Shape of Poverty in 1966," *Social Security Bulletin*, 31 (March, 1968), pp. 3–32.

of two-parent families would be appropriate for comparison? About half of the American female-headed families with minor children live in poverty. Should we compare them with equally poor intact families? We should, if we want to consider the implications of growing up in a female-headed family, *aside from income differences.* But, in reality, one of the fundamental problems of female-headed families is their poverty.

We must also recognize that a parent may be raising children without a spouse for a variety of reasons. In the case of separation or divorce, the relevant comparison group may not consist of intact families. A more relevant comparison might be with families which should be broken: those held together by mutual fear, hate, or martyred duty. After all, for persons thinking about divorce, the relevant comparison is not between an idyllic marriage and a "broken" family; the choice is between the miserable life they are enduring, and the relative peace and order that could be established without marital turmoil. If societal conditions and expectations were more supportive, that choice could be made more freely and adequately.

In one study of husbandless mothers, the mothers themselves were asked whether they thought their children would be better or worse off if the father were around.[3] Among those who thought it would make any difference, almost one in five thought the children would be worse off. As one mother said about her son:

> George lived in fear of his father. His father ignored him. His father didn't finish high school, is a vegetable; he didn't help with school work but was displeased when the report card came. His father has a good mind but doesn't use it. He has no real drive or stick-to-itiveness. He didn't do anything with George. Raising the children was 100 percent my job.

Undoubtedly, the presence of a parent who is disruptive to family life – or antagonistic to the children or who sets a poor example may be more handicapping to the children's educational attainments than would be his absence.

Most of the evidence about the effects of broken families upon the educational achievement of children refers to female-headed families and the attainments of sons. The focus upon the sons' educa-

[3]Kriesberg, Louis. *Mothers in Poverty: A Study of Fatherless Families.* Chicago: Aldine Publishing Co., 1970, pp. 201–203.

tional and occupational achievements reveals an implicit expectation about the careers of boys and girls. Yet women work and their occupational success has great significance for themselves and their families. Furthermore, the consequences of growing up in a fatherless family may be different for daughters than for sons. Daughters may be especially likely to be autonomous and undertake occupational careers. We need to know more about the implications of being raised in female-headed broken families and male-headed broken families for both boys and girls. We know very little about the consequences of growing up in a broken, male-headed family. Yet, this is not so rare. In a national study, American males of nonfarm background, aged twenty-five to sixty-four, were asked if they had lived with both parents "most of the time" until they reached age sixteen. Six percent of the men reported they had been raised in a male-headed broken family, 12 percent in a female-headed broken family, and 82 percent in a family with both parents.[4]

Examining the consequences of growing up in a broken family is further complicated because the differences between complete and broken families are multiple and often a matter of degree. Nearly all single-parent families were once two-parent families and most will become so again; many two-parent families *were* one-parent for a while. Being a single parent or a married parent is not an unchanging life characteristic; it is part of a life cycle. Therefore, comparisons of two-parent and one-parent families divide people into categories which are less distinctive than we usually think them to be. Furthermore, it is not always true that there are two parents in a "complete" family and one in a "broken" family. The former spouse or a substitute for him may be readily available in broken families, particularly in relationship to the children. On the other hand, in complete families, the spouse may be away from the family most of each day and even for extended periods when employed elsewhere, or in prison, or in the Army. In both broken and intact families, moreover, it is the father who is most often absent.

Now let us turn to the findings which we have about the educational achievement of children from single-parent families. Many studies report that children of broken families are more likely to be

[4]Duncan and Duncan, *op. cit.*, p. 275.

high school dropouts than are children of complete families.[5] They are less likely to go on to college. There is also evidence that sons of male-headed broken families do not differ in occupational success from sons of female-headed broken families.[6] Most of the evidence, however, is about female-headed families compared to two-parent families. As noted earlier, interpreting such findings requires care, in particular to avoid biased assumptions.

Female-headed families are much more likely to be poor than are complete families. One reason for this is that poor families are more likely than others to be broken by divorce, separation, desertion, death, and long-term institutionalization. In addition, without the resources which previous high income provides and which can continue through children's support money, insurance, or other payments, a female-headed single-parent family faces severe financial difficulties. Although male-headed broken families are more often in poverty than are two-parent families, their chances of being poor are less than among female-headed families.[7] Presumably, despite possible support from the former husband, a female family head cannot earn as much as a male; she is less likely to be able to earn enough to purchase child-care services. This inability is largely due to differences in occupational training and experience, and an occupational system which heavily favors males.

We know that educational achievement is less among poor families than among those who are not poor. This is true for several reasons. First of all, poor parents may tend to think and act in ways which do not help their children educationally. Like other parents, they may wish their children would do somewhat better educationally than they did. But among the economically well-off, as much or a little more education is more than the poor parents' hopes. Furthermore, poor parents may not only pass on lower absolute expectations but, having less experience with educational institutions, may be less able to help their children in school.

Income is related to many other factors which affect educational attainments. Children's educational achievement is affected by their teachers, fellow students, and the educational facilities available to

[5]Miller, S. M.; Saleem, Betty; and Bryce, Harrington. *School Dropouts: A Commentary and Annotated Bibliography.* Syracuse, N.Y.: Syracuse Youth Development Center, 1964.
[6]Duncan and Duncan, *op. cit.*, Table 2, p. 277.
[7]Inferred from Orshansky, *op. cit.*, Table 6, p. 11.

them. If teachers expect a student to go on to college, they will encourage the student to do so and guide him or her into work which will prepare him. Insofar as they do not expect children who are poor (or black, or female) to go on to college or to get professional training, they will discourage the student from attempting and will be less likely to provide the appropriate intellectual preparation. The teachers' expectations and conduct is also affected by the general tone in the classroom, which is, in turn, largely affected by the educational aspirations of students in the class. Whether or not most of them expect to finish high school, go on to college, or enter any professional training affects the teachers, and also affects the students themselves. The students are very important guides to each other's educational efforts and expectations. They teach each other how worthwhile it is to do well in school and stick it out.

The facilities which affect the educational achievement of students range broadly. Facilities such as special programs, books and educational materials, and place to study vary in availability. High-income families can provide their own facilities or purchase them for their children. But too often these facilities are more available in areas in which high-income families rather than low-income families live. Other kinds of facilities may markedly affect educational achievement, but are not so closely linked with the economic level of the residential area. Thus, attendance at college is affected by the availability of colleges near home with little or no tuition. Obviously the more income a family has per child, the less dependent they are upon such access.

Family income, then, directly affects educational achievement in many ways. Divorced, separated, or widowed mothers, because they often have low incomes, tend to have children with lesser educational attainments than children of two-parent families. Are children of broken families adversely affected educationally, even taking into account their socioeconomic conditions? There are only a few studies which give us any information in this regard. In a national study of adult males, it was found that sons from broken families completed fewer years of education than did sons of unbroken families, even taking into account the fathers' own occupation and education.[8] In a study of first- and fifth-grade pupils, the researchers found

[8]Blau, Peter, and Duncan, Otis Dudley. *The American Occupational Structure.* New York: John Wiley, 1967, p. 336; Duncan and Duncan, *op. cit.,* pp. 273–85.

that children from families without a father present had slightly lower I.Q. scores than did those in families with a father.[9] The difference was greater within the lower socioeconomic stratum that within the higher strata. This suggests that the adverse effects of poverty and single-parenthood aggravate each other when combined.

Much of the explanation for the lesser educational attainments of children of broken families is to be found in the general socioeconomic conditions of most such families. Nevertheless, there is some evidence that the lesser educational attainment of children from broken families is not fully explained by those conditions. Actually, no study can take into account all the aspects of family income mentioned here. Still, let us grant that there is some handicap, in general, for children of broken families, aside from their current financial conditions and socioeconomic background. What is it about growing up in a single-parent family which may be educationally handicapping?

Before we attribute responsibility to the parent, we should consider how others outside the family might treat the child of a disrupted marriage. It may be that teachers and others expect less achievement of children from single-parent families. It would be interesting to know to what extent such expectations exist and what their bases are. It may be that some stigmatization is made of single-parent families and perhaps particularly of female single parents. In any case, expectations that children will not have high educational achievement handicaps their achievement. There is also evidence that the marital status of the child's parents often affects how the police handle and dispose of juveniles with whom they have contact.[10]

Now let us consider the effects the parents themselves may have. Effects may arise from two sources. First, the absence of the father or of the mother may adversely affect a child's education. Secondly, the way the remaining parent handles the absence of a spouse and second parent may harm the child. As we have noted, the evidence

[9]Deutsch, Martin, and Brown, Bert. "Social Influences in Negro-White Intelligence Differences." *Social Issues* (April, 1967), p. 27.
[10]Shannon, Lyle W. "The Distribution of Juvenile Delinquency in a Middle-Sized City." *The Sociological Quarterly*, 8 (Summer, 1967), pp. 365–83, note 9; Kriesberg, *op. cit.*, p. 201, note 6.

demonstrating that there are any such adverse effects is only indirect. Evidence about how such effects may come about is also
scanty.

We can best begin to see how the absence of one parent and the
accommodation of the other parent to the situation may affect the
child's education by examining how parents generally can affect the
educational achievements of their children. There is evidence that
children's educational aspirations are greatly affected by parental
expectations and encouragement of educational attainment.[11] Several studies report that the parents of dropouts compared to parents
of high school graduates, seem to be indifferent to continuing education.[12] They are also less likely to believe that the lack of a high school
education is a disadvantage.[13] Another study found that parents'
"achievement press," aspirations for the child and for themselves,
their interest in, knowledge of, and standards of rewards for the
child's educational achievement are correlated highly with grade
achievement test scores.[14]

There is also evidence that parental activities provide an environment which affects the children's educational achievement.
Thus, parents of high school dropouts are less likely to participate
in school activities than are parents of children who have completed
pleted high school. Dropouts less often report having reference
books, newspapers, or a quiet room for study at home than do
graduates.[15] In one study, a whole set of characteristics were used to
construct an index of educational environment. In addition to the
"achievement press" cited above, the index included the following:

[11]Herriott, Robert E. "Some Social Determinants of Educational Aspiration." *Harvard
Educational Review*, XXXIII, 2 (1963), pp. 157–77; Sewell, William H., and Shah,
Vimal P. "Social Class, Parental Encouragement and Educational Aspirations." *The
American Journal of Sociology*, 73 (March, 1968), pp. 559–72.
[12]Evariff, William. "How 'Different' Are Our Dropouts?" *Bulletin of the National
Association of Secondary-School Principals*, XLI (February, 1957), pp. 212–18, cited
in Miller, Saleem, and Bryce, *op. cit.*
[13]Bertran, Alvin L. "School Attendance and Attainment: Function and Dysfunction
of School and Family Social Systems." *Social Forces*, XL (March, 1962), pp. 228–53.
[14]Dave, Ravindrakumar H. "The Identification and Measurement of Environmental
Process Variables That Are Related to Educational Achievement." Unpublished Ph.D.
dissertation, Department of Education, University of Chicago, 1963, cited in Benjamin
S. Bloom, *Stability and Change in Human Characteristics*. New York: John Wiley,
1963, pp. 124–25.
[15]Moore, Parlett L. "Factors Involved in Student Elimination from High School."
Journal of Negro Education, XXIII (1954), pp. 117–22.

1. language models (the quality of parents' language and the standards they expect in the child's language)
2. academic guidance (the availability and quality of educational guidance provided in the home)
3. activeness of the family (the extent and content of indoor and outdoor activities of the family)
4. intellectuality in the home (the nature and quality of toys and the opportunity provided for thinking in daily activities)
5. work habits in the family (the degree of routine in home management and the preference for educational activities)

This index of educational environment correlated very highly with the fourth-grade achievement test scores (+.80).[16] Interestingly, the correlation between social status and the achievement test scores was much lower (about +.50). Presumably, the often found relationship between the socioeconomic status of the parents and the educational achievement of their children is mediated by the existence of favorable educational environments in the home.[17] Such home environments, however, are not perfectly associated with socioeconomic status.

Keeping in mind what parents *can* do to affect the educational achievement of their children, we can turn to an examination of what single parents actually tend to do. The discussion will focus on husbandless mothers, because the divorced or separated mother is more likely to be raising the children than is her former husband, and because the little evidence which is available is mostly about single mothers rather than fathers.

Let us begin by considering the husbandless mothers' values, hopes, and expectations regarding their children's education. One might argue that husbandless mothers would tend to devalue education and lower their expectations for any of several reasons. For one thing, they might recognize the educational obstacles their children face, and lower their educational hopes and demands to be more "realistic." Or, concerned about their own welfare, they may wish their children to be economically independent as soon as possible.

[16]Dave, *op. cit.*
[17]For further discussion of the relationship between socioeconomic status and educational achievement see Kahl, Joseph A. *The American Class Structure*. New York: Rinehart & Co., 1953; and Lipset, S. M., and Bendix, R. *Social Mobility in Industrial Society*. Berkeley: University of California Press, 1960, pp. 227–59.

Or, feeling some sense of failure themselves, they might simply project and extend that to their children.

On the other hand, one might argue that husbandless mothers would tend to have extraordinarily high expectations and desires regarding the educational attainments of their children. It may be that they see the extra obstacles their children face in life and feel that their children must do particularly well and go especially far in school in order to overcome the extra burdens. Or, they may be more involved with their children than married mothers are and express this by greater attention and concern with their children's educational efforts; this might even extend to wishing that their children do well as a form of compensation for other disappointments. One other possibility should be considered. That is that the absence of a husband does not affect the mother's feelings and expectations about her children's educational achievement.

As a matter of fact, on the whole there is little difference between husbandless and married mothers in the educational desires and expectations they have for their children. The findings are from a study conducted of families in and around four public housing projects and a review of other pertinent research.[18] If anything, husbandless mothers are more likely than married mothers to want their children to get more education than they have, even if this means that their children become estranged from them. Husbandless mothers also are less likely to think their children would become estranged even if the children did get more education than they had.

The level of children's attainments which would disappoint the mothers is a little more complicated. Husbandless mothers do not differ from married mothers in aspirations about school marks. Husbandless mothers, however, are less likely than married mothers to aspire for more than a high school education for their sons. If, however, we compare husbandless and married mothers with about the same incomes, we find that husbandless mothers are *more* likely to have high aspirations about the school marks and just as likely to want their sons to go beyond high school. Moreover, we can compare husbandless and married mothers living in neighborhoods with different educational environments. Some neighborhoods have schools which are generally regarded as better and in which students are

[18]Kriesberg, *op, cit.*, pp. 249–89.

more likely to complete high school and continue their education. It was found that in a neighborhood which was particularly poor as an educational environment, the aspirations of husbandless mothers regarding years of school to be completed were particularly depressed. In neighborhoods with better educational environments, their aspirations were relatively high or the same as those of married mothers.

These findings indicate that under conditions which are conducive to the educational attainment of their children, husbandless mothers are at least as likely as married mothers to aspire high. In the case of educational achievements which are less obviously dependent upon external circumstances, as in the case of school marks, they are more likely to aspire high than are married mothers of the same income. But under conditions which are educationally handicapping, husbandless mothers' aspirations are depressed, as in the case of not feeling disappointed if their children do not go beyond high school.

Now let us consider the educationally relevant conduct of the mothers. Whatever the desires and hopes of parents may be, their actual conduct may differ. Wanting to be supportive and encouraging of a child's educational efforts may in actuality be unrealized for a variety of reasons. The pressure of competing demands may be too great. Encouragement may turn out to be undue pressure to achieve. Or the desire to be supportive and helpful is poorly implemented because the necessary skills and knowledge are unavailable.

The study of married and husbandless mothers in and around four public housing projects has some relevant findings. The respondents were asked to report whether they or their child decided upon the time to be spent on homework. Husbandless and married mothers did not differ in this regard. There is some evidence, however, that husbandless mothers are more likely to pressure their children about educational attainment than do married mothers. Given the same school marks, husbandless mothers are somewhat more likely than married mothers to say that they are dissatisfied with the marks received by their children. If dissatisfied with their children's school work, however, husbandless mothers are more likely to simply urge their child to do better, while married mothers more often directly aid the child in the school work or intervene with the school.

The general activity in the home pertaining to school and education also has relevance for the educational achievement of children. One indication of this is participation and involvement in school affairs such as parent-teacher meetings. Husbandless mothers may tend to be less involved in such activities than married mothers. This varies considerably, however, depending upon other circumstances. On the whole, husbandless mothers compared to married mothers are just as likely (or unlikely) to read books or magazines, to say that reading is their most preferred leisure-time activity, or to have an encyclopedia at home; but they are less likely to go to concerts, plays, and museums. The lack of facilities for single parents and the organization of social life in terms of couples thus not only is personally unsatisfactory to single parents but may also have adverse effects upon their children.

On the whole, husbandless mothers seem to be very concerned about the educational achievement of their children. However, low income or residence in neighborhoods which provide poor educational environments particularly depresses husbandless mothers' aspirations about how long their children should go to school. On the other hand, husbandless mothers who are employed are particularly likely to have high aspirations.

The aspirations and hopes, however, are not always sustained in actual conduct. Lacking some of the indirect and informal supports for themselves and for influencing their children, and also lacking a secure base for future support, they may often push too hard. This pressure may sometimes be excessive, despite the good will. Furthermore, the competing demands on husbandless mothers for time and effort may interfere with engaging in activities which would be educationally supportive for the children. Thus, working husbandless mothers, despite their higher aspirations generally, are slightly less likely than other husbandless mothers to participate in school events. On the other hand, the involvement and independence of working helps provide a more stimulating environment and serves as a model for the children. The daughters are more likely to work themselves when they grow up, and the sons are more likely to have higher educational and occupational attainments.[19]

In short, there may be ways in which single parents think and act which impede the educational attainment of their children.

[19]Kriesberg, *op. cit.*, pp. 157–58; Duncan and Duncan, *op. cit.*, pp. 283–84.

These ways are also dependent, however, upon certain social conditions. Under other circumstances, such ways would be rare and their effects would be less.

In the light of the evidence reviewed here, several suggestions can be made regarding how single parents should raise their children to help them do as well as possible educationally. Let us consider first what the parent can do personally, and then consider what he or she can do as a member of society to alter the circumstances within which the single-parent family lives.

One message should be clear. A husbandless mother or a wifeless father is more likely to err in raising children by being overly concerned and pushing too hard than in the contrary. The children do not, in general, suffer such great educational handicaps as a result of growing up in a broken family. Insofar as there are handicaps, they largely derive from circumstances over which the individual parent has little control. Sound advice would be to relax and not worry. Feeling guilty does not motivate helpful conduct in relationship to the child.

Having said that, we should also consider what the individual parent *can* do to help a son's or daughter's education. One thing is to search out supportive environments; for example, to live in neighborhoods where the schools and the other children encourage and support good education. This, like so many other educationally relevant circumstances, is facilitated by money. In this regard, as in others, parental employment can be beneficial for the child. This also suggests one of the ways in which a separated or divorced parent who does not have the day-to-day responsibility of caring for a child can make a significant contribution.

One of the most important ways in which a parent can aid the education of a child is by providing an intellectually stimulating environment at home. In part, this is done by using the skills the child might otherwise think are only classroom exercises. This includes such elementary things as reading when and where the child knows about it. The intellectually stimulating environment is also partially provided by engaging the child in conversations and activities which are intellectually appropriate and interesting. Finally, the parent can be a source of information and a guide to the school system if the parent keeps himself or herself involved and informed. Parental wisdom should be available when sought, not thrust upon the child.

As we have noted, many of the most severe difficulties a child of a broken family faces are not amenable to individual actions. Some aspects of the society should be modified to reduce the handicaps which a child from a broken family otherwise experiences. Single parents, prospective parents, and former parents, as well as the parent not raising the children all have a special interest in furthering some societal changes.

Social policies which provide more income for children should be enacted. This might be in the form of a family allowance—a fixed amount of money allocated for each child. This would remove some of the stigmatization of receiving public funds. Furthermore, such income would encourage employment because it would make it easier to earn enough money so that it would be worthwhile to pay a baby sitter and earn more than public assistance payments. A general income maintenance plan would also have these benefits.

Day-care centers and boarding schools should be more available, and the costs of child-care centers should be borne by the society as a whole. Under these conditions, more mothers would be able to work and raise themselves and their children from poverty. The recognition of societal responsibility might also encourage and facilitate the father rather than the mother to care for the children. Both parents might think this advisable, and, if social institutions made it easier for men to continue their parental responsibility, more mothers might be able to be relieved of the excess of their own responsibilities.

Since many of the problems we have considered come back to the problems of the female head of a broken family, we should discuss possible societal changes in regard to the position of women.

This means, first of all, a recognition of the actual roles assumed by women and men. Mothers are often the sole supporters of their families or along with their husbands maintain the family income. Fathers sometimes have the sole responsibility for raising the children and nearly always at least help in child-rearing. Recognition of the actual diversity of families might reduce the stigma which otherwise is attached to arrangements which do not fit the cultural "ideal."

Furthermore, what is needed are training, and social institutions which are consistent with that recognition. This means educating girls and boys for both occupational and familial responsibilities. This means insuring equal pay for equal work.

Finally, it should be observed that working for such changes may aid the education of children. The efforts will tend to involve the family in a larger circle of activities and will thus be stimulating to the children. The efforts will also provide the parent with the experience and recognition that many aspects of the problems he or she faces are not personal; consequently, inappropriate feelings of guilt may be reduced. Not least, the resulting changes may provide a future environment that will be more fitting for the new generation.

JOSEF E. GARAI, Ph. D.

Sex Education

In recent years, sex education, particularly in the schools, has been the subject of heated controversy. Practically no one denies the importance of sex education, but there is little agreement about its content, method of presentation, or outcomes. Dr. Josef E. Garai, who has written extensively on sex education, offers us a thorough and balanced treatment of this important subject. Dr. Garai provides a useful approach that takes into account the important emotional and psychological considerations that enter into imparting information, fashioning attitudes, and transmitting values.

Parents who are able to provide for their children a coherent educational framework integrating sex, love, intimacy, and marriage as prerequisites for self-fulfillment are the exception in our society. Packard[1] has described the "sexual wilderness" which is reflected by increasing confusion concerning male and female sex roles and relationships. Yet, in the midst of conflicting sex role patterns, a new model of marriage appears to be emerging among young people. It is based upon a heightened capacity for self-disclosure, honesty, and intimacy, as pointed out by Jourard[2]. It enables both spouses to regard marriage as an opportunity to promote individual growth and actualization of creative potential in an atmosphere of equality and mutual sharing in the decision-making process.

Seven basic characteristics of spouses contributing to the development of such a vital and stable marital bond are described by Packard as follows:

1. A large capacity for affection.

2. Emotional maturity.

3. The capacity to communicate effectively and appealingly each other's thoughts and feelings.

4. A zest for life.

5. The capacity to handle tensions and conflicts constructively.

6. A playful approach to sex.

7. The capacity to accept fully the other person with complete knowledge of his shortcomings. Marital breakdown usually results from the absence of several or all of these capacities.

In a study comparing children from divorced families with those from happy families, Landis[3] reports that the children of divorce got less detailed sex education from their parents. In all areas of dating, courtship, and relationships with the opposite sex, children of divorce showed less confidence and activity than those from happy families. Children of divorce dated later, less frequently, and fewer persons, went steady more often, and did not play the field. Boys made friends with girls more slowly, youngsters from divorced parents were more likely to be promiscuous, and as teen-agers they were lacking in self-confidence. They felt inferior to other children,

[1]Packard, V. *The Sexual Wilderness*. New York: McKay, 1968.
[2]Jourard, S. M. *The Transparent Self*. New York: Von Nostrand, 1964.
[3]Landis, J. T. *Building a Successful Marriage*. 5th Edition. Englewood Heights, N.J.: Prentice-Hall, 1968.

ashamed of their parents' divorce, and less attractive than children from happy families.

These findings indicate that divorced parents must place great emphasis on sound sex education in order to enable their children to establish satisfactory relationships with members of the opposite sex.

At the present time in the United States, there are approximately one and a half million families that are headed by divorced parents and these families have four million children. The available data strongly suggest the number of families with children in which one parent is absent as a result of separation or desertion (as distinct from divorce) equals the number of families of divorce. So that there are at present three million American families with eight million children that constitute one-parent families. About 90 percent of them, *i.e.*, two million and seven hundred thousand families, are headed by mothers whose children have little or no contact with their fathers. The deprivation of a paternal role model has far-reaching effects on the relative adequacy of the performance of the male role by the male children from these families.

Divorced or separated parents often perpetuate the unhealthy attitudes toward love, sex, intimacy, and marriage which may have contributed to their own marital difficulties in the past. These attitudes, whether consciously adopted or unconsciously experienced, compel them to cling to feelings of loneliness, rejection, hurt, and disappointment. Their excessive preoccupation with past failures and grievances prevents these parents from mobilizing their vital energies toward the search for more satisfactory relationships in the future. The following twelve points can serve such parents as guidelines, providing a framework to replace ineffective attitudes with a positive philosophy of life. To facilitate the discussion, the terms SDP, SDM, and SDF shall be used to designate the separate or divorced parent, mother, or father, respectively.

1. Get rid of feelings of hurt, rejection, and resentment. Stop being a man-hater or a woman-hater. Try to develop an optimistic outlook on life.

2. Clarify your attitudes toward sex, love, intimacy, and marriage. Seek competent psychotherapeutic or counseling assistance if you are unable to rid yourself of feelings of rejection. Mobilize your vital energies toward the establishment of rewarding relationships with members of the opposite sex.

3. Let your children know that they have not caused the separation or divorce. Tell them that the breakup is the result of parental incompatibility and inability to solve differences in mutually satisfactory ways. Avoid blaming your spouse or yourself. Stress the fact that you will both continue to love your children.

4. Inform yourself as intelligently as possible about all aspects of sexual behavior in relation to love and intimacy, and be aware of prevailing sexual mores among young people which may affect your children's relationships with their peers. Take into account your children's current needs and stages of development when you provide guidance and sex education. Answer all their questions honestly and truthfully.

5. Let your children know that love is possible, and that sex within the context of a genuinely loving and intimate relationship permits the full experience of growth and joy. Tell them that failure or disappointment in love does not preclude future success in love and marriage. Stress trust and hope, and discard attitudes of distrust and despair.

6. Establish conditions which permit your children to identify with suitable sex-role models.

7. Try to avoid making exaggerated demands on your children for satisfaction of your own deep longings for love, intimacy, and dependency. Develop new relationships with adults of your own age range.

8. Stop playing the role of the martyr who has to sacrifice everything for the children in order to make up for the loss of the other parent's companionship. Do not be the martyr who feels victimized by the demands of the children for constant care and support.

9. Learn to accept disagreements and conflict as a natural part of all human relationships, and develop methods of conflict-resolution which are fair and acceptable to all the members of the family.

10. Respect your children's needs for increasing privacy and self-determination with their growth toward adolescence. Refrain from excessive prying into their lives.

11. Do not establish excessively high or unrealistic standards of moral and sexual behavior. Try to provide guidance by a mature male for adolescent sons.

12. Let your children know that while you do love and respect them, you are entitled to lead a full life of your own and to seek your

own satisfaction in love and intimacy. Ask them to respect your needs for privacy as you are willing to respect theirs.

Each of these suggestions is treated in detail here to provide the basis for the type of sex education that can be used by divorced or separated parents who hope that their children may be better equipped than they to find happiness in marriage. If the children respond to this guidance, the SDP's may eventually gain enough confidence to establish satisfactory relationships with the other sex and abandon the illusion that their original failure is bound to reoccur. Let us begin to explore in depth the first of these points:

1. GET RID OF FEELINGS OF HURT, REJECTION, AND RESENTMENT

Feelings of hurt, rejection, and isolation often accompany the dissolution of a marital relationship. These feelings may turn into lasting resentment against the "guilty" spouse whose behavior or character is held responsible for the breakup of the marriage. This "blaming game" is reinforced by outdated legal practices which tend to seek the culprit and define him as the guilty party. Recent changes in the divorce laws in California have abolished the term of "guilty party" in divorce proceedings. It is extremely difficult to establish the exact distribution of responsibility for the breakdown of an intimate relationship. Most experts believe that each of the spouses makes some contribution to the dissolution of the marriage. But wounded pride and hurt feelings often seek relief in blaming the other person for the breakup.

The SDM who blames her husband may generalize that attitude to all men and tell her children that "All men are bad" or that "Women are always exploited by men." Such statements may poison her children's minds against men. Her sons may reject the masculine role as undesirable. They may begin to prefer the feminine role and identify with it as the favored role, thus setting the stage for open or latent homosexuality in later life. The more rebellious sons may turn their hatred against their own mothers whose hostility to men they reject. This attitude may lead to excessive identification with the aggressive or "bad" male role and initiate either delinquent acting out or sadistic rejection of all women.

The daughters of the men-rejected SDM who identify with their mother's hostility are likely to develop both hostility to and fear of men. This negative attitude may lead to a vicious circle of rejective and counterrejective dealings with men, a total withdrawal from relations with men, or a preference for intimacy with women, leading to overt or latent lesbianism. In some instances, these man-hating daughters may become sexually promiscuous in more or less unconscious attempts to make the "bad" men pay a high price for sexual favors. The sexual acting out is frequently the result of the belief expressed by hostile women that "All men are after one thing only: sex."

Some SDMs tend to blame "the other woman" as the mischievous seductress who used her charms as a means to "break up our happy marriage." Regardless of the accuracy of this accusation, children who are confronted by this reasoning will eventually gain the impression that women are conniving, manipulative, and treacherous. They will include their own mother in this category of untrustworthy women. The sons may adopt similar attitudes to those of sons whose mothers hate men. The daughters may either reject the feminine role as undesirable or imitate with a vengeance the role of the successful seductress to make sure that they will not lose out on the marriage market. To ascertain their powers of attraction, they may try to seduce married men and get entangled in all kinds of strange triangle situations with eventually fatal consequences for their own chances of happiness.

The SDF who remains in charge of his children may similarly imbue them with hostility to women if he has not overcome his feelings of rejection. His sons may become women-haters, too, or overidentify with the masculine role, adopting sadistic or latent homosexual patterns of interaction. His daughters may react with overidentification with the masculine role and adopt aggressive lesbian patterns, or they may turn against their fathers in attempts to get even with the male enemy. Thus they may become inveterate man-haters.

2. CLARIFY ATTITUDES TOWARD SEX, LOVE, INTIMACY, MARRIAGE

The destructive effect of man-hating or woman-hating attitudes on the sex-role development of children of SDPs can hardly be overemphasized. To avoid serious interference with the process of sexual identification and the development of appropriate same-sex and cross-sex roles, SDPs must resolve their feelings of hostility toward the opposite sex as well as their feelings of inadequacy with regard to the performance of their own sex roles.

Each person learns progressively to identify with the recognized, approved, and socially rewarded sex role of his own sex. The first impression of our sex roles are gained from our parents. The girl learns to be a woman through observation of her mother's feminine behavior, as the boy learns to be a man from observation of his father's masculine behavior. But the learning of relevant same-sex roles includes the simultaneous acquisition of an understanding of the cross-sex (opposite sex) role learning. Men must learn to like women and gain some basic understanding of the female psyche in order to be able to woo them and make a decision about a suitable mate. Similarly, women must like and understand men to make sensible marriage choices.

The SDM who projects the role of a man-hater is likely to delude her daughter into assuming that men are dangerous and untrustworthy. Such man-hating attitudes will prevent her daughter from developing sufficient trust in men to risk marriage, or may lead to the early breakdown of a marriage entered upon in a temporary suspension of this pervasive distrust.

The SDM must work through her own feelings of distrust toward men. She must learn to perceive men as potential possessors of such desirable traits as strength, courage, protectiveness, and risk-taking such as are commonly accepted as masculine characteristics in our society. She must also be sufficiently free of stereotyped thinking to realize that a genuinely strong man need not be afraid of showing sensitivity, tenderness, warmth, kindness, and love. The "flight from tenderness" which the common American stereotype has imposed upon the male seems to compel most males in our society to reject these traits as "feminine" and to conceal their presence. Jourard[4] deplores the extensive damage done to the self-image and identity of the American male as a result of this flight from tender feelings. The inability to express tender and loving feelings seriously affects the male's physical and mental health.

[4]Jourard, *op. cit.*

If the SDM is unable to divest herself of feelings of rejection and hostility toward men, she should seek competent professional help by consulting a psychiatrist, a clinical psychologist, a marriage counselor, or a certified social worker. Contrary to some mythical beliefs, the vast majority of professionals in the field of psychotherapy are not interested in either making or breaking or holding together a marriage. They provide professional skills that may assist the troubled couple in finding a resolution which is least damaging and most satisfactory for both spouses. Feeling of hurt and anger are explored and, if a separation or a divorce is regarded as necessary, ways and means are sought to terminate the relationship with a minimum of hurt feelings. In some instances, skilled professionals have even succeeded in attaining a friendly divorce or separation. The SDP alone may also find help in working out his or her problems through professional assistance.

The SDM who has worked through her feelings of resentment toward men and women can be relied upon to provide the type of sex education for her children which will permit them to approach the search for a mate with a realistic basis for trust and reciprocity. She will also be able to utilize the resolution of her own conflicts for the purpose of searching for a meaningful relationship in her own life. She may begin to trust a man and move forward toward remarriage. The unremarried SDF is similarly confronted by the necessity to resolve his own feelings of hatred toward women.

The SDF who has successfully remarried may provide the inspiration for his children to gain a positive outlook on love and marriage. They can observe their own father as taking a second chance in life and finding renewed happiness. This may convey the idea to them that divorce is not the end of life. It may supply them with a weapon against insensitive children who tease them as "the kids whose father didn't want them."

The wise SDM will encourage her children to visit the remarried father and his new family. She will seek to establish a relationship of mutual respect rather than engaging in futile rivalry with her ex-husband's second wife, if the latter agrees to it. If the SDM genuinely loves her children, she will be able to deal with temporarily emerging feelings of jealousy and resentment when her children return from the visit and report that their "new mommy" is simply wonderful.

3. LET YOUR CHILDREN KNOW THEY HAVE NOT
CAUSED THE BREAKUP

Parents frequently use children as allies or "footballs" in their violent disputes. If children are asked to become allies or referees in their parents' quarrels, they gain the impression that they possess the power to decide the outcome of the battle. This feeling of omnipotence is accompanied by strong feelings of guilt and contrition. A child may sometimes side with the parent whom he favors less for the purpose of gaining a reward or an advantage promised. When the marriage breaks up, some children may feel that their taking sides with the mother may have driven the father away from them. They tend to regard the father's intention to leave as the punishment for their support of the mother. Some parents have gone so far during quarrels as to blame their children for breaking up their marriage. At any rate, children who feel responsible for their parents' separation or divorce suffer from such strong feelings of guilt that they often engage in all kinds of magic fantasies of being able to bring their parents together again. For this reason it is very dangerous to arouse false hopes for an eventual reconciliation which may play into the hands of the children's irrational feelings of omnipotence.

One of the most unpleasant consequences of this attitude is the reenactment of constant power struggles with shifting alliances in the social life of these children. They tend to regard all human relationships as power struggles in which they can serve as allies or enlist others as allies in fierce competition for success. This competitiveness tends to disrupt their heterosexual and same-sex relationships during adolescence and adulthood. A manipulative approach is greatly detrimental to the establishment of any trusting and stable human relationship, for it relies on power rather than on love. Where the love of power prevails over all other types of interaction, the power of love is defeated.

To avoid such harmful influences in the development of children's personalities, the SDP must make certain that the children are reassured that the dissolution of the marriage was not caused by them. Parents should sit down with their children to explain to them that they have decided upon the separation or the divorce because they have met with great and, at present, insurmountable differences of opinion affecting many areas of their life. It should be pointed out that neither parent alone is to blame for the separation, but that both parents have decided to try to live apart or get a divorce. The SDPs must reassure their children that they will both continue to love them, despite their preparations for the divorce, though the children will permanently live with only one of them, usually the mother. The children must be informed of the fact that the other parent will not withdraw his support from them and that he can be seen on a regular visiting basis, if this is feasible. Parents should emphasize their conviction that the separation or the divorce will relieve the climate of constant tension which is detrimental to both the parents and the children. If a stormy marriage has finally come to an end, both parents ought to apologize to their children for having subjected them to humiliation and indignities during their quarrels, and for having tried to enlist them as allies against each other. This may clarify the reality of parent-child interaction and relieve feelings of guilt which may linger on and make the children feel overly responsible for the breakup.

4. LEARN ABOUT ALL ASPECTS OF SEXUAL BEHAVIOR IN RELATION TO LOVE AND INTIMACY.

Learning about sex can be fun and exciting. Most children exhibit signs of curiosity about the actual operation of processes of reproduction and birth in early childhood. Frequently parents fail to react to their children's questions, feeling that they cannot understand such complex processes at an early age, or because they have unresolved feelings affecting their own attitudes toward sex and intimacy. From the age of three years on, children can progressively learn to familiarize themselves with the basic processes of reproduction if they are given relevant guidance and introduced to an understanding of conception at a level appropriate to their stage of intellectual development.

A number of excellent books are available for parents who would like to give their explanations in a context of warmth, love, and acceptance. Sidonie M. Gruenberg's *The Wonderful Story of How You Were Born* and *The Wonder of Life: How We are Born and How We Grow Up* by Levine and Seligmann are probably the most outstanding books which parents can consult. For teen-agers LeShan's *Sex and Your Teen-ager: A Guide for Parents* presents a very frank and sound viewpoint. Rayner's *A Parent's Guide to Sex Education* and Reuben's *Everything You Always Wanted to Know About Sex* are obligatory reading for all parents who want to be effective sex educators. A variety of other helpful books are included in the references accompanying this chapter.

It is often difficult for the SDP to accept his own basic needs for sexual gratification. The SDM must clarify to herself her own feelings concerning satisfaction of her sexual drive. Negative attitudes toward sex, love, and marriage may lead to a rejection of evidence of sexual needs in her children. This may bring about a climate in which the children feel that any physical contact with their own bodies or any touching of other people's bodies is sinful, dirty, and forbidden. Threats of punishment following discovery of masturbatory activities increase guilt feelings surrounding sexual desires, and children exposed to such attitudes may adopt a philosophy of lifelong rejection of sexual activity. Therefore, parents who want to avoid these harmful effects of excessive standards of sexual continence or prudishness should try to resolve their feelings of rejection of sexual needs.

Premarital sex is today more widely accepted among young people then ever before. For this reason, any insistence on premarital chastity under all circumstances is unlikely to protect preadolescents or adolescents who may face virtual ostracism from participation in the activities of their peer groups if they abstain from sex. Parents who are genuinely concerned for the welfare of their children can provide sound advice if they stop adopting inflexible attitudes of opposition to any sexual involvement.

The best advice they can give is that sex should never be taken lightly or used as a means to take advantage of others or be taken advantage of. This is in line with the newly emerging sex ethics among young people who accept sex as an integral part of a genuine relationship of love and intimacy, while they tend to reject exploitative sex. The SDM sometimes shows strangely different attitudes toward the sexual behavior of her sons and that of her daughters. Whereas she appears to be proud of the early sexual conquests of her son, she may regard any early sexual activity of her daughter as inappropriate. She should remember that her son's sexual exploits always involve some other mother's daughter. The latter may have tried to dissuade her daughter from engaging in "premature" sexual experimentation just as insistently as the former daughter's mother has[5]. If we are really living in an age of increasing sexual equality, the adolescent female is just as likely to become sexually involved as the adolescent male, although she still bears the additional risk of an unwanted pregnancy.

With abortions steadily increasing among high school girls, the need for information about contraceptives is apparent. Most sex education programs provide this information too late, as a result of the unwarranted assumption that too-early information might lead to increased sexual "acting out" behavior. All available evidence points in the opposte direction, *i.e.*, that the earlier and the more correctly the information about contraceptive techniques is transmitted, the less likely are young people to engage in excessive sexual acting out, and the less likely is the adolescent girl to have an unwanted pregnancy. Most parents think that information about contraceptives should be made available only to their sons, who would then either use contraceptives or induce their partners to employ relevant contraceptive devices. These parents tend to ignore recent shifts in sexual patterns which increasingly place the responsibility for contraception on the woman. The young adolescent male expects his girl friend to "be prepared," and he assumes that she is using the pill, an IUD (intrauterine device such as the coil or the loop), or a diaphragm. Few young men come prepared with a condom. They feel that it restricts the sexual pleasure of the male.

The modern SDM who wants to prevent her daughter from incurring the risk of an unwanted pregnancy must familiarize her with the availability of suitable methods of contraception. While conveying her confidence that her daughter will know how to avoid being exploited by men who seek nothing but sex, she should also recognize the possibility that her daughter might find the type of man with whom she might seek a more intimate relationship. Trial marriages, on the increase among young people and formerly married people, always involve sexual intimacy.

The concerned mother is well advised to inform herself as adequately as possible of all available techniques of contraception. She must also be aware of incidental risks resulting from the use of certain contraceptives. Recent controversies concerning the safe application of such devices as the pill with its pervasive effects on the

[5]Garai, J. *Sex and the Single Parent.* Sexology, October, 1967, 3, 43, 148–50.

functioning of the hormonal system, and the loop or the coil with their side effects seem to recommend the diaphragm as still the least harmful and most desirable method. If the pill or any IUD is used, any side effects should immediately be brought to the attention of a competent gynecologist. The previously mentioned book by Le-Shan[6] provides extremely sound advice on this subject.

The need to provide information to the preadolescent daughter on the use of contraceptive techniques can hardly be overemphasized. In view of changing sexual standards, the education of females in this respect assumes greater importance than that of the males. Nevertheless, it is also necessary to teach preadolescent males to make certain that contraceptive devices are used during sexual intercourse. If the male no longer uses any contraceptives himself, it is still indispensable for him to accept partial responsibility for the potential effects of sexual relations.

Of course, it is desirable that this information be imparted to him as early as possible and that he be cautioned against assuming that his girl friend automatically takes care of contraception without his making sure. At any rate, it may be preferable to have the preadolescent son's father, or another warm and sympathetic male as father substitute, explain the uses of contraceptive devices to him. Such instruction must include a thorough explanation of all potential effects of male and female contraceptive techniques and the desirability of their application.

Parents should always be truthful about the advice they give. If they do not know the answer to a question, it is preferable to admit this ignorance in order to be able to retrieve the relevant information correctly or to help the young man or woman to seek it out on his own. It is even inadvisable to tell young children such slight distortions of the facts of life as "you came out of Mommy's tummy." Children, who take everything literally within their own frame of reference, may then be misled to think that such bodily functions as elimination of waste or throwing up or having a stomachache are indicative of giving birth to a child. In this instance, it is better if the mother explains that there is a special place called the womb where the mother carries the child, and that this place is not to be confused with the stomach or any other bodily organ. This will reassure the

[6]LeShan, J. J. *Sex and Your Teenager: A Guide for Parents.* New York: McKay, 1969.

questioner that he was not destined to coexist with all the "garbage" deposited in the stomach, and that he occupies a special place in his mother's esteem.

5. LET YOUR CHILDREN KNOW LOVE IS POSSIBLE, THAT SEX WITH LOVE IS A FULL EXPERIENCE OF INTIMACY AND JOY

Few people have a clear concept of what mature love implies. Too often love is confused with infatuation or dependency. Genuine love between two mature adults of the opposite sex can be defined as follows: Love is a relationship between two adults of differing sex characterized by strong desires to share experiences, to get to know, understand, and appreciate one another, to give oneself and of oneself freely and unconditionally, to accept one another as independent individuals with all assets and limitations, to create a climate in which both partners can change, grow, and develop their potentials, and in which both partners can seek the temporary overcoming of bodily separation in the act of sexual fusion achieving the fulfillment of orgastic sensations.

The test of love consists of the experience of growth and self-fulfillment. Stagnation and routine are the antitheses of genuine love. Similarly, whenever the sexual experience results in excessive preoccupation with techniques and a chasing after bodily "thrills" rather than in deepening of communication between the partners, love is on the wane. The dissociation of sex from feelings of love and intimacy leads to mechanical and meaningless preoccupation with sexual activities.

Intimacy can be defined as the type of relationship which permits both partners to feel free to reveal their "real selves" to each other. It is based on the ability to reveal one's innermost feelings, thoughts, and ideas, characterized by Jourard as the capacity for self-disclosure[7]. In intimacy one need not wear a mask. The person who seeks intimacy can reveal his identity without fear of being taken advantage of. Smoke screens erected by "role-playing" become superfluous.

Modern marriage is based on love and intimacy. Rollo May[8]

[7]Jourard, *op. cit.*
[8]May, R. *Love and Will.* New York: Norton, 1969.

believes that modern man's need for intimacy has grown, while his capacity for intimacy has been diminished. The mechanization of modern life has led to depersonalization as a result of the adoption of certain prescribed roles. Modern man acts like an automaton devoid of spontaneity and strong convictions. His marriage offers him the only opportunity to reveal his real feelings. But as a result of the taboo against showing tender and loving feelings, the American male often finds it impossible to reveal his emotional tensions, conflicts, and involvements even to his closest associate, his wife. Women outlive men in our society by seven years, on an average, and Jourard[7] thinks that this higher death toll is largely due to the American male's inability to disclose his thoughts and feelings. The popularity of encounter groups, which are currently springing up throughout the United States, is in part a result of the eagerness of males to learn again how to come to grips with their emotions. They want to learn how to express their feelings and replace stereotyped role-playing by the creation of a genuine identity[9].

The SDM must communicate to her children the firm hope that they can attain happiness in marriage, based on bonds of love and intimacy. She must be able to convey her conviction that they can overcome experiences of disappointment in love, and that feelings of rejection and despair need not linger on to prevent the search for more satisfactory bonds. She must always stress hope and trust, and counteract feelings of suspicion, fear, and despair. If she herself is able to move toward a fulfilling heterosexual relationship, her example will perhaps inspire her children to gain confidence in their own ability to attract a person of the opposite sex so as to form a bond of mutual trust and growing love.

6. SUITABLE SEX-ROLE MODELS FOR CHILDREN

We have already discussed the importance of contacts with the real father for the growing boy who is beginning to form a clearer image of the masculine role for the purpose of incorporating it into his own system of role performances. Boys learn to be men from the example of their fathers. When the father is absent, such masculine role-

[9]Burton, A. (Ed.). *Encounter: The Theory and Practice of Encounter Groups.* San Francisco: Jossey-Bass, 1969.

learning is seriously impaired. The SDM must provide her sons with frequent opportunities to meet adult males who project desirable role models. If the real father is available, her sons can form some impression of the male role from visits with him. On the other hand, it may also be desirable to establish contacts with a variety of adult men who are happily married. Such groups as "Fathers At Large" comprise many married and unmarried males who enjoy adopting boys during weekend outings or sports activities. The SDM should contact the local "Fathers At Large" group if she cannot enlist the assistance of relatives or friends. Boys also need a variety of male playmates in early adolescence as well as during their childhood years in order to establish their masculine identity on firm grounds.

Daughters living with unremarried SDFs should likewise have opportunities to get together with their real mothers whenever possible. If such contacts cannot be made on a regular basis, the SDF must seek out female relatives, friends, or teachers who can provide suitable role models. This is of particular importance for small girls who are torn away from their mothers at an early age when their needs for the nurturance of the mother are very important.

7. AVOID MAKING EXAGGERATED DEMANDS ON CHILDREN FOR SATISFACTION OF YOUR OWN NEEDS

Disappointed in love, many SDPs turn to their own children in a desperate search for fulfillment of their unsatisfied longings for closeness and intimacy. The SDM begins to show an exaggerated concern for the welfare of her children which may lead to overprotection that keeps them away from contact with children of their own age. Some mothers relate to their sons as if they were their lovers, embarrassing them with frequent demands for caresses, kisses, and intimate embraces. The son often feels his mother's strong sexual attraction, and he may be frightened of his own feelings of tenderness toward her. Although children may respond momentarily to the advances of their parents, they are too immature and carefree to accept the demands for permanent intimacy and closeness imposed upon them by the mother. Some children may react to this emotional exploitation with defiant rebelliousness, others with increasing coldness and withdrawal, and others with counterseductiveness exacting "bribes" in return for exhibitions of tender feelings toward their mothers.

Such exaggerated demands for emotional response may cripple the capacity of these children for closeness and intimacy for the rest of their lives. No son is able to serve as a substitute husband for his mother without lasting damage to his masculinity. Similarly, no daughter can serve as a substitute wife for her father without incurring a basic distortion of her feminine role. Therefore, the SDM and the SDF must avoid under all circumstances making their children the targets for their longings for intimacy. The SDP who is able to establish new relationships with adults of his own age will be less likely to persevere in making such incongruous demands on the children. But the SDM who tells her son that he is now the only person close to her after the separation or the divorce, and that she expects him to understand what this closeness means to her imposes an impossible burden on him to serve as her support and comfort when he himself is most in need of such sympathetic reassurance.

According to psychoanalytic theory, each son around the age of three to five years begins to entertain secret hopes that he can have his mother all for himself. Since she caters so lovingly to all his needs, he imagines that she might one day become his sole lover. He has only one rival for his mother's love: his father. In his dreams and fantasies, he imagines that his father has left the mother or has "died," leaving the field wide open for him to conquer his mother. Toward preadolescence, this futile hope of getting rid of his father as an unwanted competitor for the love of the mother gives way to a more realistic appraisal of the situation. The son then accepts the fact that his father will continue to be his mother's main lover. He attempts to model himself in all aspects after the example of his father, replacing rivalry with masculine identification through imitation of the role played by his father. He will endeavor to act like his father, wear his ties, and try to compete with him in sports and other activities to show his competence. The early stage when the child hopes to retain his mother all for himself is designated the "Oedipus complex" by Freud.

In the case of the SDM who experiences the separation or divorce when her children are still at a tender age, the oedipal fantasy that the father should disappear has become a reality. The son who is left alone with his mother may experience unconscious feelings of triumph mixed with guilt, stemming from his belief that he has actually caused his father's desertion. If his mother persists in exploiting him as her "main support" or "sole hope," she may be reinforcing the oedipal fantasy and setting the stage for a fixation of the oedipal complex. In his imagination, the son may accept his own role as that of his mother's only lover and cut himself off from seeking relationships with children of his own age. Excessive emotional investment in the mother-child bond leads to impoverishment of emotional responsiveness with regard to all other relations.

During adolescence when sexual maturity leads to an upsurge of sexual feelings, the oedipal conflict may be reexperienced. Many mothers keep their youthful appearance and attitudes alive during middle age so that mother and son may actually present the impression of being a young couple. Some mothers in turn tend to fall in love, as it were, with their handsome young sons of whose emerging manhood they are extremely proud. Loneliness and the inability to establish relationships outside the family reinforce this tendency. The son becomes increasingly dependent on his mother for guidance in all matters. A strong conflict between the son's growing needs for companionship with his age-mates and his attachment to his mother is likely to develop with serious consequences for the emotional equilibrium of the growing adolescent. Psychiatric help is then needed to help both mother and son to resolve this mutual dependency.

Similar difficulties may arise in the case of the daughter who remains together with her unremarried father. In either case, the young adolescent is prevented from the necessary freedom of contact with members of the peer group. Symptoms of isolation and withdrawal from socializing with members of the opposite sex reinforce tendencies to move away from people outside the family circle. The SDP who wants to avoid such isolation of the children from normal social interaction with peers must adopt an attitude which minimizes dependency on him or her. Adolescents should be encouraged to participate in social activities with their peers, and the SDP must learn to transfer the search for emotional responsiveness to persons outside the immediate family. Excessive closeness of sons to their mothers as well as daughters to their fathers is bound to lead to difficulties when young people seek to establish satisfactory heterosexual relationships. They may either get involved with unsuitable mates, or find it impossible to maintain the necessary intimacy with their spouses which demands freedom from excessive emotional dependency on one parent. As one young man stated succinctly: "You can either be married to your wife or to your mother . . . being married to both is a case of bigamy involving incest . . ." Of course, what he meant was the presence of strong unconscious incestuous impulses which are rarely translated into action.

8. STOP PLAYING THE MARTYR ROLE

Many mothers tend to resent the heavy burden which separation or divorce imposes upon them. They feel overwhelmed by the necessity to make alone all the decisions concerning the education and welfare of their children. Though they may receive alimony or child support from the father, they must often supplement their income through part-time employment. Their frustration may be released in state-ments indicating that they feel victimized and placed in the role of the suffering martyr when called upon to cater to the needs of their children. "I'm killing myself for you . . ." or "Look how hard I'm working to get you all through school. . . . The least you can do for me is to bring home top grades . . ." are frequently voiced statements by martyr mothers.

Martyrdom imposes a heavy burden of guilt on those who are told that they are profiting from it. The children of the martyred mother may feel overly responsible for her welfare and believe that they are letting her down if they place their own needs for love and intimacy first. Just as their mother apparently gives up her own life for them, they will have to repay their debt by giving up their lives for her one day. Whether they actually do so or not, they will invari-ably be caught in a vicious cycle of pity and guilt stifling their own development. The SDM who cannot abandon her attitude of being exploited by her children or sacrificing her life for her children must seek competent help to rid herself of such damaging feelings of self-pity. Carol Mindey's book *The Divorced Mother* makes a number of helpful suggestions how this can be done.[10]

[10]Mindey, C. *The Divorced Mother: A Guide to Readjustment.* New York: McGraw-Hill, 1969.

9. LEARN TO ACCEPT CONFLICTS AS PART OF ANY RELATIONSHIP

Many SDPs who experienced periods of intense fighting during their marriages may tend to advise their children to seek the type of relationship in which they will rarely or never engage in any quarrels or violent disagreements. Any relationship of intimacy includes the freedom to vent negative and hostile feelings as well as positive and friendly ones. As Bach and Wyden (5) emphasize in their delightful book, *The Intimate Enemy: How to Fight Fair in Love and Marriage,* quarreling serves as a healthy means for the venting of feelings of frustration, resentment, and hostility in any genuine relationship.[11] Most divorces result from the use of unfair tactics in marital fights. If the spouses attempt to tear down one another's self-esteem and thereby destroy their image of themselves as loving and trustworthy individuals during their violent disagreements, they are setting the stage for marital breakdown. These foul tactics include conjuring up of past disagreements or inadequacies, unfavorable comparisons with relatives or competitors, and threats of abandonment and revenge.

The SDM should tell her children that the freedom to express disagreements, anger, resentment, and dissatisfaction is just as important as the freedom to express feelings of love, intimacy, support, and nurturant care. Of course, she must be able to create a climate of frankness and openness in which this freedom of self-expression can prevail, and in which the tactics employed to provide this atmosphere are fair and adjusted to a pattern of cooperation and the preference for compromise solutions. Her own example will be serving as the best model for the establishment of such a viable interrelationship among the family members. Unfair tactics are to be discouraged, and the common interest serves as a framework within which individual needs can be satisfied.

10. RESPECT CHILDREN'S NEEDS FOR PRIVACY AND SELF-DIRECTION

Some parents assume that they ought to be informed of everything related to their children's lives. But each child acquires the need for

[11]Bach, G. R. and Wyden, P. *The Intimate Enemy: How to Fight Fair in Love and Marriage.* New York: Morrow, 1969.

privacy early in life. He must be provided with an opportunity to keep certain ideas and activities secret. This secrecy serves as a protective device which permits the growing child to try out different roles and work out his own solutions of problems or relationships with people. A child who feels constantly spied upon becomes suspicious and withdrawn, whereas a child who is permitted to be by himself at times without being asked to tell what he is doing or thinking about will feel respected as an individual. He is thus much more likely to approach his parents or siblings with the request for help when needed.

The need for privacy increased in intensity during adolescence when the growing man or woman experiences strange sexual urges and a new vitality. At this juncture the adolescent needs to be left alone and reassured that he will find his own life goals and develop suitable heterosexual relationships. The search for a viable identity includes experimentation with new and different life styles. While parents with divergent standards are not required to approve of these life styles, they should give assurance that they know that their child will eventually establish self-direction and intimacy with members of the opposite sex. The adolescent insists on being treated as a person with his own rights. He resents the opening of his letters or telephone inquiries to his friends without his knowledge as serious intrusions into his private life. The SDM should muster the patience to wait for her children to confide in her. Excessive prying will only lead to habitual lying and dissimulation on the part of the adolescents. If the SDM busies herself with establishing a gratifying social life, she will feel the need for supervising her children's social life less urgently.

11. DO NOT ESTABLISH UNREALISTIC STANDARDS OF BEHAVIOR

Sex education includes the transmission of correct information concerning menstruation, masturbation, contraception, homosexuality, lesbianism, a variety of other sexual aberrations, abortion, sterilization, and venereal diseases. The person who has a sound grasp of sexual and interpersonal problems affecting these phenomena is better equipped than the one who has been told "It is better not to know anything about all these undesirable activities." When confronted by homosexual advances, the young man had better know how to protect himself. Otherwise he might comply just for "the thrill of it." Joining the boys to engage in group sex with prostitutes may sound like fun, but the young man ought to be aware that he might contract syphilis or gonorrhea and that a checkup by a physician is necessary as soon after this experience as possible.

The worst thing that a parent can do is to use "fear appeal," threatening dire consequences resulting inevitably from premarital sex, promiscuity, or masturbation. It will lead to the development of strong feelings of guilt and shame which may prevent the adolescent from seeking sound professional or medical advice when needed. The SDM who wants to provide real protection for her children should tell her adolescent sons and daughters that they may well meet with a variety of sexual experiences and become exposed to healthy as well as to unhealthy practices and standards. Without condemning these as immoral or unethical, she should point out the potential consequences of unsound sex practices for the physical and mental health of her children. She should make certain that they know how to avoid these practices and how to find the best kind of assistance in case of any damage to their health.

12. LET CHILDREN KNOW YOU FEEL ENTITLED TO LEAD YOUR OWN LIFE

Just as you must refrain from prying into the lives of your children, you have the right and, indeed, the obligation to make certain that your children are not unduly concerned with your private life. It is not necessary to tell your children in detail what you do on your dates. If your children suspect that you engage in sex relations with your male friend, do not become apologetic or try to defend yourself as if you had committed a crime. In an age of changing sexual mores and standards, you need not stay away from any sexual enjoyment in order to provide an illustrious example for your children, who anyhow conform to the norms of their peer group with regard to sexual behavior.

Children who observe their mother as an outgoing and optimistic person who seeks a new meaningful relationship with a man are likely to gain confidence from her example that they can succeed in their own search for love and intimacy. If they ask the SDM whether she will get married again and whether her male friend will be their new father, she should give her answer as truthfully as possible to avoid arousing unnecessary fears or hopes. She should always stress the fact that she is looking for a husband for herself rather than for a father for her children to prevent them from pushing her into marriage before she is ready just because they anticipate the excitement derived from having a father again. But she should always be aware of the possibility that even the kindest and most considerate newcomer as the stepfather may be resented as an unwelcome intruder. He may reap the resentment and attempts to be "got rid of" as fast as possible, so that the children can reestablish their relationship of mutual dependency with the mother. Several sensible books providing advice on how to deal with such situations are listed in the references to this chapter.

In conclusion, the following basic rule is offered to the SDP as a guideline for the establishment of a climate of mutual hope and respect: *Try to be honest, truthful, nonjudgmental, and accepting at all times. Try to provide the type of guidance to your children which will inspire them to seek a meaningful relationship with a member of the opposite sex. Stress love, intimacy, self-disclosure, and respect for the integrity and individuality of each partner as prerequisites for any meaningful relationship.* The twelve suggestions made in this chapter should furnish the SDP with the necessary skills, knowledge, and techniques to create such a self-actualizing climate of trust and hope.

Community Resources and Assistance Available for Parents and Children

Part Six

Families in trouble need assistance and knowledge of the kinds of community resources that can help them. The following two chapters offer a representative sample of the kinds of agencies that render help to separated and divorced parents and their children. Of course, many other agencies are worthy of consideration, and it is likely that each community has its own programs.

Mrs. Lillian Oxtoby and Dr. Muriel Farrell write about day care and its implications for separated and divorced parents. It is helpful to keep in mind that the 1970 White House Conference on Children placed heavy emphasis on the expanding day care center program and stressed its importance as a social action program that has proved its merit and is in need of further development and expansion. The authors of this chapter have some interesting and helpful comments about such programs common to a large urban area.

Mrs. Eloise B. Waite presents, as an example of a program that is both national and international in scope, the important services offered to military families by the American National Red Cross. The importance of the National Red Cross family assistance program for military families is clear when we consider that there are over three million men in the U. S. Armed Forces, many married and with children.

LILLIAN OXTOBY, A. C. S. W.,
and MURIEL FARRELL, Ph. D.

Day Care and Its Implications for Divorced and Separated Parents

At the 1970 White House Conference on Children, delegates representing various women's groups were among the most vocal in their demands that child care be made available for all who wish it. Their demands are consistent with the current public understanding of the importance of the early childhood years and the experiences which day care centers offer to enrich this period. Day care is presently escaping its former stigma as a resource for indigent or minority groups, mainly because of the growing recognition that women have a right to personal fulfillment and that restriction to full-time child-rearing is not the only avenue to such fulfillment.

Mrs. Oxtoby and Dr. Farrell bring to this discussion of the philosophy, programs, and goals of day care a wealth of practical experience in organizing and directing such a center. The program of day care centers offers a viable solution for the mother seeking to restore her self-image and personal independence as she meets the demands of a single parenthood.

Today in our society, in rural as well as urban areas, there are greater numbers of individuals than ever before who are confronted with problems of child care because of separation and divorce. The working parent of small children finds that facilities for child care are limited or totally unavailable. The problem is highlighted when one looks at statistics concerning working mothers.

"Nearly half of all American mothers have jobs. Two of every five working mothers have children under six. Nearly five million children under six have part-time mothers, mothers who have full or part-time jobs. Of these children a half million are left to shift for themselves while their mothers are at work; most of the rest get what educators call 'inadequate care.'"[1]

For the divorced or separated parent or the working mother, frequently the answer to the need for responsible child care is a day care center.

What is a day care center? Many people think of the day care center as a baby-sitting service, others conceive of it as a nursery school. It is neither, but instead a program that serves both these functions. The day care center includes an enriched educational program based on the physical and emotional development of the child.

Which elements of a good nursery school are incorporated in a successful day care center? A good nursery school provides a fertile educational and social environment in which the child is able to grow at his own rate and reach his full potential. The nursery school provides an arena in which the young child can discover his inquisitiveness and his creativity. He learns much about life and specific skills.

Let us take the example of the block area in the nursery school. As they become architects with blocks, they learn about shapes, sizes, and design. They also learn many mathematical concepts, such as the ideas of halves, wholes, addition and subtraction, height, width, length, etc. An adult takes these concepts for granted, but a child has yet to develop them in meaningful situations. Meaning comes through learning by doing or, as the adult says, "through experience."

Another popular area in a nursery school is the housekeeping or

[1]Bernstein, Victor, quoted in the *New York Early Education Reporter*, February, 1970, from an article in *Redbook*, November, 1969.

doll corner, which provides a place for the acting out of the child's thoughts. The child can play the father, mother, or the baby without fear of parental punishment.

Generally speaking, the child has to conform to the large-size adult world. But in nursery school, even the furnishings are scaled to a child's size. This enables the child to see that this is his world, and thereby he can assign himself his role. He can perfect skills with materials that fit his hands, his feet, and his size. Even the toilets are scaled to his size, and he can therefore take responsibility for his habits because the equipment is at his level and within his reach.

Other nursery school activities include painting, clay work, and the use of scissors; there are areas devoted to the library, music, science, and water play; there is provision for quiet activities such as working puzzles, cognitive development, and problem-solving.

Despite the lack of open spaces in the urban setting, the nursery school always makes allowance for outdoor play, thus enabling the youngster to climb, play in the sand, to cycle, etc., in order to develop his motor coordination.

There are different kinds of nursery schools. Some are financed privately, some by public funds; some are supported by philanthropic groups; sometimes parents sponsor a nursery school cooperatively. Many nursery schools are operated on a half-day or school-day schedule, and there are others that operate only two or three times a week. Occasionally there are some short-time play groups called nursery groups. Head Start, designed for disadvantaged children, is a nursery school-type program. The prekindergarten groups in some public schools are of nursery school nature. However, the day care center that covers the educational goals of all nursery schools is operated for a long day. Too, it usually has more need for inclusive attention to eating, sleeping, elimination, and health, since it has supervision of the children for such a long time.

Let us visit a day care center in New York City. Mrs. X, a divorcee, walked into and applied at the child care center in her immediate neighborhood. A neighbor had suggested that she might find help and a place for her four-year-old daughter while she was away at work.[2]

[2]All cases and descriptive elements in this chapter have been changed and fictionalized so that only composite pictures based on many experiences in various nursery schools in a number of states are used as examples.

Mrs. X, twenty-five years old, did not have anyone to care for her child, Amy. Her parents were not living and Mrs. X was very much alone. Amy was greatly attached to her father and could not understand why Daddy was living away from home. Mrs. X had difficulty explaining the reasons for the divorce. Amy was somewhat withdrawn, ready to cry at the slightest provocation.

At the day care center Amy found a warm, sympathetic friend in each of her teachers. She found, too, that other children looked forward to spending the day at the center. Upon arriving at 8:15 A.M., Amy would immediately join her close new-found friends, Roy and Maria, at the quiet activity table doing puzzles and games. She could not wait until 9 A.M., when her second teacher arrived, to begin painting with big brushes. Besides painting, there were opportunities to play with many different toys. Sometimes she played with the big blocks, sometimes in the doll corner. Other times she hammered at the workbench and made an airplane for her mother, while her teacher stood by and encouraged her.

Weather permitting, winter or summer, all the children raced to the outdoor playground to their favorite equipment. Amy liked to play in the sandbox and ride the bike. If she could not get the bike first, she cried, but her friend Maria would comfort and reassure her that she would get a turn later.

After outdoor activity the children would go back to their classroom and sit in a circle. Here a new world would open up to Amy. The children would learn about music, hear stories, see wonderful picture books. They would even hear about numbers and the alphabet. Amy felt very grown-up when she told her mother about these activities. Her mother had known about the play facilities, but she had not known that Amy would learn the alphabet and numbers or that Amy could read her own name.

After enjoying the hot, nutritious lunch served at the center, the children lay down on cots for a nap or rest. Sometimes Amy slept, other times she rested quietly. After rest period there were many interesting activities to select from. When Amy's mother came for her at 5:30 P.M., Amy would bubble with stories of her day.

By finding a day care center for Amy, Mrs. X established a strong measure of security for herself and her daughter. Mrs. X was able to meet other people who, like herself, were divorced, working mothers, and she did not feel so lonely. She formed friendships through her associations at the center.

Mr. A., whose wife had deserted him, came to the center because he needed care for his three-year-old son, Ken. Despite the fact that he had assistance from his mother and father with his older children, he still needed care for his youngest child. By enrolling Ken in a day care center, he was able to provide the necessary activities for a normal, active, healthy youngster.

Both of these parents were seeking help because of their broken home situations which amplified the need for day care for their youngsters. They found that the day care centers could fulfill their needs. In New York City, for the admission of children to the groups, the day care program has several criteria which were established to assist those who have the greatest need for such care.

The idea of day care for young children is not a new concept. Day nurseries were established in the latter part of the nineteenth century, initiated and supported by private philanthropic and religious groups. The goal was physical safety for the children, and there was a lack of educational or planned play programs. The care of the children was mainly custodial, which meant that the children were kept off the streets. The nurseries provided meals, health examinations, and baby sitting. The facilities were staffed by adults who were not required to have any formal education. On the whole, they knew little of materials and methods for young children or of the development of the growing child.

It was not until the Depression of the nineteen thirties that specific standards and educational requirements were established for day care groups. During this period the Federal government supported all day care centers for preschool children under the supervision of the Works Program Administration. This was the first time that the day care programs were financed by public moneys. In addition, it was the first time that individuals who worked with the children were required to be teachers who met professional standards on a par with those of the public schools. This contrasted with the old concept that the day care worker need only be an adult.

The day care movement received additional impetus during World War II when many mothers were employed in war industries because of the manpower shortages. The day care philosophy of employing and retaining educationally qualified staff was continued. After the war, as a result of the experience, some state and municipal governments continued to fund programs for children.

Most day care centers in New York City today provide early childhood educational programs. The typical center is a nursery school whose program extends all day from 8 A.M. to 6 P.M. The children's ages usually include three year olds, four year olds, and five year olds. Sometimes provision is made for the first and second-grade child to attend the center after school. On the whole, the schedules are planned so that the child has appropriate equipment for worthwhile learning experiences in both indoor and outdoor play. The child has opportunities for intellectual stimulation through play, participation in music, and other activities at his level. In addition, he learns to get along with others through social interchange with other children and the adult staff of the day care center. Events and holidays within the child's interest and understanding are noted.

The day care centers provide a balanced lunch, nutritious snacks, rest periods, and attention to toileting. There also is a preventive health program which provides a pediatrician from the New York City Health Department who visits and examines each child yearly. There is a physician on call, and arrangements have been made with the neighboring hospital for emergency services.

All nursery schools, including day care centers, must be licensed by the Department of Health in New York City, and all teachers must be certified by the New York State Department of Education. The Department of Health provides consultants and actively supervises the centers after they have been licensed.

The day care centers in New York City endeavor to provide total family services, with the child as the focal point. However, the family's problems, including those with older children, are always taken into consideration. The day care center staff know of other community services which can be of assistance to the parent, including summer day camps, remedial school help, and assistance in relocating. In addition, the day care center encourages parent activities—working for community improvements, sanitation, new schools, better lighting, police protection, etc. Parents can help inform the community about new health advances, current ideas on child-rearing, and similar trends. They often find the day care center a clearinghouse for the exchange of ideas affecting many facets of their lives.

The day care center can be of special importance to the one-parent family. Let us look at the case of Mrs. Y, a divorcee with two children in Los Angeles County.

She and her husband married at an early age—Mrs. Y was seventeen and Mr. Y twenty-one. The older child, Richard, was conceived within the first year. The second child, Ruth, followed after eighteen months. There were constant bickering and recriminations plus many financial problems, since Mr. Y was not a skilled worker. He had a difficult time in getting and holding any job that would pay him wages sufficient to support his family. Therefore, Mrs. Y, who had taken typing in high school, went to work to help out financially.

Mrs. Y enrolled Richard in a private day care center while her mother took care of Ruth. Mrs. Y's mother complained that Mrs. Y was not properly caring for her children because she went to work. Mr. Y resented his wife's working, and there were continuous arguments on this point. The situation, aggravated by the immaturity of the couple and their personality differences, became so severe that a divorce followed. The lack of finances and the inability to cope with reality also helped to destroy the marriage.

When Ruth reached age two, she was enrolled in the same day care center with her brother. Both Mr. and Mrs. Y were working at the time. After about six months, the teachers at the center noted that Ruth was not reacting as were the other children. The teachers requested that the mother take the child to a physician to be tested for hearing loss. The subsequent examination showed that Ruth was partially deaf.

This was the point which Mr. Y picked up to accuse Mrs. Y of neglecting her children by going to work. Somehow he associated the child's deafness with his wife's working, although there was absolutely no basis for it.

The prognosis for Ruth was a hearing aid that enabled her to function with a 20 percent hearing loss rather than the 50 percent hearing deficiency. The day care center assisted the child in coping with her handicap and in making life easier for her. In addition, her mother realized that she herself would need some kind of help in adjusting to the divorce and to her feelings as a mother and as a woman. By meeting others with problems similar to hers, she gained more inner security and felt better about herself.

FINDING A DAY CARE CENTER

There are several places to inquire about the local day care center, including the local Health, Education and Welfare Departments, as well as the local fire department.

It is important to keep in mind that day care centers, nursery schools and day nurseries vary in educational programs, length of day, physical settings, philosophy, and goals. They also vary in the quality of staff, activities, and achievements. Before enrolling a child in any of these preschool settings, one should explore and investigate the program that seems most suitable and acceptable.

What should one look for in a day nursery, day care center, or nursery school?

1. Does it have the approval of appropriate agencies? Is it necessary to have a license from the health, fire, education, or welfare departments? Is the license on display? Does the building conform to fire and building regulations? Are the premises safe for children?

2. Does the staff have the necessary educational qualifications? Do the teachers seem responsive to the children's needs? Are other staff members interested and competent in their areas?

3. Are parents welcomed in the school? Are they encouraged to visit?

4. Are there intellectual and educational stimulation in the program? Are all children treated alike? Is there allowance for individualization? Are children allowed to express themselves? Does the school respect the parents' concern for their children?

5. Is the furniture child-sized? Are there sufficient numbers of play materials for the children enrolled?

6. Is there provision for the children to go out-of-doors?

7. Is the school alert to the child's health and physical well-being?

What should be avoided in any nursery school setting?

1. An unlicensed school.

2. An unsafe building.

3. A school that discourages parent visits.

4. Programs that keep children sitting still for periods of time; programs that provide no activities of childlike nature.

5. Schools that do not have child-sized furniture, and do not have appropriate, numerous play materials.

6. Schools that have no access to outdoor facilities, whether these be on the premises or a nearby park.

7. Schools that show a lack of concern for the child's health.

Day care centers are funded and sponsored in different ways in different parts of the country. For example, in New York City there are approximately 125 centers funded by the New York City Department of Social Services and sponsored by some voluntary incorporated groups. There are also some profit-making private day care centers. In California, there are day care centers operated by the California State Department of Education. Because of the large population of working women, there are a great number of private, profit-making day care centers.

The philosophy of day care is changing rapidly not only in New York City but throughout the country. Day care offers opportunities for children from all walks of life, whether they be rich, poor, or middle class. Private industry has already begun to provide day care for the children of their employees. It is possible that, due to the increasing number of working women, there will soon be more day care facilities to meet the greater demands for such centers.

ELOISE B. WAITE

Red Cross Services to
Military Families

This chapter discusses the influence and effect on American
family life. Many married servicemen are presently trying to
carry on a normal family life within the confines of their military responsibilities. Hundreds of thousands of dependents
now follow American servicemen all over the globe, even more
remain at home waiting for their fathers and husbands to return after foreign tours of duty. The stresses and strains of
waiting at home are paralleled by the pressures American families abroad encounter in strange and often antagonistic cultures.

The American Red Cross is the only official agency approved by the United States government to deal with the family
problems of servicemen in the Armed Forces. Mrs. Waite, National Director of the Red Cross Services to Military Families,
discusses the goals of her organization and the techniques it has
found effective in maintaining good family relationships.
Typical problems are discussed, and solutions suggested, for the
benefit of all families, whether or not they are connected with
the military, with particular emphasis on problems of children.

For more than fifty years, the Red Cross has been serving military families in communities, military installations, and hospitals around the world. Domestically, Red Cross chapters offer a well-rounded program of welfare services to military families and act as the channel of communication between the family and the serviceman when problems arise. Families come to the Red Cross for help during crises involving illness, death, or accident; when financial assistance is needed for basic maintenance or an unanticipated emergency; when family communications have broken down; or when there is occasion to file claims for the variety of benefits for which military families are eligible. Inherent to all these services is the counseling often given to troubled families and to wives left alone with burdensome responsibilities.

With almost four million men and women in military service, it can be expected that many problems will arise that cannot be considered military responsibility. The service branches are exceedingly concerned about the morale and well-being of the troops and their families, and go to great lengths to provide for their welfare. Since the military establishment is not constituted to function as a social agency, provisions have been made for families to obtain welfare services elsewhere. The Red Cross, military welfare societies, and military organizations serving families are looked to as resources to supplement help available through community agencies to servicemen and their families.

Since military families are, in fact, part of the community, whether they live on post or off, and since it is the wish of the military that families identify themselves with the civilian community, Red Cross workers make maximum utilization of community resources to meet military client needs. Generally, families needing specialized services for physical or emotional problems are referred to appropriate agencies for long-term services. When servicemen do not support their families adequately and do not respond to attempts to elicit their positive and sustained financial participation, referral to public welfare is explored.

Red Cross experience over the years has established the need of military families for practical and tangible help with environmental problems and crisis intervention. Equally important is the sustaining support and reassurance that strengthens domestic life and helps families to survive frequent separations for reasons of military service. In conducting a welfare program for service families, Red Cross workers must be very knowledgeable about military life styles and attitudes, and about practices of all branches of service. The Service to Military Families procedural manual is designed to help servicemen and their families through the maze of regulations relating to emergency leaves and extensions, dependency or hardship discharges, family benefits, pay and allowances due, etc. Because of the necessity of working within the military frame of reference and authority, workers often have the difficult task of helping families to understand actions and decisions that seem unfeeling or arbitrary. There are times, alas, when the clients must wonder whose side the Red Cross is on—the family's or the military's.

Experiences gained from working with service families in Red Cross chapters form the basis for the general observations made here about the problems of children in families separated for reasons of military service.

MILITARY LIFE TODAY

Unaccompanied tours of short or long duration are an established fact of military family life, as is the hazard that may be an integral part of this separation. Career military families recognize that separation and hazard are basic to achievement of career goals and that they must be considered a part of the normal military life pattern and culture. The absence of the father to fulfill worldwide military commitments has always been a problem for military families and is becoming a greater concern in this day of rapid mobilization and of increased use of short tours of duty without families.

Predictability and preservation of the *status quo* in the national defense is a thing of the past. Accelerated communications have made the world a small place, and technical and scientific developments are daily changing the styles of defense and waging of wars. When consideration is given to changes that affect the military, most of us think of the well-publicized and documented aspects of the nuclear age and of resulting changes in military management. Submarines are diving deeper and staying longer. Navy families of submariners frequently experience regularly recurring three-month separations for a total of six to eight months a year. Ranger and airborne training are part of the program to develop a new fighting man. For frogmen and para medics, hazard is a built-in feature that becomes a routine.

Our country's ten-year involvement in Southeast Asia has been a cruel strain on military family life. Some in the military, especially career men, have already served twice in Vietnam and can anticipate additional tours should there be no sudden victory or negotiated peace. The troops in this war—which has no battlefields or battle fronts, and is so diffuse and ill defined—may be out of touch with comrades and families for days or weeks at a time while on patrol boats in the Delta or on jungle missions. To compound anxieties, for the first time in any conflict, families may have instant war in the living room every night on TV. Reports are received frequently from wives of servicemen who have, or think they have, seen their husbands lying wounded or killed in combat. Similarly, wives frequently identify their husbands in newspaper and magazine photos. The graphic stories and pictures in full living color that are featured in news magazines leave nothing to the imagination and contribute nothing to the tranquility of military families left behind.

Mention must also be made of the families of the four hundred and fifty prisoners of war and the fifteen hundred men declared missing in action. For the prisoners' families, there is the agony of not knowing what kind of treatment the men are receiving or when they will be released and in what condition. For the families of the servicemen reported missing, there is the additional anxiety of not knowing whether they will ever be reunited—whether there is even a father or a husband to come home.

Added to all this is the growing public disenchantment with military involvement in foreign countries. The community support that families have received in past conflicts is not forthcoming now. Cruel hoaxes are played on them—phone calls announcing the death of a husband or son, poison pen letters, outright hostility to military wives and children, etc. In previous wars, families could view their sacrifices as valid patriotic effort. Not so any more. Negative national attitudes are a phenomenon unique to this time.

PROFILE OF THE MILITARY FAMILY

As of May, 1970, there were 3,083,686 American men and women in military service in one hundred countries around the world. The median age of all officers is 29.7 years; 76.3 percent of them are

[1]Statistics obtained from Information Office, Secretary of Defense.

married with 2.24 children on the average. The median age of the enlisted men is 22.2, and 46 percent of them are married with 1.28 children. Although career military personnel—volunteers who enlist for three or more years—are more likely than are other personnel (mainly draftees) to be married, the difference is smaller than would be anticipated—45 percent versus 29 percent. The total of military dependents amounts to approximately 4,359,652.

One of every two married enlisted men and one of every three married enlisted men with children are in the lower pay grades. The eighty-five thousand enlisted men with children include between thirty thousand and forty thousand who earned less than the Census Bureau's 1968 estimate of a poverty income. The quarters allowance is limited to $60 per month for one dependent; for the second, $15 a month; for the third, $30.60; and nothing thereafter.

Occupying many of the low-ranking positions are the draftees and men who have enlisted for short tours in a service of their choice to avoid being drafted. Many of these are young single men, not in military service by their choice, who are counting the days until they are discharged. The ones who are married fit the general description of the career military family man and encounter many of the same problems. They are undoubtedly less committed to military family values and, while the duration of their stress at time of separation is no briefer, they know that they do not have to look forward to a lifetime of it.

Statistics show young, maritally stable, growing families. Every child living in a military family has a father or stepfather in good health and of average intelligence, steadily employed, and legally married to the mother or stepmother. Since military salaries are common knowledge, competitive financial strivings are diminished, and there is really not much pressure for conspicuous consumption nor for living up to the Joneses. Because of the medical benefits available to military children, they are generally in good health. The military expects its men to assume responsibility for their families and to meet their financial obligations. When breakdowns occur, the command feels free to counsel these men and demand that the delinquencies be remedied—with varying degrees of success, needless to say. Discipline of children, especially in career families, is often authoritarian. The values of obedience, politness, decorum, and neatness are stressed.

Since servicemen are a young group and since men customarily marry women younger than themselves, there exists what amounts to a dropout problem among the many young girls who have left school for marriage. An increase in the number of necessitous marriages has also been noted. Many young wives are too immature to be wives and mothers, which they generally become very quickly, and too inexperienced or uninterested to be housewives and managers of incomes often inadequate to meet the basic necessities of life. Since World War II, social and military mobility have produced many marriages with partners outside one's own religious, ethnic, or racial group. As military commitments seem to be increasing and expanding to all corners of the globe, to countries some have barely heard of, it can be expected that servicemen will continue to find wives in every part of the world.

The combination of military life and the ordinary complexities of our society make marital roles very difficult. The military wife must be a competent housewife, mother, and companion, and, in the absence of the husband, a business manager and father substitute for the children. Not always are the skills and personality of the wife suited to these demanding roles. The serviceman, on the other hand, must be the breadwinner, husband, and father, even though much of his time is spent away from home on matters not even remotely concerned with home and family. In the highly technical and mobile military organization of today, he often earns his living in a place remote from his home (in terms of miles, states, or continents) and by a skill so technical or confidential as not to be understandable to or not sharable with his wife. The artificially created environment in which the serviceman lives offers him no opportunity for sharing practical, everyday aspects of family living, and it tends to blunt his awareness of the need to share himself with his family. Servicemen separated from their families share leisure-time activities with other servicemen in similar circumstances. It can be expected that some of these men will find themselves with distractions and wandering thoughts, with the resulting temptation to put to one side responsibilities for home and family—or to lose interest entirely.

In spite of the most vigorous efforts by military leaders, it is often impossible for those involved to know why certain changes or transfers are being made. The factors of impersonality in decision-making and seemingly arbitrary actions (and the question of good intentions) often makes the serviceman and his family feel that they are being pushed around. When a serviceman receives orders for an unaccompanied tour of duty, his family must generally move off post if they have been occupying military-sponsored housing. Such a move, which may occur every several years or oftener, involves deciding where to go, packing, taking children out of school, arranging the move, resettling, getting used to new friends, neighbors, and community, registering the children in a new school—much of this without the serviceman and often with several small children who need constant attention.

For the military family that has a home community to return to or relatives to settle near, the stresses of separation and mobility are diminished for wives and children. The presence of familiar sources of obtaining help—sources of strength which families receive from relatives, friends and neighbors, the church, and the familiar social and economic milieu—must not be underestimated. For the mother, there is someone to share the daily burdens of life, to help with decision-making, to come to the rescue in time of crisis, to be companionable. For the children, there are others who are involved and interested in the family, and there is an escape from the sameness and too muchness of the mother. Red Cross workers have generally observed substantially fewer child behavior or family problems in those families who return to familiar surroundings and waiting relatives.

For the military family that does not have a familiar community to which to return, the decision must be made as to whether to stay in the vicinity of the installation where perquisites (PX, military medical care and hospitalization, movie, club, commissary, etc.) are available and help to ease the financial strain. The towns adjoining many large military installations are small, isolated, unappealing, often hostile to the military, and unable to cope with the housing and commercial demands of large numbers of military dependents. Regrettably, local residents may not see the young service families as being like those in their community. Too often they are viewed as outsiders who have been brought in as a result of a national decision over which the local community has no control. The alternative frequently is a metropolitan area where—if they are large, low-ranking families, members of minority groups, or poor—they will likely end up in a marginal or ghetto section in which the children are the victims of unsafe neighborhoods, poor schools, and unsuitable companions. The family may be charged high prices for substandard and crowded housing. Scarcity of adequate child care facilities make it difficult or impossible for the mother to work to supplement the income. Opportunities abound for all the family to get into trouble. While many in the military know racial discrimination, all know the discrimination that many landlords, employers, and merchants practice against transient military families—high rents for poor housing, reluctance to employ servicemen or their wives, and stringent credit requirements for those who, it is known, will be moving on.

While the ranks of commissioned and noncommissioned officers may not feel the financial press so severely as the large low-ranking, enlisted families, all find that moves are expensive and that it is more costly to maintain two households than one. Recent studies made in several Red Cross chapters surprisingly revealed that the majority of the emergency financial assistance had been given as loans and grants to officers and men in the higher pay grades who had indebtedness which committed all of their monthly pay and left nothing for savings or unanticipated emergencies. Whatever the rank, financial status, or new living arrangements, certain common problems exist in all military families—the difficulty of the two-parent role for even the most competent mother; the expense of maintaining two households; the finding of new social outlets for mother and children; and the reestablishment of the family equilibrium as quickly as possible.

PROBLEMS OF MILITARY LIFE AND THEIR EFFECT ON CHILDREN

Since military families are part of society and the communities in which they live, the particular problems they face cannot be viewed out of the context of the world in which we all live—a world that is becoming increasingly crowded, complicated, dangerous, impersonal, frustrating, and ill functioning. Many of us, from personal or family experience, have been touched by the current military involvement. Many feel the demoralizing aspects of discrimination. All know the pinch of inflation. The restlessness, revolt, and alienation of youth is a modern phenomenon. Drugs and crime in the streets hang over us like a dark cloud, frightening everyone. Urban sprawl, substandard or insufficient housing, deteriorating public transportation facilities, and scarcity of decent-paying jobs for unskilled workers are problems approaching crisis proportions. For those of us who are stable, fully employed, united families, getting from one day to another seems sometimes like a major achievement. Imagine how these universal problems must complicate the lives of military families who in addition are frequently separated, must move often, have unusual demands on their incomes, and are subject to special kinds of discrimination because of their military status.

It is this extra layer of stress on top of the universal problems that makes the lives of military families potentially precarious, and that makes it necessary to be alert to ways by which tensions and pressures can be alleviated and crises averted. Of the thousands of military families never seen by social agencies, many have resources of emotional strength, durability, fortitude, courage, and optimism, and perhaps the support of the extended family, that see them safely through frequent moves and separations. Others have needs for help but never get to social agencies. They muddle along as best they can with results that vary from marginal, unhappy adjustments to family breakup and dissolution. The families that are discussed in this paper are those who identify their problems or are made sufficiently uncomfortable by them to seek professional help.

No matter what his role or his strengths in the family grouping, the father provides an equilibrium that is absent with his departure for whatever reason. In order to understand the adjustments families must then make, it is necessary to understand the roles the father plays in the family. For his wife, he is a source of support and reassurance, helping with decision-making, offering a strong shoulder to lean on, serving as companion and lover, sharing responsibilities. For his children, he is a protector, companion, and hero who helps both sons and daughters through the process of socialization. For all he is the financial provider.

The fatherless family has suffered a loss, no matter how temporary his absence or how effectively he has filled his role as protector, provider, and head of the household. It can be anticipated that families will react in certain ways—with a sense of loss, anxiety, anger, fear of desertion, withdrawal, aloneness, etc. Since periodic separations are part of the military family life style, reactions should be expected to be less severe than had death, for example, occurred, because there has been time to prepare for the departure. Those who stand separations well anticipate them and have plans ready to put into operation.

Separation from the father appears to be one of the most stressful situations for children in military families. They are affected even before the father departs and the actual move takes place. Fear is inherent in many military moves and realistically so in the cases of fathers who are being assigned to combat zones. News media stories and TV coverage have exposed the real bloody horrors of war to total public view. War is no longer bands playing martial music and men marching to battles fought far from home. All family members know what can happen to Daddy. If nowhere else, this will be discussed at school. Since children pick up parents' anxieties, sharing of concerns and talking about them is a very important emotional release. Children should be allowed to express their feelings, helped to be realistic about dangers rather than to deny them, and encouraged to consider the positive aspects of the transfer. In career families, duty, loyalty to country, and the importance to the father's career of the moves are well understood.

After the father's departure and during the move, activities are likely to become family-centered as the mother starts to take over her husband's role. Some wives experience increased competence in managing home and business affairs, and feel that the husband's absence and the lessening of his demands affords them opportunities for personal growth and self-realization. Some realistic and insightful wives acknowledge that it is the periodic separations that hold the marriage and family together, and that prolonged proximity is fatal where emotional conflicts and tense interpersonal relationships exist. As one wife said, "Happy to see him come and happy to see him go." Another stated, "It's like a honeymoon every time he comes home."

Many wives see a proper husband as one who comes home at five, puts on slippers and watches TV or works around the house and yard. Often these are the ones who make marginal adjustments at the best, delaying decision-making and plans toward the day when the serviceman returns, moving about in a state of mild depression or resignation, irritable and unsure of themselves, prey to a succession of psychosomatic illnesses. Some wives blame a mobile situation for difficulties which have long been present in their relationships with others. The routine problem or minor emergency that a wife takes in her stride and solves with a minimum of stress under normal conditions may, in the absence of her husband, take on a significance way beyond the limits of reality. This is the point at which a new problem may be introduced—how to get the serviceman home to help. Failure to accomplish this and the fustration that results may produce other problems, perhaps unconsciously developed to create, ultimately, a problem of sufficient gravity to necessitate the serviceman's return. The complexity of the problem, then, does not necessarily determine the degree of stress on the wife separated from her husband.

Until the mother has gotten into the dual role of mother and father and into the swing of being the disciplinarian, she will have her ups and downs with the children, whatever their ages, since, with the departure of the father, changes in their behavior can be anticipated. Typical are the comments of mothers after the departure of the serviceman: "The boys are saucy and naughty," "My four year old started wetting the bed again," "I catch the older boys in minor delinquencies," "They test me to see how far they can go." It is likely that the children's behavior during this period reflects the lowered tolerance threshold to the mother. If the mother feels put upon and overburdened and alone, the children are likely to be resentful that their father has gone away and left them.

It is not uncommon to see a wife, reacting to a particularly stressful event or even to the routine everyday problems of rearing a family, strike out at her absent husband for real or imagined indignities. By shifting the blame to an absent husband who cannot defend himself, she avoids facing her own inadequacies. This kind of behavior and denigration of the father, carried on in the presence of the children, can result in their gaining a negative father image or in their being scornful of him. In instances of long separation, these attitudes can grow in the wife and children until fantasy is accepted for reality.

This technique of hitting out is one method of meeting stress. Such behavior can have serious effects on the normal growth patterns of children and may result in serious emotional problems. To caution a wife to keep such feelings to herself is unrealistic. What is needed at this point, before this self-defeating behavior becomes solidified, is a referral for counseling that will help the wife to understand what she is doing to herself, the children, and the marriage. Unless there is intervention at the appropriate time, the return of the serviceman may serve only as a stopgap measure, bringing only temporary relief, and a return to repetitive behavior at the time of the next separation.

If the mother takes the separation in her stride and is able to remain calm, cheerful, and optimistic, the children will probably respond similarly.

When the father leaves, children should be expected to assume additional responsibilities appropriate to their ages and sex. However, caution is needed so that the mother does not expect support from a child—he should not be expected to fill a role other than his own. For a boy, this role reversal can cause more harm than the absence of the father does, especially when the mother consciously or unconsciously expects him to take the place of the father. The observation that girls make out better than boys in a female-dominated home is certainly borne out by Red Cross workers, and emphasizes the importance of providing suitable role models and father substitutes for the boys. When adult male relatives or neighbors are not nearby, opportunities should be sought to enroll boys in classes with male teachers or in recreational centers that have diversional programs led by men. Rough masculine activities that promote development of skills and muscle and that test ruggedness, self-assertiveness, and self-confidence are advised.

Many chapter workers have recruited Red Cross Youth volunteers of high school or college age to be companions to young boys, especially those who are growing up in all-female homes. A commitment is made by the Youth volunteer to spend one or more days each week of the summer holiday with the youngster, exploring the community and its culture and recreational advantages, going on outings and to shows and entertainments. Emphasis is put on free or inexpensive outings but there is money provided for hot dogs and ice cream. This summer program has proven to benefit everyone—the son who has fun and gets a rest from home, siblings, and mother; the mother who likewise gets a rest from son and freedom from responsibility for him for a while; and the Youth volunteer who is early in life learning the pleasures of helping others.

Summer camp is another resource that families should be alerted to, as well as to swimming or boating lessons. Parenthetically, it has been observed that the mothers of large, multiple-problem families whose children are involved in such programs keep closely in touch with their workers the year-round rather than just when they need emergency help. They are receptive to outreach and preventive casework and have commented that father substitutes are helpful in modifying the behavior of the boys.

To maintain the image of the father as the head of the household facilitates and reinforces the mother's ability to keep control. She will want to find time to spend with the children, to talk with them, and to involve them in the decision-making process by discussing what the father would think, how he would act, what he would propose. An open channel of communications is essential to success. The children, even the small ones, should be encouraged or helped to write to or draw pictures for their father. It must not be assumed that all separated families take naturally or easily to letter writing. Many are marginally educated and have never even learned to read very well, much less express themselves in writing. Some can hardly write the daily events on a piece of paper and can barely express in writing their thoughts, feelings, fears, or aspirations. Red Cross workers find many a communications breakdown because of lack of facility with the written word, which has resulted in bewilderment, anger, or family estrangement. Alert workers serve both as letter readers and writers; when appropriate they provide help in making a tape recording for a wife who may be able to resolve a problem by "talking" a letter to her husband. Tapes have proven to be a very effective casework tool in serious communications breakdowns.

Tapes and records (talking letters) are also a means of communication that the whole family can share. Many Red Cross chapters have a holiday and/or a year-round Voice from Home program in which families can talk, sing, or play to their fathers and have a picture made to send him. Many families come dressed in costumes sent from foreign lands with instruments to play and songs to sing. Even the dog is encouraged to bark his bit. Increasing numbers of families have their own recorders and exchange tapes regularly. One father disciplined his young son by tape, cautioning him to behave himself and be a gentleman. His mother played this when the boy had been naughty.

Photographs of children sent at frequent intervals when they are growing and changing rapidly will help to diminish the strangeness that results when a father has left a sweet baby and comes home to an active, boisterous youngster.

Although the need for family communication may appear to be so self-evident as not to warrant such emphasis, experience has shown the extent to which this is critical to the family's welfare. Just as wife and children can feel lost by the serviceman's absence, so can he. His family may be his most important concern, and a letter even hinting at such problems as illness, money, poor grades, may cause such anxiety as to be demoralizing or potentially injurious to a soldier in battle. A simple problem, alarmingly presented, inadequately stated, or merely hinted at, can set off a chain reaction far greater than the problem warrants. Equally upsetting to the serviceman may be the failure of the wife to share any problems. Any husband knows that all is not sweetness and light to a mother who is left by herself to rear a growing family. To leave details to his imagination in an effort to spare his worry can be much worse than writing the awful reality. Frustration at separation, worry about alarming news, conjecture about the lack of news, and inability to rush to the family, results frequently in carelessness in performance of duty, unwarranted risk-taking in hazardous situations, and even AWOL's, all of which adversely affect total family welfare.

Whatever the marital and family relationships, the financial management, and the individual strengths or problems, most women —from the general's lady to the private's wife—have to make a decision about a new home location, and move. For many, especially the young and lower-ranking, the trouble starts right then, especially when the serviceman is not present to help. The three-month pay advance drawn to facilitate the move is soon gone, often to make essential purchases or to pay debts so that the post can be cleared. Transfers in and out of a combat zone and changes of address cause allotment delays for families of all ranks, sometimes for so long as three or four months. So, the family is short even before they make their move, and they can anticipate a wait of several months until the serviceman can send money from his pay to supplement the family's allowance.

Social workers have observed that help given promptly at the time of moving or separation often enables a family to establish its equilibrium on a sound basis and to maintain itself in a healthy, stable condition. One Red Cross worker mentioned the number of families he had seen only once, who had been given a number of emergency services and financial assistance sufficient to meet needs until the reestablishment of allowances. His opinion was that this help got the family off to a good start and established a momentum that they were able to sustain thereafter.

As has been mentioned, many of the lower-ranking families move into the only place they can afford—substandard housing in a poor area of town. Being away from the military base and its privileges, plus having only one income for a divided family, make it necessary for many a wife to provide a supplemental income to make ends meet. Large families, small children, shortage of child care facilities, and inadequate transportation often make this difficult, if not impossible. Furthermore, many of the young wives have had no training that equips them for any but the most menial, low-paying jobs in a market that has very little room for the unskilled.

Life in all parts of town, but especially in the poor areas, is full of hazards for children, who have to be watched every minute to see that they are not under cars or buses, who have to be taken everywhere because of the dangers that abound. Mothers learn that behavior problems of children generally tend to be less easily accepted by neighbors and others in a new community than they were back home in familiar surroundings.

Women alone in a strange place or a large urban environment are prey to hazards that a few years ago were not generally noted. Red Cross workers are now seeing the service wife who comes to ask Red Cross to help in obtaining the consent of her husband overseas for an abortion, because she has been raped; the wife who is shot or stabbed in a neighborhood argument; the wife who is robbed as she sits in her own living room—all are victims of their surroundings.

And there is many a young, immature wife, overwhelmed with problems, who needs no invitation to trouble. In her need to escape her ever-present responsibilities, and in her loneliness, she will find a strong shoulder to lean on whom she hopes will provide her with the reassurance and diversion she has been missing. This is the military wife to whom educational and preventive services must be offered in anticipation of the stress-producing events already mentioned, for whatever troubles the mother has will most certainly be reflected in the behavior of the children. A recent professional article reviewed a study about military children who were not doing well in school because of emotional disturbances. Interestingly, it was found that these disturbances were not brought on so much by frequent moves as by the responses of the parents to the moves and to separation.

Since learning and past successful experience in getting through similar situations lessen the stress of separation, it is to be expected that the greatest need for support will be among the young wife group, those most economically deprived, women lacking in life experience, and poorly educated members of minority groups. Red Cross social workers find that they have the job of mothering these young wives to maturity, of teaching them housekeeping skills, money management, and child care. Many need help over a considerable period of time; they are seen in their homes so that observations can be made about how they relate to their children, how the children relate to each other and to their friends, how home and money are managed, and how leisure time is spent. A great deal of the need is for practical help with getting things done (finding a better house to live in, applying for a job, arranging for the care of the children, getting necessary repairs, etc.) and part is for encouragement, reassurance, and interest. The fact that, in the absence of the husband, a mother has someone stronger and wiser to turn to with everyday problems is a very stabilizing influence.

Aside from practical help to young wives, there should be attention paid to the changing or modifying of attitudes and values, and to the setting of standards and goals. It is very important to a young family to draw strength from past successes and to develop a sense of the relatedness of life events in order to avoid repetition of unproductive behavior. Separated or together, families should have clearly defined and mutually understood goals toward which they are working, since military life offers an abundance of temptation to drift along, because so many decisions are made for servicemen and their families.

In serving military families, social workers learn to go beyond the immediate request which may ask for a simple, easily rendered service, and they learn to explore for other, deeper problems. For instance, an alert Red Cross worker, interviewing a mother who has asked that a message be sent to her husband announcing the birth of a new baby, will ask for vital statistics and the health of both. She will also find out if there are a layette and a crib for the baby at home, and if the medical benefits for payment of the hospital bill have been applied for. If the mother wishes, the Red Cross will help with the application for the baby's allowance. The Red Cross worker will also ask these questions: Is there someone to help when the mother goes home? Are there other children? Who is taking care of them? How are they responding to the arrival of the new baby? Since young mothers often feel a sense of aloneness and helplessness, it is important that assistance be offered so that anxieties will be allayed and serious emotional problems will not develop. The help of a strong person at a critical stage is a single preventive technique whose benefit should not be underestimated.

For the young wife on a limited budget, alone in a strange town with several small children who are her constant companions and care, the need for a chance to get away periodically, to have some fun, is often overlooked. Unless socially acceptable, wholesome opportunities are available, she may find other diversions that could end in calamity for the whole family. Military wives' clubs are being formed in many communities, sponsored by the Red Cross, military organizations, and community agencies. Such clubs offer opportunities for companionship with young women who share similar problems and have similar backgrounds. In some places there are clubs for foreign-born wives. Some clubs are diversional, some stress cultural enrichment, some offer opportunities for volunteer and civic service. Others emphasize group therapy with professional leadership—a chance for problem-solving and an exchange of ideas with wives who understand and who have been through the same experiences. The problems of the single parent and of child-rearing are two of the most commonly discussed.

The young wife living with or near relatives may need a social outlet as much as her counterpart who is away from all the normal sources of help. In one club when the proposal was made that the mothers of servicemen be admitted, the wives declined, on the basis that they needed opportunities to talk about their mothers-in-law and problems with adult relatives, and that they would not feel free to do this were the membership rules changed.

One of the ever-present worries of many young wives is what their husbands are doing when they are away. A wives' club recently visited the office of a well-known Congressman who had just returned from Vietnam. He was emphasizing the fine training their husbands had received, the concern of the military for their welfare and safety, and the efforts that were made to minimize risks. The wives revealed that they had come to terms with the dangers to their husbands' lives. Their pressing concern was what were their husbands' extracurricular activities. Did the Congressman think that the Vietnam girls were pretty? Did he think that their husbands would come back home still loving them? Such realistic fears, plus problems of expressing feelings in writing, are real contributions to communications breakdowns and to misunderstandings.

Many wives also fear that their husbands will come home addicted to drugs. Again the news media has made wives all too aware of the availability of drugs, especially in Southeast Asia, and their usage that is alleged to exist in the military.

Wives worry about the drug problem not only in relation to their husbands but in relation to their teen-age children also. In fact, teenagers cause military families of all ranks a great deal of concern and anguish. The conflict between military family values—loyalty, obedience, discipline, cleanliness, decorum—and today's youth behavior and values—restlessness, hostility toward the war and military service, truancy, running away, casual attitudes toward dress and toilet, unwed pregnancy, drug usage—is resulting in substantial estrangement of military children from their families. Red Cross workers are noting an increase in leave requests for servicemen to come home to deal with emergencies related to alienated and rebellious children. An article in a local Washington paper recently stated that 50 percent of the youngsters who were in a "runaway house" maintained for children who could no longer live with their parents, were from military families.

It should be noted that not all problems are miraculously resolved when the serviceman's tour of duty ends and the family is reunited. The readjustment process may be hard on everyone. If the mother has successfully taken her responsibilities in stride, she may find it difficult to relinquish her authority and some freedoms she has had, as happy as she is to have her husband back. The children may have found their mother understanding and flexible in her requirements of their conduct, or they may have had a free rein. Father comes back and demands for discipline and restrained behavior become more stern. He may, in fact, attempt to correct all permissiveness overnight. Hopefully, the serviceman can tolerate his gradual reintroduction to the family and to his place as the head of the house, and can understand his wife's lapses when she tries to take charge—

or his children's attitudes when they sense that they are no longer the center of attention and feel relegated to the background. All in the family must realize that time has passed and all have changed in some ways that will take getting used to.

SUMMARY

While separated military families may have many problems, it should be remembered that the problems of living in a complicated, technical, and mobile society are not theirs exclusively. Many civilians, too, have chosen to be similarly mobile and subject to family separations. The military families have in their favor youth and resilience. They are a group whom we expect to be able to survive adversity, to set standards and goals, to modify behavior, and to learn from experience.

Existing social agencies can help by reevaluating their programs, policies, and practices to be sure that they are problem-solvers and not just symptom-treaters. Civilian and military, social and health agencies should coordinate their programs, make their services widely known and responsive to client needs, and have staff available to give help when it is needed. In order that families not be "lost" between stations, a referral system should be developed so that there will be a receiving agency prepared to welcome the family and to help them to settle into the new community. The military has, in a few locations, allowed families whose sponsors are overseas to remain in their post housing. To stay in a familiar community of united families where one is established and safe is a substantial contribution to the stability and happiness of the separated family.

It is important that each person seeking help from a social agency be received in a friendly, relaxed atmosphere, and that time be adequate for a thorough exploration of needs and resources. The importance of going beyond the presenting problem cannot be stressed too emphatically. Each crisis that a family is helped to anticipate and avert offers an opportunity for learning and growth. Workers should be prepared to stay with crisis-prone families for the protection of the children, who are the natural victims of their parents acting-out, impulsive behavior.

To fully serve the whole military family, it is important to have a thorough knowledge of military and civilian resources—medical, educational, recreational, and religious. It is equally important that the staffs of these agencies know one another and their agency programs, and maintain amiable working relationships in order that the referral process be efficient and productive. Agency workers should be prepared to act in the advocacy role to help families accomplish what they are not able to do for themselves.

Careful attention should be paid to the children at home and in school in order to detect disturbances in their early stages. Father substitutes and role models for boys are advisable. Planning for use of free time after school and on weekends is essential. A variety of interests and wholesome activities for the whole family are contributory to well-being and good mental health. Diversional, educational, and cultural activities appropriate to each member should be available and their utilization encouraged; for the children, recreational activities as well as ways to earn money or to participate in community service; for the mother, a wives' club, volunteer service, or community involvement; for the whole family, church or activities that educate, relax, and sustain. All of these offer opportunities for early case finding—for spotting behavior and attitudes that signal problems in the making.

Emphasis in all contacts with separated families should be on helping wives and children to find personal and family satisfactions while they are alone with added responsibilities. This may be a matter of simple practical help, or it may require extreme sensitivity in the area of interpersonal relationships and a thorough knowledge of community resources. There must be a genuine concern for the separated family and a feeling of urgency that they must be afforded the best possible service, given with love and imagination.

REFERENCES

PART IV, CHAPTER 1.

1. Barclay, A.G., and Cusumano, D.R. "Testing masculinity in boys without fathers." *Trans-action*, 1967, 15, 33–35.
2. Berle, Beatrice B. *80 Puerto Rican Families in New York City*. New York: Columbia University Press, 1958, 138–39.
3. Campos, L. "Developing eight therapeutic communities at a school for boys." *Youth Auth. Quarterly*, 1967, 20, 20–31.
4. ——"Personality needs of Latin-American and North American students." *In Proceedings of XI Interamerican Congress of Psychology*, Mexico City, 1968.
5. Clark, Margaret. *Health in the Mexican-American Culture*. Berkeley: University of California Press, 1959
6. Deutsch, M., and Associates. *The Disadvantaged Child. Studies of the social environment and the learning process*. New York: Basic Books, 1967.
7. Diaz-Guerrero, R. "Neurosis and the Mexican family structure." *American Journal of Psychiatry*, 1955, 112, 411–17.
8. ——*Estudios de psicología del Mexicano*. Mexico, D.F., Antigua Libreria Robredo, 1961.
9. ——"Sociocultural and psychodynamic processes in adolescent transition and mental health." In Sherif, M., and Sherif, Carolyn (Eds). *Problems of Youth: transition to adulthood in a changing world*. Chicago: Aldine Publishing Co., 1965.
10. Dohen, Dorothy. *The Background of Consensual Union in Puerto Rico*. Unpublished M.A. thesis, New York: Fordham University, 1959.
11. Dunteman, G., and Wolking, W. "Relationship between marital status and the personality of mothers of disturbed children." *Journal of Consult. Psychol.*, 1967, 31, 220.

12. Dworkin, A.G. "Stereotypes and self-images held by native-born and foreign-born Mexican-Americans." *Sociol. & Social Res.* 1965, 49, No. 2.

13. Field, P.B.; Maldonado-Sierra, E.; Wallace, S.; Bodarsky, C.; and Coelho, G. "An other-directed fantasy in a Puerto-Rican." *Journal of Soc. Psychol.* 1962, 58, 43–60.

14. Fitzpatrick, J. "Intermarriage of Puerto Ricans in New York City." *American Journal of Sociology.* 1966, LXXI, 395–406.

15. Flomenhaft, K., and Kaplan, D. "Clinical significance of current kinship relationships." *Social Work,* 1968, 13, 68–75.

16. Forbes, J.D. *Mexican Americans: A handbook for educators.* Berkeley, California. Far West Laboratory for Educational Research and Development, 1968.

17. Geismar, L.L., and Gerhart, Ursula. "Social class, ethnicity, and family functioning: exploring some issues raised by the Moynihan report." *Journal of Mar. & Fam.* 1968, 30, 480–87.

18. Glazer, N., and Moynihan, D.P. *Beyond the Melting Pot.* Cambridge: Harvard University Press, 1963, pp. 86–142.

19. Goode, W.J. "Marital satisfactions and instability: a cross-cultural analysis of divorce rates." *Int. Soc. Sci. J.,* 1962, 14, 507–26.

20. Gonzalez, Nancie L. *The Spanish American of New Mexico: a destructive heritage.* Advance Report #9, M.A. Study Project, Div. Res. Graduate School, Business Administration, University of California, L.A., 1967.

21. Gordon, M. *Assimilation in American life: the roles of race, religion and national origins.* New York: Oxford University Press, 1964.

22. Green, Helen B. "Comparison of nurturance and independence training in Jamaica and Puerto Rico, with consideration of the resulting personality structure and transplanted social patterns." *Journal of Soc. Psychol,* 1960, 51, 27–63.

23. Gurin, G.; Veroff, J.; and Field, Sheila. *Americans View Their Mental Health.* New York: Basic Books, 1960.

24. Heller, Celia S. *Mexican American Youth: forgotten youth at the cross roads.* New York: Random House, 1966.

25. Herzog, Elizabeth, and Sudia, Cecilia. "Fatherless homes: A review of research." *Children,* 1968, 15, 177–82.

26. Jones, R.C. "Ethnic family patterns: the Mexican family in the U.S." *American Journal of Sociology,* 1948, 53, 450.

27. Kelly, F.J.; North, J.; and Zingle, H. "The relation of the broken home to subsequent school behavior." *Alberta J. Educ. Res.,* 1965, 11, 215–19.

28. Kluckhohn, F., and Strodtbeck, F.L. *Variations in Value Orientations.* Evanston, Ill.: Row, Peterson and Co., 1961.

29. Kushner, Sylvia. "The divorced, non-custodial parent and family treatment." *Social Work,* 1965, 10, 52–58.

30. Lance, Evelyn A. "Intensive work with a deprived family." *Social Casework,* 1969, 50, 454–60.

31. Landis, J.T. "The trauma of children when parents divorce." *Marriage and Family Living,* 1960, 22, 7–13.

32. ——"Dating maturation of children from happy and unhappy marriages." *Marriage and Family Living*, 1963, 25, 351–53.
33. Langner, T. "Psychophysiological symptoms and the status of women in two Mexican communities." In Murphy, Jane, and Leighton, A.H. (Eds.) *Approaches to Cross-Cultural Psychiatry*. New York: Cornell University Press, 1965, pp. 360–92.
34. Lewis, O. *Five Families*. New York: Basic Books, 1959.
35. ——*La Vida: a Puerto Rican family in the culture of poverty—San Juan and New York*. New York: Random House, 1965.
36. Loeb, Janice and Price, J. "Mother and child personality characteristics related to parental marital status in child guidance cases." *Journal of Consult. Psychol.*, 1966, 30, 112–117.
37. Love, J. L. "La Raza: Mexican Americans in rebellion." *Transaction*, 1969, 6, 35–41.
38. Madsen, W. *Mexican Americans of South Texas*. New York: Holt, Rinehart and Winston, 1964.
39. Maldonado-Sierra, E.; Fernandez-Marina, R.; and Trent, R. D. "Three basic themes in Mexican and Puerto-Rican family values." *Journal of Social Psychol.*, 1958, 48, 167.
40. Maldonado-Sierra, E.; Trent, R. D.; and Fernandez-Marina, R. "Neurosis and traditional family beliefs in Puerto Rico." *International Journal of Soc. Psychol.*, 1960, 6, 237–46.
41. Malzberg, B. "Mental disease among Puerto Ricans in New York City." *Journal of Nerv. and Ment. Disease*, 1956, 123, 263–69.
42. Manuel, Herschel, T. *Spanish-speaking Children of the Southwest: their education and the public welfare*. Austin: University of Texas, 1965.
43. McCormick, P., and Campos, L. *Introduce Yourself to Transactional Analysis*. Authors, Stockton, Calif., 1909.
44. Minuchin, S.; Montalvo, G., Jr.; Rosman, B., and Schumer, Florence. *Families of the Slums*. New York: Basic Books, 1967.
45. Mittlebach, F.G., and Moore, Joan W. "Ethnic endogamy—the case of Mexican Americans." *American Journal of Sociology*, 1968, 74, 50–62.
46. Mittelbach, F.G.; Moore, Joan W.; and McDaniel, R. *Intermarriage of Mexican Americans*. Mexican-American Study Project, Advance Report #6. Graduate School of Business Administration. University of California, L.A., 1966.
47. Moore, Joan W. *Mexican Americans: problems and prospects*. Madison: University of Wisconsin Institute for Research on Poverty, 1967.
48. Moustafa, A.T., and Weiss, Gertrude. *Health Status and Practices of Mexican Americans*. Mexican American Study Project, Advance Report II. School of Public Health, University of California, L.A., 1968.
49. O'Neil, Elizabeth. *Acculturation of Mexican American children*. Unpublished M.A. Thesis, University of Pacific, Stockton, Calif., June, 1968.
50. Padilla, Elena. *Up from Puerto Rico*. New York: Columbia University Press, 1958.
51. Peck, R. F. "A comparison of the value systems of Mexican and American youth." *Revista Interamericana de Psychologia*, 1967, I, 41–50.

52. Peck, R. F., and Diaz-Guerrero, R. "The meaning of love in Mexico and the United States." *American Psychol.*, 1962, 17, 329.

53. Penalosa, F. "The changing Mexican American in southern California." *Sociol. and Social Res.*, 1967, 51, 405–17.

54. ——. "Mexican family roles." *Journal of Mar. & Fam.*, 1968, 30, 680–89.

55. Radin, Norma. "Some impediments to the education of disadvantaged children." *Children*, 1968, 15, 171–76.

56. Rainwater, L. "Marital sexuality in four cultures of poverty." *Journal of Mar. and Fam.*, 1964, 26, 457–66.

57. Rand, C. *The Puerto Ricans.* New York: Oxford University Press, 1958.

58. Rogler, L. H., and Hollingshead, A. B. *Trapped: Families and Schizophrenia.* New York: John Wiley & Sons, Inc. 1965.

59. Rosenberg, C. "Young alcoholics." *British Journal of Psychology*, 1969, 115, 181–88.

60. Rosenberg, M. *Society and the Adolescent Self-image.* New Jersey: Princeton University Press, 1965.

61. Rubel, A. *Across the Tracks: Mexican Americans in a Texas city.* Austin: University of Texas Press, 1966.

62. Samora, J. (Ed.) *La Raza: forgotten Americans.* Notre Dame: University of Notre Dame Press, 1966.

63. Samora, J., and Lamanna, R. A. *Mexican Americans in a Midwest Metropolis: a study of East Chicago.* Advance Report No. 8, Graduate School of Business Administration. University of California, L.A., 1967.

64. Satterfield, Donna M. "Acculturation and marriage role patterns: a comparative study of Mexican American women." *Dissert. Abstracts*, 1967, 27, 2517.

65. Schwartz, Anne C. "Reflections on divorce and remarriage." *Social Casework*, 1968, XLIX, 4, 213–17.

66. Sexton, Patricia C. *Spanish Harlem.* New York: Harper & Row, 1965.

67. Srole, L.; Langner, T.; Michael, S. T.; Opler, M.; and Rennie, T. A. *Mental Health in the Metropolis: the Midtown Manhattan Study.* New York: McGraw-Hill, 1962.

68. State of California Department of Industrial Relations, Division of Fair Employment Practices. *Californians of Spanish Surname.* San Francisco, May, 1964.

69. Steiner, C. *Script Analysis in Alcoholism.* Unpublished manuscript, 1969, p. 105.

70. Stycos, J. M. *Family and Fertility in Puerto Rico.* New York: Columbia University Press, 1955.

71. Tharp, R.; Meadow, A.; Lennhoff, Susan; and Satterfield, Donna. "Changes in marriage roles accompanying the acculturation of the Mexican American wife." *Journal of Mar. and Fam.*, 1968, 30, 404–12.

72. Trent, R.D. "Economic development and identity conflict in Puerto Rico." *Journal of Soc. Psychol.*, 1965, 65, 293–310.

73. Tumin, M.M., and Feldman, A.S. *Social Class and Social Change in Puerto Rico.* New Jersey: Princeton University Press, 1961.

74. U.S. Children's Bureau. *Cuba's Children in Exile.* U.S. Department of

Health, Education and Welfare. Social and Rehabilitation Services, 1967.
75. Valdes, D. T. "The U. S. Hispano." *Social Educ.* 1969, 33, 440–42.

PART V, CHAPTER 4.

Books helpful to parents in effective sex education

Anderson, W. J. *Design for Family Living: A Guide From Childhood to Old Age*. Minneapolis: Denison, 1966.
——*How to Discuss Sex with Teen-agers*. Minneapolis: Denison, 1969.
——*How to Understand Sex: Guidelines for Students*. Minneapolis: Denison, 1969.
Arnstein, H. S. *What to Tell Your Child About Birth, Death, Illness, Divorce, and Other Family Crises*. New York: Bobbs-Merrill, 1962.
Cox, F. D. *Sex, Marriage, and the Seductive Society*. Dubuque, Iowa: Brown, 1969.
Eichenlaub, J. E. *New Approaches to Sex in Marriage*. New York: Dell, 1967.
Fromm, E. *The Art of Loving: An Enquiry into the Nature of Love*. New York: Harper, 1956.
Gottlieb, B. S. *What a Girl Should Know About Sex*. Indianapolis: Bobbs-Merrill, 1961.
Gruenberg, S. M. *The Wonderful Story of How You Were Born*. Garden City, N.Y.: Doubleday, 1959.
Hunt, M. M. *Her Infinite Variety: The American Woman as Lover, Mate, and Rival*. New York: Harper & Row, 1962.
Jones, K. L.; Shainberg, L. W.; and Byer, C. O. *Sex*. New York: Harper & Row, 1969.
LeShan, E. J. *Sex and Your Teenager: A Guide for Parents*. New York: McKay, 1969.
Levine, M. I. and Seligmann, J. H. *The Wonder of Life: How We are Born and How We Grow Up*. New York: Golden Press, Rev. Ed., 1964.
McCary, J. L. *Human Sexuality: Physiological and Psychological Factors of Sexual Behavior*. Princeton, N. J.: Van Nostrand, 1967.
Rayner, C. *A Parent's Guide to Sex Education*. Garden City, N.Y.: Doubleday, 1969.
Reuben, D. *Everything You Always Wanted to Know About Sex*. New York: McKay, 1969.
Saxe, L. P. and Gerson, N. *Sex and the Mature Man*. New York: Gilbert Press, 1964.
Strain, F. B. *Being Born*. New York: Appleton-Century-Crofts, Rev. Enl. Ed., 1954.
Winter, G. *Love and Conflict*. Garden City, N. Y.: Doubleday, 1962.

Books dealing with the relationships of single parents and their children

Champagne, M. *Facing Life Alone: What Widows and Divorcees Should Know.* Indianapolis: Bobbs-Merrill, 1964.
Donelson, K. and Donelson, I. *Married Today, Single Tomorrow: Marriage Breakup and the Law.* Garden City, N. Y.: Doubleday, 1969.
Hunt, M. M. *The World of the Formerly Married.* New York: McGraw-Hill, 1966.
Mindey, C. *The Divorced Mother: A Guide to Readjustment.* New York: McGraw-Hill, 1969.
Neisser, E. *Mothers and Daughters, a Lifelong Relationship.* New York: Harper & Row, 1967.
Simon, A. *Stepchild in the Family.* New York: Odyssey Press, 1964.
Steinzor, B. *When Parents Divorce: A New Approach to New Relationships.* New York: Random House, 1969.
Waller, W. *The Old Love and the New: Divorce and Readjustment.* Carbondale, Ill.: Southern Illinois University Press, 1958.

PART VI, CHAPTER 1.

BOOKS:

Gans, Roma. "Young Children at the Turn of This Era." *Early Childhood Education*, Forty-sixth Yearbook, Part I. Chicago: National Society for the Study of Education, 1947.
Hechinger, F.M. *Preschool Education Today.* Garden City, N.Y.: Doubleday, 1966.
Hymes, James L. *The Child Under Six.* New Jersey: Prentice Hall, 1963.
Read, Katherine. *The Nursery School.* Philadelphia: Saunders, 1966.
Rudoplh, M., and Cohn, D. *Kindergarten.* Boston: Appleton, 1964.
Todd, V.E., and Heffernan, H. *The Years Before School.* New York: Macmillan, 1964.

ASSOCIATIONS (to write to for pamphlets)

Association for Childhood Education International, 3615 Wisconsin Ave., N.W., Washington, D.C. 20016.
Bureau of Child Development and Parent Education, New York State Department of Education, Albany, N.Y.
Child Study Association of America, 9 East 89 St., N.Y., N.Y. 10028.
Child Welfare League of America, Inc., 44 East 23 St., N.Y., N.Y. 10010.
National Association for the Education of Young Children, 1834 Connecticut Ave., N.W., Washington, D.C. 20009.
Play Schools, Inc., 120 West 57 St., N.Y., N.Y. 10019.
U. S. Government Printing Office, Division of Public Documents, Washington, D.C. 20402.

BIBLIOGRAPHY*

Arnstein, H. S. *What to Tell Your Child*. Indianapolis: Bobbs-Merrill and Co., 1962.
> This book was written with the cooperation of the staff of the Child Study Association of America.

Bernard, Jessie. *Remarriage*. New York: The Dryden Press, 1956.
> One of the many universities at which Dr. Bernard has taught is the Pennsylvania State University. She is both a statistician and a sociologist.

Blaine, Graham J., Jr. "The Children of Divorce," *Atlantic Monthly*, CCXI, March, 1963, p. 100.
> Dr. Blaine is a psychiatrist at University Health Services at Harvard and Radcliffe and an assistant psychiatrist at Children's Hospital in Boston.

Bossard, James. *Parent and Child*. Philadelphia: University of Pennsylvania Press, 1956.
> Dr. Bossard is a sociology teacher at the University of Pennsylvania and also the director at the William T. Carter Foundation for Child Development.

Bowerman, Charles E., and Donald P. Irish. "Some Relationships of Stepchildren to Their Parents," *Marriage and Family*, XXV, May, 1962, pp. 113–21.
> Both Bowerman and Irish were professors of sociology at the University of North Carolina at the time they conducted this particular study.

Despert, Louise. *Children of Divorce*. New York: Doubleday, 1955.
> Dr. Despert, a child psychiatrist, was head of the Children's Service of the New York State Psychiatric Institute.

Egleson, James and Egleson, J. *Parents Without Partners*. New York: E. P. Dutton, 1961.

*The editors are indebted to Mrs. Gertrude Green of Baldwin, New York, for the development of this bibliography.

308] BIBLIOGRAPHY

Authors based their conclusions on two main sources: testimony of experts in such fields as pediatrics and psychiatry; interviews with representative divorced and separated parents.

English, O. Spurgeon. *Fathers Are Parents Too*. New York: C. P. Putnam's Sons, 1951.
Dr. English is head of the Department of Psychiatry of Temple University Medical School.

Goode, William J. *Women in Divorce*. New York: The Free Press, 1965.
——*After Divorce*. Glencoe, Illinois: The Free Press, 1956.
Dr. Goode is a sociology professor at Columbia University.

Greenberg, Kenneth R. "Dating and the Single Parent." *The Single Parent*, XII, September, 1969, pp. 9–11.
Dr. Greenberg is Associate Professor of Psychology at the University of Maryland, and is also in private practice.

Grollman, Earl A. (Ed.). *Explaining Divorce to Children*. Boston: Beacon Press, 1969.
Nine experts on divorce from the fields of sociology, psychiatry, law, and child study have contributed to this book, which was edited by Rabbi Grollman.

Hunt, Morton M. *The World of the Formerly Married*. New York: McGraw-Hill, 1966.
A free-lance writer whose subjects deal most often with psychology, love and sex, and marriage, Hunt's articles have appeared in most of the major national magazines.

Hurlock, Elizabeth. *Child Development* (4th ed.). New York: McGraw-Hill, 1964.
Dr. Hurlock teaches at the Graduate School of Education at the University of Pennsylvania.

Jones, Eve. *Raising Your Child in a Fatherless Home*. New York: Macmillan, 1963.
The author is a member of the faculty at the University of Chicago, where she obtained her doctorate in clinical psychology. She is also a consultant in psychodiagnostics for emotionally disturbed children.

Landis, Judson T. "The Trauma of Children When Parents Divorce." *Marriage and Family Living*, XXII, February, 1960, pp. 7–12.
Dr. Landis has taught sociology at many universities including Berkeley, California. He has also been on the editorial board of the magazine *Marriage and Family Living*.

Nye, Ivan F. "Child Adjustment in Broken and Unhappy Unbroken Homes." *Marriage and Family Living*, XIX, November, 1957, pp. 356–61.
Dr. Nye has been an Associate Professor of Sociology at Bucknell, Florida State, and Washington State. He has been the editor of *Marriage and Family Living*.

Perry, Joseph B., and Pfuhl, Erdwin H. Jr. "Adjustment of Children in 'Solo'

and 'Remarriage Homes.' " *Marriage and Family Living*, XXV, May, 1963, p. 221.
Dr. Perry is a sociologist at Louisiana State University, and Dr. Pfuhl teaches at Whitman College.

Polatin, Phillip, and Philtine, Ellen C., *Marriage in the Modern World*. New York: J.B. Lippincott, 1956.
Dr. Polatin is Professor of Clinical Psychiatry at the College of Physicians and Surgeons, Columbia University.

Rochford, Elbrun. *Mothers on Their Own*. New York: Harper and Brothers, 1953.
Mrs. Rochford is a free-lance writer who wrote this book after interviewing doctors, ministers, lawyers, teachers, and mothers. She drew her conclusions from stories, facts, and opinions imparted to her.

Sherwin, Robert Veit. *Compatible Divorce*. New York: Crown, 1969.
Mr. Sherwin is a practicing attorney in New York City who specializes in domestic relations. He belongs to the American Academy of Matrimonial Lawyers.

Simon, Anne. *Stepchild in the Family*. New York: The Odyssey Press, 1964.
The author is a psychiatric social worker who acknowledges the help of directors of family services, psychiatrists, and pediatricians in writing this book.

Spock, Benjamin. *Problems of Parents*. New York: Houghton, 1962.
Dr. Spock is a pediatrician famous for his book *Baby and Child Care*.

Taves, Isabella. *Women Alone*. New York: Funk and Wagnalls, 1968.
Mrs. Taves is a free-lance writer of books and a contributor to many magazines. She gathered her material for this book through personal interviews, group interviews, and questionnaires.

Thomson, Helen. *The Successful Stepparent*. New York: Harper and Row, 1966.
Mrs. Thomson has written many magazine articles on social questions. For this book she has called on the services of Mrs. Erna R. Bowmer of the Family Service of Rochester, New York, and the Department of Health, Education and Welfare.

INDEX

This book has been set on the Photo Composition in Video Gael.

The display type is Baskerville.

The paper is Sebago-Antique, supplied by the S. D. Warren Company.

The composition, printing and binding is by Haddon Craftsmen, Inc., New York.